TOPICS IN PRODUCTION THEORY

This volume is devoted to current topics in production theory. The papers are organized under four headings. Part I deals with *technical change*. *Jorgenson* reports on econometric research on production functions for a large number of production sectors as part of a general equilibrium model of an economy. *Førsund* and *Jansen* focus on *one* industrial sector and study structural and technical change within the Norwegian aluminum industry, using Leif Johansens's concept of a short-run industry function. *Kopp* and *Smith* measure the effects of technical change on an even more disaggregated level. Two large-scale process analysis models provide a description of the production technology with the possibility of applying six specific process innovations. *Baumol* and *Wolff* outline a model which takes into account not only the contributions of R & D to the rate of growth of an economy's productivity, but also the likelihood that there is a relationship in the other direction.

Part II is devoted to *efficiency*. *Diewert* uses a comparative static framework and duality theory to characterize two measures of the loss to the economy brought about by distortions in the resource allocation in the production sector. *Färe, Grosskopf* and *Lovell* start out from Farrell's measure of productive efficiency and study nonparametric measurements of efficiency under less restrictive assumptions on technology.

The papers in Part III deal with *aggregation, quasi-fixed factors* and *cost of adjustment*. *Epstein* addresses the problem of aggregating quasi-fixed factors in the context of an adjustment-cost model. *Blackorby* and *Schworm* investigate the conditions under which – in adjustment-cost models – aggregates for heterogeneous capital and investment exist for individual firms and the conditions under which the sum of wealth functions over firms depends only on aggregate capital. *Pindyck* and *Rotemberg* model the industrial demand for structures, equipment and blue- and white-collar labor in a manner consistent with rational expectations and stochastic dynamic optimization in the presence of adjustment costs. *Brown* and *Greenberg* investigate the conditions under which the Divisia index of total factor productivity for all production units is path independent within a general equilibrium framework.

Other aspects of production theory are present in Part IV. *Vislie* analyzes the optimal use of inputs for producing goods which take a long time to complete, when prices of inputs may change at some unknown future date. *Bosworth* and *Pugh* deal with the degree of capital utilization. In particular, increased utilization results in more rapid depreciation of the capital stock. *Hamlin* and *Heathfield* analyze consequences of the rate of profit being the maximand for a firm and examine *ex ante* employment, investment and shiftwork decisions in a putty-clay model when output and prices are given. *Mizon* and *Nickell* present estimates of a vintage production model for the U.K., with the aim of discovering whether it is possible to explain satisfactorily the output of manufacturing industries as a simple, stable function of a small number of input aggregates.

TOPICS IN PRODUCTION THEORY

Edited by

Finn R. Førsund
Department of Economics
University of Oslo, Norway

St. Martin's Press   New York

ISBN 0-312-80914-X

Library of Congress Cataloging in Publication Data
Main entry under title:

Topics in production theory.

Originally published as v. 85, no. 2, 1983 of The
Scandinavian journal of economics.
Includes bibliographies and index.
1. Production (Economic theory)—Addresses, essays,
lectures. 2. Technological innovations—Addresses,
essays, lectures. 3. Efficiency, Industrial—Addresses,
essays, lectures. I. Førsund, Finn R. II. Scandinavian
journal of economics.
HB241.T66 1984   338.5   83-40610
ISBN 0-312-80914-X

Contents

Contributors' Affiliations

Dale W. Jorgenson	Harvard University, Cambridge, MA
Finn R. Førsund	University of Oslo, Norway
Eilev S. Jansen	Central Bureau of Statistics, Oslo, Norway
Raymond Kopp	Resources for the Future, Washington, DC
V. Kerry Smith	University of North Carolina, Chapel Hill, NC
William J. Baumol	Princeton University, Princeton, NJ and New York University, NY
Edward Wolff	New York University, NY
W, Erwin Diewert	University of British Columbia, Vancouver, BC
Rolf Färe	Southern Illinois University, Carbondale, IL
Shawna Grosskopf	Southern Illinois University, Carbondale, IL
C. A. Knox Lovell	University of North Carolina, Chapel Hill, NC
Larry G. Epstein	University of Toronto, ON
Charles Blackorby	University of British Columbia, Vancouver, BC
William Schworm	University of British Columbia, Vancouver, BC
Robert S. Pindyck	M.I.T., Cambridge, MA
Julio J. Rotemberg	M.I.T., Cambridge, MA
Murray Brown	State University of New York, Buffalo, NY
Richard Greenberg	State University of New York, Buffalo, NY
Jon Vislie	University of Oslo, Norway
Derek Bosworth	Loughborough University, Leicestershire, England
Clive Pugh	Loughborough University, Leicestershire, England
Alan Hamlin	University of Southampton, England
David Heathfield	Unversity of Southampton, England
Grayham Mizon	University of Southampton, England
Stephen Nickell	London School of Economics and Political Science, London, England

PART I TECHNICAL CHANGE

Modeling Production for General Equilibrium Analysis

Dale W. Jorgenson

Harvard University, Cambridge, MA, USA

Abstract

The purpose of this paper is to present econometric models of producer behavior suitable for incorporation into a general equilibrium model. Implementation of these models requires a time series of inter-industry transactions tables. Second, implementation requires methods for estimation of parameters in systems of nonlinear simultaneous equations. Finally, the economic theory of producer behavior implies equality and inequality restrictions on the parameters that must be incorporated into the estimation. We discuss an empirical application to modeling producer behavior in thirty-six industrial sectors of the U.S. economy.

I. Introduction

The purpose of this paper is to present nonlinear econometric models of producer behavior suitable for incorporation into a general equilibrium model of the U.S. economy. General equilibrium modeling originated with the seminal work of Leontief (1941), based on empirical implementation of a static input-output model for the U.S. economy. Leontief (1953) gave a further impetus to the development of general equilibrium modeling by introducing a dynamic input-output model.

The usefulness of the "fixed coefficients" assumption that underlies input-output analysis is hardly subject to dispute. By linearizing technology Leontief was able to solve at one stroke the two fundamental problems that arise in the practical implementation of general equilibrium models. First, the resulting general equilibrium model could be solved as a system of linear equations with constant coefficients. Second, the unknown parameters describing technology could be estimated from a single data point.

The first successful implementation of an applied general equilibrium model without the fixed coefficients assumption of input-output analysis is due to Johansen (1960). Johansen retained the fixed coefficients assumption in modeling demands for intermediate goods, but employed linear logarithmic or Cobb-Douglas production functions in modeling the substitution between capital and labor services and technical change.

Linear logarithmic production functions imply that relative shares of inputs in the value of output are fixed, so that the unknown parameters characterizing substitution between capital and labor inputs can be estimated from a single data point. In describing producer behavior Johansen employed econometric methods only in estimating constant rates of technical change.

To implement models of producer behavior that are less restrictive than those of Johansen, it is essential to employ econometric methods. A possible econometric extension of Johansen's approach would be to estimate elasticities of substitution between capital and labor inputs along the lines suggested by Arrow, Chenery, Minhas, and Solow (1961). Unfortunately, constant elasticity of substitution production functions cannot easily be extended to encompass substitution among capital, labor, and intermediate inputs or among different types of intermediate inputs. With more than two inputs Uzawa (1962) and McFadden (1963) have shown that constant elasticities of substitution imply, essentially, that all elasticities of substitution must be the same.

An alternative approach to modeling producer behavior for general equilibrium models is through complete systems of input demand functions for each industrial sector. Each system gives quantities of inputs demanded as functions of prices and output. This approach to modeling producer behavior has been implemented by Berndt and Jorgenson (1973), Hudson and Jorgenson (1974), and Jorgenson and Fraumeni (1981). As in the description of technology by Leontief and Johansen, production is characterized by constant returns to scale in each sector. As a consequence, commodity prices can be expressed as functions of factor prices, as in the general equilibrium model of Samuelson (1953). This greatly facilitates the calculation of a set of equilibrium prices by permitting a substantial reduction in dimensionality of the space of unknown prices.

The implementation of econometric models of producer behavior requires a time series of inter-industry transactions tables. By comparison the noneconometric approaches of Leontief and Johansen require only a singel inter-industry transactions table. Second, the implementation of systems of input demand functions requires methods for the estimation of parameters in systems of nonlinear simultaneous equations. Finally, the incorporation of restrictions implied by the economic theory of producer behavior requires estimation under both equality and inequality constraints.

II. Producer Behavior

In this section we present an econometric model of producer behavior that has been implemented for thirty-six industrial sectors of the U.S. economy by Jorgenson and Fraumeni (1981). This model is based on a production function for each sector, giving output as a function of inputs of intermediate goods produced by other sectors and inputs of the primary factors of production, capital and labor services. Output also depends on time as an index of the level of technology. Producer equilibrium under constant returns to scale implies the existence of a sectoral price function, giving the price of output as a function of the input prices and time. To incorporate the restrictions implied by the economic theory of producer behavior we generate our econometric model from a price function for each sector.

Sectoral price functions must be homogeneous of degree one, nondecreasing, and concave in input prices. In addition, we assume that these price functions are homothetically separable in the prices of capital, labor, energy, and materials inputs. Under homothetic separability our model of producer behavior is based on a two-stage allocation process.[1] In the first stage the value of sectoral output is allocated among capital, labor, energy, and materials inputs. In the second stage the value of each of the inputs is allocated among individual types of that input. Two-stage allocation makes it possible to determine the rate of technical change and the shares of thirty-six intermediate goods and two primary factors of production in the value of output as functions of input prices.

Our most important conceptual innovation is to determine the rate of technical change and the distributive shares of productive inputs simultaneously as functions of relative prices. While technical change is endogenous in our models of production and technical change, these models must be carefully distinguished from models of induced technical change, such as those analyzed by Hicks (1932), Kennedy (1964), Samuelson (1965), von Weizäcker (1962) and many others.[2] In those models the biases of technical change are endogenous and depend on relative prices. In our models the biases of technical change are fixed, while the rate of technical change is endogenous and depends on relative prices.

As Samuelson (1965) has pointed out, models of induced technical change require intertemporal optimization, since technical change at any point of time affects future production possibilities. In our models myopic decision rules can be derived by treating the price of capital input as a rental price for capital services, even though the rate of technical change is endogenous.[3] The rate of technical change at any point of time is a function of relative prices, but does not affect future production possibilities. This

---

[1] Two-stage allocation is discussed by Blackorby, Primont and Russell (1978), especially pp. 103–216; they give detailed references to the literature.

[2] A review of the literature on induced technical change is given by Binswanger (1978 a). Binswanger distinguishes between models, like ours and those of Ben-Zion and Ruttan (1978) Lucas (1967) and Schmookler (1966), with an endogenous rate of technical change and models, like those of Hicks (1932), Kennedy (1964), Samuelson (1965), von Weizsäcker (1962) and others, with an endogenous bias of technical change. Additional references are given by Binswanger (1978 a).

[3] For further discussion of myopic decision rules, see Jorgenson (1973).

vastly simplifies the modeling of producer behavior and greatly facilitates the implementation of our econometric models.

Given myopic decision rules for producers in each industrial sector, we can describe all of the implications of the theory of production in terms of the sectoral price functions.[4] The sectoral price functions must be homogeneous of degree one, nondecreasing and concave in the prices of the four inputs. A novel feature of our econometric methodology is to fit econometric models of sectoral production and technical change that incorporate all of these implications of the theory of production.

To represent our models of producer behavior we first require some notation. There are I industrial sectors, indexed by $i = 1, 2, \ldots, I$. We denote the quantities of sectoral outputs by $\{Z_i\}$ and the quantities of sectoral capital, labor, energy, and materials inputs by $\{K_i, L_i, E_i, M_i\}$. Similarly, we denote the prices of sectoral outputs by $\{q_i\}$ and the prices of the four sectoral inputs by $\{p_K^i, p_L^i, p_E^i, p_M^i\}$. We can define the shares of inputs in the value of output for each of the sectors by:

$$v_K^i = \frac{p_K^i K_i}{q_i Z_i}, \quad v_L^i = \frac{p_L^i L_i}{q_i Z_i}, \quad v_E^i = \frac{p_E^i E_i}{q_i Z_i}, \quad v_M^i = \frac{p_M^i M_i}{q_i Z_i}, \quad (i = 1, 2, \ldots, I).$$

Outputs are valued in producers' prices, while inputs are valued in purchasers' prices. In addition we reguire the notation:

$v_i = (v_K^i, v_L^i, v_E^i, v_M^i)$—vector of value shares of the ith industry $(i = 1, 2, \ldots, I)$.

$\ln p_i = (\ln p_K^i, \ln p_L^i, \ln p_E^i, \ln p_M^i)$—vector of logarithms of prices of sectoral inputs of the ith industry $(i = 1, 2, \ldots, I)$.

t—time as an index of technology.

We assume that the ith industry allocates the value of its output among the four inputs in accord with the price function:

$$\ln q_i = \alpha_0^i + \ln p_i' \alpha_p^i + \alpha_t^i \cdot t + \frac{1}{2} \ln p_i' \beta_{pp}^i \ln p_i \qquad (1)$$
$$+ \ln p_i' \beta_{pt}^i \cdot t + \frac{1}{2} \beta_{tt} \cdot t^2, \quad (i = 1, 2, \ldots, I).$$

For these price functions, the prices of outputs are transcendental or, more specifically, exponential functions of the logarithms of the prices of inputs. We refer to these forms as *transcendental logarithmic* price functions or, more simply, translog price functions,[5] indicating the role of the variables

[4] The price function was introduced by Samuelson (1953).

[5] The translog price function was introduced by Christensen, Jorgenson, and Lau (1971, 1973). The translog price function was first applied at the sectoral level by Berndt and Jorgenson (1973) and Berndt and Wood (1975). References to sectoral production studies incorporating energy and materials inputs are given by Berndt and Wood (1979).

that enter the price functions. In this representation the scalars $\{\alpha_0^i,\ \alpha_t^i,\ \beta_{tt}^i\}$ the vectors $\{\alpha_p^i,\ \beta_{pt}^i\}$, and the matrices $\{\beta_{pp}^i\}$ are constant parameters that differ among industries, reflecting differences among sectoral technologies. Differences in technology among time periods within an industry are represented by time as an index of technology.

The value shares of the i'th industry can be expressed in terms of the logarithmic derivatives of the sectoral price function with respect to the logarithms of the prices of the corresponding inputs:

$$v_j = \frac{\delta \ln q_i}{\delta \ln p_i}, \qquad\qquad (i = 1, 2, \ldots, I). \qquad (2)$$

Applying this relationship to the translog price function, we obtain the system of sectoral value shares:

$$v_i = \alpha_p^i + \beta_{pp}^i \ln p_i + \beta_{pt}^i \cdot t, \quad (i = 1, 2, \ldots, I). \qquad (3)$$

We can define the *rate of technical change* for each of the sectors, say $\{v_t^i\}$, as the negative of the rate of growth of the price of sectoral output with respect to time, holding the prices of sectoral capital, labor, energy, and materials inputs constant:

$$v_t^i = -\frac{\delta \ln q_i}{\delta t} \quad (i = 1, 2, \ldots, I). \qquad (4)$$

For the translog price function this relationship takes the form:

$$-v_t^i = \alpha_t^i + \beta_{pt}^{i\,'} \ln p_i + \beta_{tt}^i \cdot t, \quad (i = 1, 2, \ldots, I). \qquad (5)$$

Given the sectoral price functions, we can define the *share elasticities with respect to price*[6] as the derivatives of the value shares with respect to the logarithms of the prices of capital, labor, energy, and materials inputs. For the translog price functions the matrices of share elasticities with respect to price $\{\beta_{pp}^i\}$ are constant. We can also characterize these functions as *constant share elasticity* or CSE price functions, indicating the role of fixed parameters that enter the sectoral price functions.[7] Similarly, we can define the *biases of technical change with respect to price* as deriva-

---

[6] The share elasticity with respect to price was introduced by Christensen, Jorgenson, and Lau (1971, 1973) as a fixed parameter of the translog price function. An analogous concept was employed by Samuelson (1973). The terminology is due to Jorgenson and Lau (1983).

[7] The terminology "constant share elasticity price function" is due to Jorgenson and Lau (1983), who have shown that constancy of share elasticities with respect to price, biases of technical change with respect to price, and the rate of change of the negative of the rate of technical change are necessary and sufficient for representation of the price function in translog form.

tives of the value shares with respect to time.[8] Alternatively, we can define the biases of technical change with respect to price as derivatives of the rate of technical change with respect to the logarithms of the prices of capital, labor, energy and materials inputs.[9] These two definitions of biases of technical change are equivalent. For the translog price functions the vectors of biases of technical change with respect to price $\{\beta_{pt}^i\}$ are constant. Finally, we can define the *rate of change of the negative of the rate of technical change* as the derivative of the rate of technical change with respect to time.[10] For the translog price functions these rates of change $\{\beta_{tt}^i\}$ are constant.

Our model of producer behavior consists of a system of equations giving the shares of all inputs in the value of output and the rate of technical change as functions of relative prices and time. To formulate an econometric model we add a stochastic component to these equations. Since the rate of technical change is not directly observable, we consider a form of the model with autocorrelated disturbances. We can transform the data to eliminate the autocorrelation. We treat the prices as endogenous variables and estimate the unknown parameters by means of econometric methods appropriate for systems of nonlinear simultaneous equations. Estimates of the unknown parameters of our econometric model of producer behavior are based on the nonlinear three-stage least squares estimator introduced by Jorgenson and Laffont (1974).[11]

Our next objective is to describe the empirical results of implementing the model of producer behavior presented above for thirty-six industrial sectors of the United States. This model is based on a two-stage process for the allocation of the value of output in each sector among capital, labor, energy, and materials inputs. The value of inputs from these four commodity groups exhausts the value of the output for each of the thirty-six sectors. We limit our presentation of empirical results to the first stage of the two-stage process.

---

[8] The bias of technical change was introduced by Hicks (1932). An alternative definition of the bias of technical change is analyzed by Burmeister and Dobell (1969). Binswanger (1974) has introduced a translog cost function with fixed biases of technical change. Alternative definitions of biases of technical change are compared by Binswanger (1978 *b*).

[9] This definition of the bias of technical change with respect to price is due to Jorgenson and Lau (1983).

[10] The rate of change of the negative of the rate of technical change was introduced by Jorgenson and Lau (1983).

[11] Estimators for systems of nonlinear regression equations with additive errors are presented by Malinvaud (1980), Chapter 9. Nonlinear two-stage least squares estimators were introduced by Amemiya (1974). Subsequently, nonlinear three-stage least squares estimators were introduced by Jorgenson and Laffont (1974). For detailed discussion of nonlinear three-stage least squares estimators, see Amemiya (1977), Gallant (1977), and Gallant and Jorgenson (1979). Estimators for systems of nonlinear simultaneous equations are discussed by Malinvaud (1980), Chapter 20.

To implement our econometric models of production and technical change we have assembled a time series data base for thirty-six industrial sectors of the United States. For capital and labor inputs we have first compiled data by sector on the basis of the classification of economic activities employed in the U.S. National Income and Product Accounts. We have then transformed these data into a format appropriate for the classification of activities employed in the U.S. Interindustry Transactions Accounts. For energy and materials inputs we have compiled data by sector on interindustry transactions on the basis of the classification of activities employed in the U.S. Interindustry Transactions Accounts.[12]

The endogenous variables in our models of producer behavior are value shares of sectoral inputs for four commodity groups and the sectoral rate of technical change. We can estimate four equations for each industry, corresponding to three of the value shares and the rate of technical change. As unknown parameters we have three elements of the vector $\{\alpha_p^i\}$, the scalar $\{\alpha_t^i\}$, six share elasticities in the matrix $\{\beta_{pp}^i\}$, which is constrained to be symmetric, three biases of technical change in the vector $\{\beta_{pt}^i\}$, and the scalar $\{\beta_{tt}^i\}$, so that we have a total of fourteen unknown parameters for each industry. We estimate these parameters from time series data for the period 1958–1974 for each industry, subject to the inequality restrictions implied by monotonicity of the sectoral input value shares.

Our interpretation of the empirical results begins with an analysis of estimates of the parameters $\{\alpha_p^i, \alpha_t^i\}$. If all other parameters were set equal to zero, the sectoral price functions would be linear logarithmic in prices and linear in time. The parameters $\{\alpha_p^i\}$ would correspond to constant value shares of inputs and the negative of the parameters $\{\alpha_t^i\}$ to constant rates of technical change. The parameters $\{\alpha_p\}$ are nonnegative for all thirty-six sectors included in our study and are estimated very precisely. The parameters $\{\alpha_t^i\}$ are estimated less precisely and are negative in sixteen sectors and are positive in nineteen sectors. The rate of technical change is identically zero in the Miscellaneous sector.

The estimated share elasticities with respect to price $\{\beta_{pp}^i\}$ describe the implications of patterns of substitution for the distribution of the value of output among capital, labor, energy, and materials inputs. Positive share elasticities imply that the corresponding value shares increase with an increase in price; negative share elasticities imply that the value shares

---

[12] Data on energy and materials are based on annual inter-industry transactions tables for the United States, 1958–1974, compiled by Jack Faucett Associates (1977) for the Federal Emergency Management Agency. Data on labor and capital are based on estimates by Fraumeni and Jorgenson (1980).

decrease with price; zero share elasticities correspond to value shares that are independent of price. The concavity constraints on the sectoral price functions contribute substantially to the precision of our estimates, but require that the share of each input be nonincreasing in the price of the input itself.

By imposing monotonicity on the sectoral input value shares or concavity of the sectoral price functions, we have reduced the number of share elasticities to be fitted from three hundred sixty or ten for each of our thirty-six industrial sectors to one hundred fifty-six or an average of less than five per sector. All share elasticities are constrained to be zero for eleven of the thirty-six industries, so that our representation of technology reduces to a price function that is linear logarithmic in the input prices at any given time for these industries. For thirteen of the thirty-six industries the share elasticities with respect to the price of labor input are set to equal to zero. Finally, for thirty-three of the thirty-six industries the share elasticities with respect to the price of capital input are set to equal to zero.

Our empirical findings on patterns of substitution reveal some striking similarities among industries. We find that the elasticities of the shares of capital with respect to the price of labor are nonnegative for thirty-three of our thirty-six industries, so that the shares of capital are nondecreasing in the price of labor for these thirty-three sectors. Similarly, elasticities of the share of capital with respect to the price of energy are nonnegative for thirty-four industries and elasticities with respect to the price of materials are nonnegative for all thirty-six industries. We find that the share elasticities of labor with respect to the prices of energy and materials are nonnegative for nineteen and for all thirty-six industries, respectively. Finally, we find that the share elasticities of energy with respect to the price of materials are nonnegative for thirty of the thirty-six industries.

We continue the interpretation of our empirical results with estimated biases of technical change with respect to price $\{\beta_{pt}^i\}$. We can interpret these parameters as changes in the sectoral value shares (3) with respect to time, holding prices constant. This component of change in the value shares can be attributed to changes in technology rather than to substitution among inputs in response to price changes. For example, if the bias of technical change with respect to the price of capital input is positive, we say that technical change is capital-using; if the bias is negative, we say that technical change is capital-saving.

Considering the rate of technical change (4), we can interpret the biases of technical change $\{\beta_{pt}^i\}$ in a completely different way. These parameters are changes in the negative of the rate of technical change with respect to changes in prices. As substitution among inputs takes place in response to price changes, the rate of technical change is altered. For example, if the bias of technical change with respect to capital input is positive, an increase

Table 1. *Classification of industries by biases of technical change*

Pattern of biases	Industries
Capital using Labor using Energy using Material saving	Agriculture, metal mining, crude petroleum and natural gas, nonmetallic mining, textiles, apparel, lumber, furniture, printing, leather, fabricated metals, electrical machinery, motor vehicles, istruments, miscellaneous manufacturing, transportation, trade, finance, insurance and real estate, services
Capital using Labor using Energy saving Material saving	Coal mining, tobacco manufactures, communications, government enterprises
Capital using Labor saving Energy using Material saving	Petroleum refining
Capital using Labor saving Energy saving Material using	Construction
Capital saving Labor saving Energy using Material saving	Electric utilities
Capital saving Labor using Energy saving Material saving	Primary metals
Capital saving Labor using Energy using Material saving	Paper, chemicals, rubber, stone, clay and glass, machinery except electrical, transportation equip- ment and ordnance, gas utilities
Capital saving Labor saving Energy using Material using	Food

in the price of capital input reduces the rate of technical change; if the bias is negative, an increase in the price of capital input increases the rate of technical change. Biases of technical change establish a direct link between price changes and the rate of technical change.

A classification of industries by patterns of the biases of technical change is given in Table 1. The pattern that occurs with greatest frequency is capital-using, labor-using, energy-using, and materials-saving technical change. This pattern occurs for nineteen of the thirty-five industries for which we have fitted biases. Since the rate of technical change is identically zero for the Miscellaneous sector, all biases of technical change are set equal to zero. We find that technical change is capital-using for twenty-five of the thirty-five industries, labor-using for thirty-one industries, energy-using for twenty-nine industries, and materials-using for only two industries.

The patterns of biases of technical change given in Table 1 have important implications for the relationship between relative prices and the rate of economic growth. An increase in the price of materials increases the rate of technical change in thirty-three of the thirty-five industries we have considered. By contrast, increases in the prices of capital, labor, and energy reduce the rate of technical change in twenty-five, thirty-one, and twenty-nine industries, respectively. The substantial increases in energy prices since 1973 have had the effect of reducing sectoral rates of technical change, slowing the aggregate rate of technical change, and diminishing the rate of growth for the U.S. economy as a whole.[13]

The final parameter in our models of producer behavior is the rate of change of the negative of the rate of technical change $\{\beta^i_{tt}\}$. We find that the rate of technical change is decreasing with time for twenty-four of the thirty-five industries and increasing for the remaining eleven. While the biases of technical change with respect to the prices of capital, labor, energy, and materials inputs are estimated very precisely, we find that the rates of change are estimated with much less precision. Overall, our empirical results suggest a considerable degree of similarity across the industries, especially in the qualitative character of the distribution of the value of output among inputs and of changes in technology.

III. Conclusion

Our empirical results for sectoral patterns of production and technical change are very striking and suggest a considerable degree of similarity across industries. However, it is important to emphasize that these results have been obtained under strong simplifying assumptions. First, for all industries we have employed conditions for producer equilibrium under perfect competition; we have assumed constant returns to scale at the industry level; finally, we have employed a description of technology that leads to myopic decision rules. These assumptions must be justified primarily by their usefulness in implementing production models that are uniform for all thirty-six industrial sectors of the U.S. economy.

Although it might be worthwhile to weaken each of the assumptions we have enumerated above, a more promising direction for further research appears to lie within the framework provided by these assumptions. First we can provide a more detailed model for allocation among productive inputs. We have disaggregated energy and materials into thirty-six groups

---

[13] Implications of patterns of biases of technical change are discussed in more detail by Jorgenson (1981).

—five types of energy and thirty-one types of materials—by constructing a hierarchy of models for allocation within the energy and materials aggregates. For this purpose we have assumed that each aggregate is homothetically separable within the sectoral production function. We assume, for example, that the share of energy in the value of sectoral output depends on changes in technology, while the share of, say, electricity in the value of energy input does not.

The second research objective suggested by our results is to incorporate the production models for all thirty-six industrial sectors into a general equilibrium model of production in the U.S. economy. An econometric general equilibrium model of the U.S. economy has been constructed for nine industrial sectors by Hudson and Jorgenson (1974). This model is currently being disaggregated to the level of the thirty-six industrial sectors included in our study. A novel feature of the thirty-six sector general equilibrium model will be the endogenous treatment of the rate of technical change for thirty-five of the thirty-six industries we have analyzed. A general equilibrium model will make it possible to analyze the implications of sectoral patterns of substitution and technical change for substitution and technical change in the U.S. economy as a whole.

References

Amemiya, T.: The nonlinear two-stage least squares estimator. *Journal of Econometrics 2* (2), 105–110, 1974.
— The maximum likelihood estimator and the nonlinear three-stage least squares estimator in the general nonlinear simultaneous equation model. *Econometrica 45* (4), 955–968, 1977.
Arrow, K. J., Chenery, H. B. Minhas, B. S. & Solow, R. M.: Capital–labor substitution and economic efficiency. *Review of Economics and Statistics 43*, (3), 225–50, 1961.
Ben-Zion, U. & Ruttan, V. W.: Aggregate demand and the rate of technical change. In. *Induced innovation*, (ed. H. P. Binswanger and V. W. Ruttan), pp. 261–275. Johns Hopkins University Press, Baltimore, 1978.
Berndt, E. R., & Jorgenson, D. W.: Production structure, Chapter 3 in D. W. Jorgenson and H. S. Houthakker, eds., *U.S. energy resources and economic growth*. Energy Policy Project, Washington, 1973.
Berndt, E. R. & Wood, D. O.: Technology, prices, and the derived demand for energy. *Review of Economics and Statistics 56* (3), 259–268, 1975.
— Engineering and econometric interpretations of energy–capital complementarity. *American Economic Review, 69* (3), 342–354, 1979.
Binswanger, H. P.: The measurement of technical change biases with many factors of production. *American Economic Review 64* (5), 964–976, 1974.
— Induced technical change: Evolution of thought. In *Induced innovation*, (ed. H. P. Binswanger and V. W. Ruttan), pp. 13–43. Johns Hopkins University Press, Baltimore, 1978 *a*.
— Issues in modeling induced technical change. In *Induced innovation*, (ed. Binswanger and V. W. Ruttan), pp. 128–163. Johns Hopkins University Press, Baltimore, 1978 *b*.
Blackorby, C., Primont, D. & Russell, R. R.: *Duality, separability, and functional structure*. North-Holland, Amsterdam, 1978.
Burmeister, E. & Dobell, A. R.: Disembodied technological change with several factors. *Journal of Economic Theory 1*, (1), 1–8, 1969.
Christensen, L. R., Jorgenson, D. W.& Lau, L. J.: Conjugate duality and the transcendental logarithmic production function. *Econometrica 39* (4), 255–256, 1971.

The purpose of this paper is to establish short-run industry functions for the Norwegian primary aluminum industry and to utilize these in analyzing technical progress and structural change over the period 1966–1978.

II. The Short-run Industry Production Function

For an industry consisting of a certain number of micro units, the short-run industry production function is established by maximizing output for given levels of current inputs. Thus, it corresponds to the basic definition of a production function when the industry is regarded as *one* production unit.

The *ex post* micro functions are assumed to be of the following limitational type:

$$x = \min\left[\frac{v_1}{\xi_1}, \ldots, \frac{v_n}{\xi_n}, \bar{x}\right],$$ (1)

where x is the rate of output, $\bar{x}$ the capacity limit, v_j current input no. j, and the input coefficients $\xi_j = \bar{v}_j/\bar{x}$ $(j=1, \ldots, n)$ are assumed to be constant, i.e. independent of the rate of capacity utilization.

The short-run industry function $X = F(V_1, \ldots, V_n)$ is obtained by solving the following linear programming problem:

$$\text{Max } X = \sum_{i=1}^{N} x^i \text{ subject to}$$ (2 a)

$$\sum_{i=1}^{N} \xi_j^i x^i \leq V_j \quad j = 1, \ldots, n$$ (2 b)

$$x^i \in [0, \bar{x}^i]$$ (2 c)

where X denotes output and $V_1, \ldots, V_n$ current inputs for the industry as a whole and where $i = 1, \ldots, N$ refers to plants.

The short-run function explicitly recognizes that the technology of the individual micro units differs. It utilizes all these technologies when establishing, by explicit optimization, the relationships between the aggregate industry output and inputs. Thus, in a putty-clay world, the short-run function is the true function for the *industry* as a whole. Due to the unique relationship between actual technologies and the short-run function, this function and its derived relationships provide us with a well-defined concept of industrial structure.

In particular, the following three aspects of technical change can be studied empirically on the basis of a succession of short-run production functions: (i) factor bias, i.e. shift of the substitution region; (ii) productivity change, i.e. shift of the isoquants towards the origin; (iii) changes in the shape of the isoquants, i.e. change in substitution properties.

Since the form of the short-run production function is nonparametric, how should the function be represented? This, of course, depends on the use for which the function is intended. In order to analyze long-run technical progress and structural change, we need a complete representation of each isoquant of the set found suitable for analyzing the three aspects: factor bias, productivity change and change in substitution properties.

Instead of explicitly solving linear programming problems (2), our approach yields—for the two-factor case—a *complete* description of the isoquants by locating all the cornerpoints geometrically. This enables us to provide a full characterization of the production function via marginal productivity, marginal rates of substitution, elasticities of substitution and elasticities of scale. Even for problems with a large number of production units, the computation of isoquants is performed within a very reasonable amount of computer time. For a further description of the algorithm and an empirical analysis of the cement industry, see Førsund & Hjalmarsson (1983).

III. The Data

We had access to data for the Norwegian aluminum industry for the years 1966–1978 from the Norwegian Industrial Statistics for that period. The unit of observation is a plant, which may contain several vintages of smelters. (The ideal unit for our approach would have been the smelter itself.) Additional information was gathered on the capacity output of each plant, which is well-defined for this sector. Moreover, *a priori,* there is good reason to believe that the clay part of our putty-clay assumption, which is the important aspect in this context, is also an appropriate and realistic assumption for this particular industry. The industry is extremely energy intensive, and the technology is almost exclusively based on electric power. Engineering information indicates that raw materials can be treated as shadow factors of production and this is clearly supported by the data. Thus, the current factors under study are labor and electricity. The number of production units is relatively small, varying from 7 to 9 units during the period.

When describing structural changes in the aluminum industry, we focus on four equidistant years: 1966, 1970, 1974 and 1978.

The notation employed is: $N1 =$ labor (hours), $EL =$ electricity (kWh), $X =$ output (tonnes), $K\text{-cum} =$ cumulated shares of capacity. $N1/X$ and EL/X are input coefficients, measured by observed inputs and outputs.

The observed input coefficients for labor and energy for the years 1966 and 1978, are compiled in Figure 1, which also shows the change in the

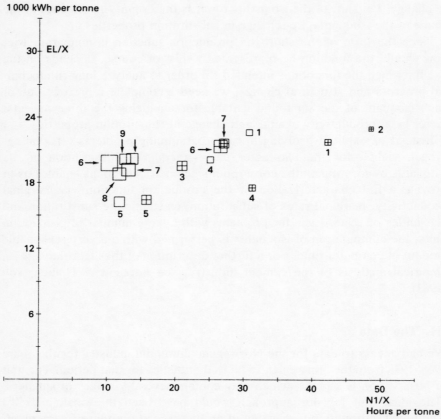

Fig. 1. The capacity distribution in 1966 (cross squares) and in 1978 (empty squares).

capacity distribution. The size of the squares is proportional to capacity. The units are identified by numbers. In general, the production capacity of each unit, except the smallest ones, increased throughout the period. The relatively much greater reduction in labor input coefficients than energy input coefficients is clearly depicted by the almost horizontal shift of the capacity distribution. All units reduced the labor input coefficient, while some smaller units increased the electricity coefficient.

Partial distributions could be used to clarify the development of each of the input coefficients; see Førsund and Jansen (1983). As seen in Figure 1, the range of the labor input coefficient decreased significantly from 1966 to 1978. This concentration and productivity improvement actually took place gradually between 1966 and 1974; the latter year was the last peak year for the Norwegian aluminum industry. Labor productivity had been almost at a standstill between 1974 and 1978.

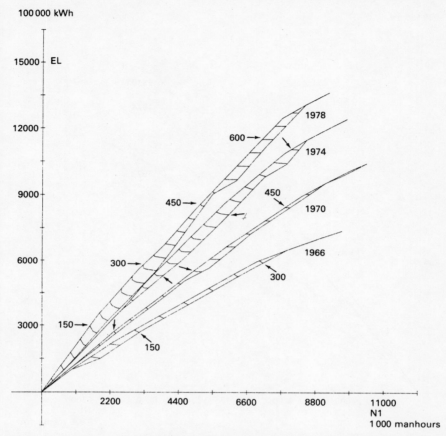

Fig. 2. The development of the short-run industry production function between 1966 and 1978. (The interval between the isoquants represents 30 000 tonnes.)

The range of variation in the electricity coefficient is considerably smaller than for the labor coefficient, and the downward trend over time is very small. In the peak year of 1974, the electricity coefficients were, on the whole, actually somewhat smaller than in 1978. The explanation for this seems to be some variation in the electricity coefficient due to capacity utilization.

Structural changes and introduction of new production techniques are usually regarded as closely related to investment in new capital equipment. In the short run, real capital may be considered fixed, but it may of course change over time.

There was a marked shift upwards over time in the distribution of real capital per tonne of aluminum. This was to be expected due to the vintage

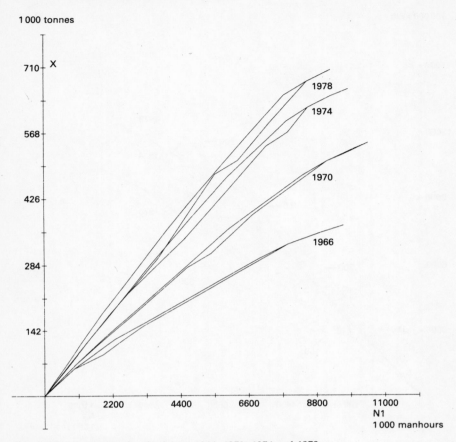

Fig. 3. The demand region for labor, 1966, 1970, 1974 and 1978.

nature of the aluminum industry and *a priori* knowledge about long-run substitution possibilities between the variable inputs—labor and energy—and capital. The correlation across firms between the capital/output coefficients and the input coefficients of energy and labor, respectively, have changed considerably over time. Both correlation coefficients were clearly negative in 1966, thus confirming the possibility of *ex ante* substitution between capital and energy-labor.

In 1978, the energy coefficient was uncorrelated with the capital/output ratio, while the correlation between the labor input coefficient and the capital/output ratio was positive. Further technological improvement as regards electricity consumption had come to a standstill at the same time as labor productivity, due to lower capacity utilization and the difficulties of short-run adjustment of labor.

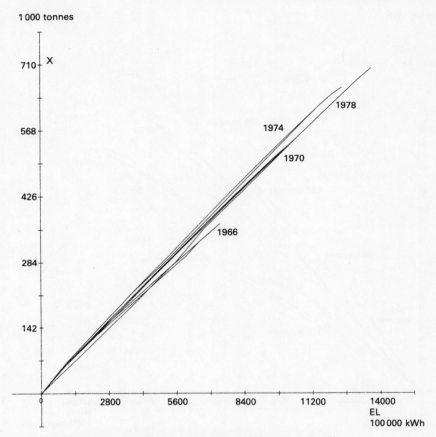

Fig. 4. The demand region for electricity, 1966, 1970, 1974 and 1978.

IV. Empirical Results on the Short-run Industry Production Function

Information about the *ex post* micro production functions must be available in order to derive the short-run industry function. The production capacity of each unit is directly observed, and the fixed current input coefficients are simply calculated by using observed amounts of current inputs and output. This procedure is in accordance with the assumptions made about the *ex post* technology.

The Region of Substitution

The region of substitution and isoquant map of the short-run industry production function for the selected years are set out in Figure 2. The substitution regions are rather narrow for all years, which reflects the uniformity of the technique utilized in Norwegian aluminum plants. The

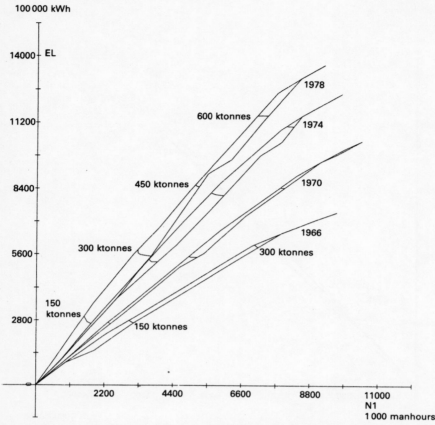

Fig. 5. The short-run industry production functions for the years 1966, 1970, 1974 and 1978 with the isoquants for 150 000, 300 000, 450 000 and 600 000 tonnes.

collapse of the substitution region into one line, as is the case for the tail end in 1966, 1974 and 1978, and for the front end in 1966, 1970 and 1974, corresponds to assigning the same rank number to one unit in the two partial input coefficient distributions. (The probability that this will occur is, of course, higher the smaller the number of production units. Recall that there are only between 7 and 9 units). The remaining scope for substitution on the industry level is markedly largest for labor, as should be expected from the structural description in the preceding section.

The last observation is also valid for the steady shift towards the energy axis revealed in Figure 2. It should also be noted in this context that there are strict physical limitations on the improvement in electricity productivity. According to Johansen & Thonstad (1979) there is—within the existing technology—very little feasible improvement left of the best practice elec-

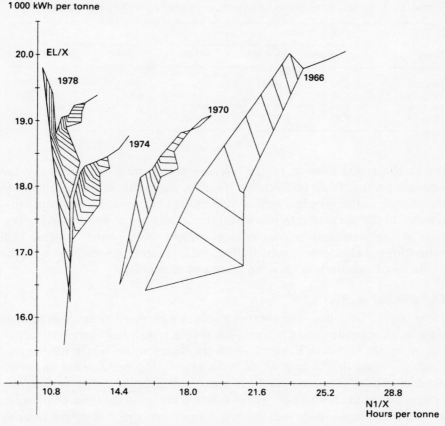

Fig. 6. The development of the capacity region of the short-run industry production function, 1966, 1970, 1974 and 1978.

tricity input coefficient at the 1978 level, while the reduction in labor input coefficients does not contradict any such physical law.

These shifts of the substitution region towards the energy axis are consistent with the changes observed in the relative input prices. The development of these prices shows, with few exceptions, a steady increase in the price of labor relative to the price of electricity; the relative price is nearly doubled during the period of observation.

We note that the isoquants are almost straight lines with only a *few cornerpoints*. Generally, the curvature of an isoquant is characterized by the *elasticity of substitution*. Short-run elasticities can be approximated by analogy with the definition in the case of smooth isoquants.[1] The change in

---

[1] See Table III in Førsund & Hjalmarsson (1983).

Table 1. *Technical progress. Reduction in unit costs; 1978 prices*

| Years | Output level | | | | |
	Frontier	150 000	300 000	450 000	600 000
1966–70	0.95	0.86	0.78	–	–
1970–74	0.86	0.84	0.85	0.83	–
1974–78	1.04	1.01	0.98	0.98	0.96
1966–78	0.85	0.72	0.65	–	–

the factor ratio, relative to the average factor ratio measured for the extreme points of two consecutive isoquant segments, is set in relation to the change in the marginal rate of substitution between the two segments, relative to the average rate of substitution. Contrary to the visual impression of the isoquants approximating straight lines, which implies high values for the elasticity of substitution, we find rather low estimates for the elasticity of substitution between labor and electricity.[2]

The demand regions

What implications does the short-run industry production function have as regards industry demand for inputs? A simple transformation of the substitution regions shown in Figure 2 yields the region within which the demand functions must lie for any set of input prices. Figures 3 and 4 show the demand regions for labor and electricity, respectively. The regions are projections of the borders of the substitution region in the three-dimensional output and input space into the two-dimensional space of output and one input in turn.

The upward shift of the labor demand regions is marked. The demand regions for electricity are extremely narrow and ray-like, and stable over time.

Productivity changes

The productivity improvements for various levels of output can be studied in Figure 2 by following the movement of the isoquants in question. The interval length in Figure 2 is 30 000 tonnes. The levels of 150 000, 300 000, 450 000 and 600 000 tonnes are shown separately in Figure 5. The almost exclusively labor-saving movement is clearly portrayed. Energy productivity even decreased from the high capacity utilization year 1974 to the lower rate of capacity utilization year 1978 for all levels of output.

The movement towards the electricity axis is also clearly observable by

---

[2] Low values for the elasticity of substitution, however, are in accordance with the conjectures in Hildenbrand (1981).

Table 2. *Factor bias. Change in the optimal electricity/labor factor ratios* $(EL/N1)_{t+1}/(EL/N1)_t$; *1978 prices*

Years	Output level				
	Frontier	150 000	300 000	450 000	600 000
1966–70	1.10	1.25	1.31	–	–
1970–74	1.19	1.22	1.32	1.36	–
1974–78	1.01	1.16	1.16	1.13	1.18
1966–78	1.32	1.77	2.02	–	–

looking at the isoquant maps within the substitution regions transformed from the input space of Figure 2 to the input coefficient space, carried out in Figure 6. These transformations represent the feasible regions of input coefficients for the short-run industry function, and must then necessarily show more limited variations than the capacity distributions of individual units shown in Figure 1.

As regards energy usage, Figure 6 shows that the frontier values of the electricity input coefficients were quite stable, except for an extra low value for one unit in 1974. Industry improvement amounted to the other units catching up with best practice performance. This trend was weakened from 1974, the year with high capacity utilization, to 1978, a year with a less than average rate of capacity utilization. The transformation of the isoquants to the input space brings out these movements more sharply over time. The downward movement to the southwest in 1974 and the increase again in electricity coefficients in 1978 to about the same level as in 1970 are clearly portrayed.

Measures of technical progress

Following Salter (1960), the significance of technical change can be assessed by computing the relative change in unit costs at constant input prices and output levels. We have chosen to use the average observed

Table 3. *Development of the scale elasticity along the average factor rays*

Year	Output levels in 1 000 tonnes							Energy/labor: Average factor ratio
	100	200	300	400	500	600	700	
1966	0.89	0.86	0.89	–	–	–	–	0.76
1970	0.91	0.94	0.94	0.92	0.94	–	–	1.00
1974	0.96	0.98	0.94	0.96	0.95	0.91	–	1.26
1978	0.94	0.93	0.95	0.97	0.94	0.95	0.42	1.47

N.kr per tonne

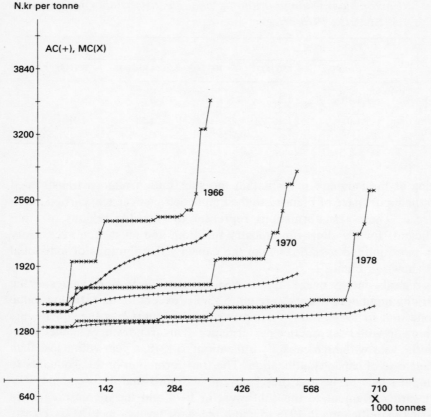

Fig. 7. The marginal and average cost functions, MC (×) and AC (+), respectively, for 1966, 1970 and 1978 in 1978 prices.

prices in the last year, 1978. The results for output intervals of 150 000 tonnes, including the frontier, i.e. the best practice performance, are shown in Table 1.

The unit cost reduction from 1966 to 1978 varies significantly from the frontier at about 85 percent to much higher reductions in unit costs at higher output levels, e.g. 65 percent at 300 000 tonnes. Corresponding to what was revealed by Figure 6, the only significant improvement of the frontier was from 1970–1974. But this was due to only a single individual unit, and performance slipped again, resulting in an *increase* in unit costs at best practice from 1974 to 1978. The average "catching up" with best practice performance appears in Table 1, with the greatest unit cost reductions at higher output levels. The technical advance from 1974 to 1978 was very small indeed; the reduction in labor input coefficients just offset *increases* in electricity input coefficients. The technical progress measure is in terms of reductions in current costs. In order to obtain a complete picture, the capital costs should also be taken into account.

The degree of factor-saving bias can be expressed by computing Salter's (1960) measure of bias, i.e. the change in the cost-minimizing factor ratios for consecutive time periods, *keeping factor prices constant* at the 1978 level. At the frontier, the electricity/labor ratio increased by 32 percent for the whole period; the change took place between 1966 and 1974. The labor-saving bias is greater the higher the output level, and is 102 percent for the whole period for an output level of 300 000 tonnes (see Table 2).

Only a few points on the average cost curves were utilized in Table 1. The complete average cost curves for 1966, 1970 and 1978 are set out in Figure 7 along with the marginal cost curves, all based on 1978 average observed input prices. (The curves for 1974 are excluded because they are so close to the 1978 curves, as is evident from Table 1.)

Salter measures at various output levels may be calculated by comparing average costs in Figure 7. As regards the shape of the average cost curve, it has flattened out.

The form of the marginal cost curves add to the structural picture. They have become increasingly similar to the average cost curves, and the tail on the J-shape applies to smaller and smaller shares of the output capacity. This development supports the impression of growing uniformity in the structure of aluminum smelters.

This uniformity is caused by both labor-saving investments undertaken by all plants more or less at the same time, and small improvements over the period in the basic process of smelting the raw material input alumina.[3] The structure is very similar to that which appears in long-run steady state with no technological change. From an economic policy point of view, the structure in 1978 implied that the *whole* industry could incur a loss, at the same time that the aluminium price was falling on the world market.

The elasticity of scale

Additional structural features can be brought out by looking at values of the elasticity of scale (i.e. an increase in output on the short-run function by a proportional increase in current inputs). The development of the scale elasticity for the average factor ratio is shown in Table 3. (When the factor ray is outside the substitution region, the scale elasticity on the bordering isoquant segment in question is used.)

The maximal value of the scale elasticity in short-run industry functions of the type constructed is 1.0. The level of the elasticities increased from 1966 to 1974. The high values in 1974 and 1978 again reflect the technical

---

[3] A brief description of the production technology is given in Førsund & Jansen (1983).

uniformity of the units. The extremely low value for the highest output level in 1978 is due to the fact that the least efficient unit was utilized, corresponding to the top of the tail of the J-shaped marginal cost curve for that year.

V. Concluding remarks

The short-run industry production function for aluminum is characterized by narrow substitution regions for all years, reflecting a high degree of technical uniformity among Norwegian aluminum smelters.

There was a marked shift of the substitution region towards the electricity axis. Direct substitution between electricity and labor is possible only to a very limited extent when capital is a variable factor. Thus we interpret the results as clear evidence of labor-saving technical change over the period of observation, probably induced by the rise in the relative price of labor as compared to electricity (by a factor of about 2 over the period 1966–1978) and the technical possibilities for cost reduction.

References

Førsund, F. R. & Hjalmarsson, L.: Technological progress and structural change in the Swedish cement industry 1955–1979. Forthcoming, *Econometrica*, 1983.

Førsund, F. R. & Jansen, E. S.: Analysis of energy-intensive industries—the case of Norwegian aluminium production. In *Analysis of supply and demand of electricity in the Norwegian economy* (ed. O. Bjerkholt et al.). Social Economic Studies, 53, Central Bureau of Statistics, Oslo, 1983.

Hildenbrand, W.: Short-run production functions based on microdata. *Econometrica 49*, 1095–1125, 1981.

Johansen, L.: *Production functions*. North Holland Publ. Co., Amsterdam, 1972.

Johansen, P. & Thonstad, J.: Aluminium processing, technology and prospects. Final report (in Norwegian). *SINTEF-rapport STF 34*, Trondheim, 1979.

Salter, W. E. G.: *Productivity and technical change*. Cambridge University Press, Cambridge, UK, 1960.

Neoclassical Modeling of Nonneutral Technological Change: An Experimental Appraisal*

Raymond J. Kopp

Resources for the Future, Washington, DC, USA

V. Kerry Smith

University of North Carolina, Chapel Hill, NC, USA

Abstract

The results of an experimental evaluation of the performance of neoclassical models, using alternative indexes of the pace of introduction of innovations to measure the effects of technical change on the patterns of factor input usage, are reported. The analysis maintains that production processes should be viewed as engineering activities, so that neoclassical characterizations of them and of any innovations to them are best treated as approximations. Two large-scale process analysis models provide the description of the "true" production technology with and without access to six specific process innovations. The analysis considered both input aggregation and the index of the extent of technical innovation. The results suggest that indexes which are explicitly tied to the technical features of the innovations involved perform better in isolating the direction of the input effects associated with each innovation. Moreover this conclusion was found to hold with differing levels of input aggregation.

I. Introduction

Several recent studies, e.g. Berndt & Khaled (1979) and Jorgenson & Fraumeni (1981) as notable examples, have attempted to decompose and measure the contribution of technical change to economic growth over the recent past. While these papers represent important contributions to our understanding of the effects of technical change, they have had to rely on a crude index of the pace of technological innovation—a time trend.[1] Recent-

---

* Thanks are due an anonymous referee for most constructive comments on an earlier draft of this paper. This research was partially supported by grants from the National Science Foundation (DAR-7921-805), the Mellon Foundation, and a contract with the Electric Power Research Institute.
[1] The difficulties in deriving independent estimates of technological change have been recognized for nearly twenty years. Stigler (1961) was among the first to question the change and scale effects with time series information. The recent literature has drawn quite similar conclusions. Berndt and Khaled (1979) and Lopez (1980) have both reported difficulty in accurately distinguishing nonneutral technical change and non-homothetic production structures.

ly, Denny et al. (1981) have found that explicit indicators of the pace of introduction of technological changes perform better in estimating the effects of innovations on a neoclassical cost function for the Bell Canada telecommunications network. Further support can also be found in Christensen et al. (forthcoming). That is, their analysis of scale economies for the U.S. telecommunications industry indicated that a time trend did not provide a useful index of changes in this technology. Both of these studies used specific indexes of innovations to the production activities involved, such as measures of the access to modern switching facilities and the percentage of long distance calls directly dialed.[2]

Unfortunately, to appraise the implications of using these more specific indexes of innovations to describe the influence of technological change for these production activities, these studies have had to rely on *a priori* beliefs with respect to the influence of new technologies together with judgemental comparisons of the quality of all the estimated parameters with alternative indexes of technological change.

The purpose of this paper is to report the findings of the first evaluation of alternative indexes of the rate of introduction of production innovations for the measurement of the nonneutral changes in input usage as a result of technical change. Our analysis utilizes an experimental framework with control over the conditions under which new innovations are added to a given set of production activities and with the ability to measure the pace of their introduction. In Section II we outline the framework used in our analysis and describe the experimental design. Our results for a variety of indexes of technical change, using each of five input aggregations, are described in Section III. The implications of these findings for measuring the pace of technical change within conventional neoclassical models of production activities are discussed in Section IV.

II. The Conceptual Framework and Experimental Design

Ideal measures of the implications of technical change for each input's usage would distinguish the substitutions between inputs within a given technology (as a result of changes in relative factor prices) from those arising thru a nonneutral displacement in the isoquant map. This distinction was first emphasized by Salter (1960) and more recently has been opera-

---

[2] Randy Nelson, in on-going empirical research, has also found evidence consistent with these conclusions. Using data for fossil-fuel fired steam generating firms, he finds that the index of technological change has a significant impact on the changes in input usage attributed to technical innovations. His results compared a time trend with an index computed as the weighted average age of each firm's steam generating equipment, with the weights based on each BTG unit's contribution to total steam generating capacity.

tionalized by Binswanger (1974). His framework assumes that it is possible to estimate the extent of input substitution for a static set of production activities.[3] If these features are described using cost share elasticities,[4] then the effects of static input substitution on changes in inputs' cost shares can be characterized as in (1):

$$dM_i = \sum_{j=1}^{n} \varepsilon_{ij} \frac{dP_j}{P_j}, \quad i = 1, 2, \ldots, n \tag{1}$$

where:

dM_i = price induced change in the ith input's cost share

ε_{ij} = ith input's cost share elasticity with respect to the jth input's price (i.e., $\varepsilon_{ij} = \partial M_i / \partial \ln P_j$).

P_j = jth input's price

n = number of factor inputs.

Given measures of the change in each factor's actual cost shares over time along with the corresponding pattern of changes in inputs' prices, it is possible to measure the nonneutral changes in input usage due to technical change as the unexplained residual defined in (2) below.

$$dR_i = dM_i^A - dM_i = dM_i^A - \sum_{j=1}^{n} \varepsilon_{ij} \frac{dP_j}{P_j} \tag{2}$$

where:

dR_i = index of nonneutral technical changes for the ith factor input

dM_i^A = actual change in the cost share of the ith factor over some time interval in which the changes in factor prices were observed.

Unfortunately, we do not generally have access to an independent estimate of the features of the static technology (i.e. the ε_{ij}'s). Since we observe the effect of both static input substitution possibilities and nonneutral changes in input usage due to innovations in actual measures of the changes in inputs' cost shares, we must introduce additional information to the model in order to separate the respective contributions of each. That is, a specific role must be assigned to some index of the pace of technical change in a neoclassical cost or profit function. For example, using a translog cost function corresponding to a nonhomothetic technology, tech-

---

[3] Binswanger (1974), (1978) actually proposed two methods—the unrestricted indexes of nonneutral changes in factor shares and a parametrization of the neoclassical cost function similar to Eq. (3) for those cases where the static technology could not be estimated directly.
[4] This terminology was introduced in Christensen, Jorgenson and Lau (1980) and has been used by Samuelson (1973) in his discussion of the relationship between elasticities of substitution. The share elasticity, ε_{ij}, is defined as the change in the ith factor's cost share with respect to the natural log of the jth factor's price.

nical change has often been introduced with additional first and second-order terms in an index of the extent of introduction of the new technologies as in (3).[5] The variable T is the index of the pace of technical change and Q represents output.

$$\ln C = \alpha_0 + \alpha_1 \ln Q + \alpha_2 (\ln Q)^2$$
$$+ \sum_{j=1}^{n} \beta_j \ln P_j + \frac{1}{2} \sum_{i=1}^{n} \sum_{j=1}^{n} \varepsilon_{ij} \ln P_i \cdot \ln P_j$$
$$+ \sum_{j=1}^{n} \Theta_j \ln Q \cdot \ln P_j + \delta_1 T + \delta_2 (T)^2$$
$$+ \sum_{j=1}^{n} \gamma_j T \cdot \ln P_j \tag{3}$$

This specification is equivalent to assuming that the general index of nonneutral input usage defined above, dR, was a multiple of dT (i.e., for (3) $dR_i = \gamma_i dT$). While there may be some reasons to question this particular specification,[6] it is clear that the definition of T is central to the plausibility of the estimates of the effects of technical change.

As we noted at the outset, most past analyses of the magnitude and pattern of technical change in production activities have used a time trend (or its natural log) for T. This choice is simply a crude proxy for the unknown pace with which new technologies have been introduced into existing production processes. The work of Fuss et al. and Christensen et al. represents the first attempts to provide an alternative characterization of the pace of technological change by using measures of diffusion of specific innovations in Canadian and U.S. telecommunications firms.

Our analysis evaluates the performance of alternative indexes of the rate at which new technologies are being introduced within a given hypothetical firm. These indexes include measures tied to specific innovations (analogous to those used by Denny et al. and Christensen et al.) as well as an

---

[5] There are several different treatments of T which have been used with the time trend as the index of the pace of introduction of new innovations. These include: the use of the trend directly, i.e., $T = 1, 2, 3, ..., N$; the natural logarithm of the trend, i.e., $T = \log (t)$; and each of these additional specifications with restrictions on the parameters for the second order terms in T and the logs of factor prices; see Wills (1979) as an example.

[6] For example, Kamien and Schwartz's (1968) analysis of the patterns of induced technical change concluded that:

> "the preferred technical change need not be exclusively of one sort (e.g., 'neutral' change). Once 'neutral' technical change becomes optimal, however, it remains so until there is a change in relative factor prices. On the other hand, the adoption of a 'biased' technical change may eventually cause 'neutral' advance to become desired even in the absence of relative factor price changes." (Kamien & Schwartz (1968), p. 16)

overall measure for all innovations that would be more closely aligned to what an ideal time trend might attempt to measure. The analysis does maintain a particular view of neoclassical models of production activities. We assume that neoclassical models are best interpreted as approximate descriptions of the complex engineering activities present in actual production processes; see Marsden et al. (1974) and Kopp & Smith (1980 *b*). Technical change arises thru the adoption of process innovations involving new capital equipment.[7] This perspective implies that a fully disaggregated description of the static production activities would *not* include the factor inputs (i.e., types of capital equipment) associated with future process innovations. Thus both the Binswanger decomposition, given in Eq. (2), and the more structured approach, as in Eq. (3), for measuring nonneutral technical change would be incomplete. These problems do not arise in practice because inputs are not described in fully disaggregated form. Nonetheless these differences in the composition of the factor inputs available under the static and innovation augmented technologies have significant implications for the procedures that can be used to evaluate the performance of alternative indexes of the pace of technological change, and will be described below.

The logic underlying our experimental analysis is somewhat detailed. Two large-scale process analysis models have been used to depict the static production technology and the technology augmented with six process innovations. Both models are based on the work of Russell & Vaughan (1976), and Vaughan et al. (1976). Each offers a complete technical description of the physical activities involved in steel production within a cost-minimizing, linear programming framework. One of the models was used to describe static *ex ante* production decisions, allowing any one or all of three types of steelmaking processes (i.e., basic oxygen (BOF), open hearth (OH), and electric arc) to be utilized for steel production. The second version model expanded the tecchnology matrix for the static production processes from 694 to 826 columns to include the six innovations, each described in specific engineering terms. At 1973 input prices, these innovations reduce the model's estimate of unit costs by 10.4%. In each case the innovations provide the ability to replace or supplement existing processing activities. They include: (1) scrap preheating before its introduction in a BOF furnace to increase the cold metal that can be used in the charge; (2) direct reduction of iron ore for use in the electric arc furnace; (3) coal gasification to provide an alternative source of fuel for the direct reduction; (4) cryogenic shredding for automobile derived scrap to reduce the portion of nonferrous materials in the scrap; (5) continuous casting to replace

---

[7] This framework is consistent with the embodiment hypothesis for modeling the introduction of technological innovations into existing production technologies.

several stages in conventional finishing activities; and (6) extended fuel injection to replace some coke in the blast furnace.

Our experiments utilize both models. Our objective is to use the Binswanger idealized index of nonneutral technical change, defined in Eq. (2), as a benchmark for evaluating each of four indexes of the pace of technical change. This requires that estimates of the features of the static *ex ante* technology, i.e., the ε_{ij}'s in Eq. (2), be used to decompose changes in each factor input's cost share in the sample of solutions derived from the innovation augmented model. Using these estimates of the direction of nonneutral input usage implied by each innovation, we can evaluate the neoclassical models that attempt to measure the patterns of input substitution and nonneutral technical change simultaneously, as described in Eq. (3). Our evaluation has considered two aspects of such a model's specification: (a) the definition of the factor inputs to production; and (b) the index of the pace of technological change.

To implement this logic one sample was drawn from each model (i.e., static *ex ante* and innovation augmented), by using the models' respective solutions for variations in each factor input's price over four multiples (k) of the base 1973 prices with $k=0.1$, 0.75, 1.45 and 3.0. In designing these solutions we have defined 31 separate factor inputs in order to provide the basis for the alternative input aggregations and to allow each innovation to be identified by the capital equipment associated with it. Consistent aggregation of the subcomponents of each of the 31 inputs is assured by varying the price of each member of each input in the same proportion; see Diewert (1974) for discussion of this production analog to the Hicks composite commodity theorem.[8] With the base case solution and the four variations in each factor's price our samples consist of 125 solutions for each model.[9]

To develop our benchmark evaluation of the implications of the innovations we estimated a nineteen factor translog cost function using a sample composed of the solutions to the static *ex ante* process model.[10] To summarize the properties of our estimates of the Binswanger indexes we

---

[8] With process models as large and complex as the Russell-Vaughan models, there are likely to be a large number of inputs to production. The reason for the large number of inputs follows from the development of these models. Process detail is introduced, in part, by distinguishing inputs according to their attributes. For example, separate types of Iron Ore might be identified according to the Fe content, sulfur content, and size of the ore particles. For discussion of the implications of input and technology aggregation for neoclassical model see Kopp & Smith (1980*a*), (1980*b*). Smith and Vaughan (1981) discuss the implications of input and process detail for model complexity.

[9] The actual sample used for the estimation of all models eliminated the solutions (4) for price variation in liquid nitrogen, because this input is exclusively associated with the innovation cryogenic shredding which was never adopted in any of the solutions to the innovation augmented model.

[10] A more detailed discussion of the properties of the nineteen factor cost function is given in Kopp & Smith (1981).

regressed each factor input's index on the shares of capital expenditures associated with each of the innovations adopted in these solutions. A comparison of these indexes with the engineering features of the innovations indicated that they consistently describe the primary factor usage effects of each innovation; see Kopp & Smith (1981). Thus, they offer an appropriate benchmark for evaluating the estimated nonneutralities in input usage derived from models such as Eq. (3) under alternative definitions of *T*.

Before proceeding to a discussion of the performance of neoclassical models which attempt to distinguish input substitution and nonneutral technical change by specifying a role for an index of the pace of technological change in a cost function, we should consider another potential standard for evaluating such models. An obvious standard would seem to be available directly from our data. That is, one might suppose it would be possible to match observations from the two samples (i.e. static *ex ante* and innovation augmented) by the specified factor price change and calculate the true change in each input's cost share due to technological change from the cost share changes observed in each of the two samples. The change in cost share in the static *ex ante* sample due to the factor price change would measure the effects of input substitution. The change observed in the innovation augmented model would represent the effects of both input substitution and innovation induced changes. Thus the difference between these measures would (for the *same* change in factor prices) appear to provide an ideal standard to use in the evaluation of the neoclassical model's parameterization of technical change within a cost function.[11]

Unfortunately, this approach is not feasible, because there are never circumstances where the price changes for the factor inputs involved are comparable (despite the comparability in the initial design at the 31 input level). The reason for this incompatibility arises from the need to model innovations within a framework that includes their equipment as part of specific aggregated factor inputs. The price index for these aggregated factors will not be comparable between solutions from the static *ex ante* and innovation augmented models with the same specified variation in input prices at the thirty-one input level. For example, selecting a form of Tornqvist approximation to a Divisia price index in the two cases, will require not only the price of all the components to the inputs to change in the same proportion for the two models, but in addition the shares of total expenditures on the specific aggregate omit accounted for by each factor must remain invariant. The very process of adopting an innovation changes these shares for those aggregate factor inputs which include innovation related equipment among their components. Hence we cannot define solu-

---

[11] We are grateful to an anonymous referee for drawing our attention to this issue.

Table 1. *Definition of factor inputs for experimental design*

Input number	Input description
1	Maintenance
2	Metallurgical and Eastern coal
3	Western coal
4	Natural gas
5	Fuel oil
6	Iron ore
7	Purchased scrap
8	Labor
9	All other operating inputs
10	Silicon carbide
11	Lime
12	Liquid nitrogen
13	Coking capital
14	Boiler-turbine generator capital
15	Sinter capital
16	Blast furnace capital
17*	Extended fuel injection capital (innovation)
18	BOF steelmaking furnace capital
19*	Scrap preheating capital (innovation)
20	OH steelmaking furnace capital
21	ARC steelmaking furnace capital
22	Finishing capital
23*	Continuous casting capital (innovation)
24*	Direct reduction capital (innovation)
25*	Coal gasification capital (innovation)
26	Scrap processing capital
27*	Cryogenic shredding capital (innovation)
28	Air pollution control equipment capital
29	Air pollution by-product recovery equipment capital
30	Water pollution control equipment capital
31	Water pollution by-product recovery equipment capital

* Indicates a process innovation measure.

tions with "comparable" changes in relative factor prices. The nature of our measures of the price change for aggregated factors will be affected by the presence of the innovation. This point also serves to highlight the possibility of an interrelationship between the definition of factor inputs (i.e. level of input aggregation) and the performance of indexes of the pace of technological change.

Since only three of the six innovations were adopted in the solutions to the innovation augmented model, our specific indexes of the pace of technological change will be confined to them. They were scrap preheating, continuous casting, and direct reduction. In each case we used the fraction of total capital expenditures associated with the equipment for each innovation (with all capital priced using service prices).[12] These capital shares

---

[12] The base period prices for the noncapital inputs are estimates of 1973 producer's prices for each factor. The base period prices for capital services follow the neoclassical tradition of Hall

were ranked to provide an ordinal index for each of the three innovations. Our general index follows the same procedure but uses the sum of expenditures on all innovations relative to capital expenditures for the ranking. Each of these indexes was used individually with each of five translog cost functions corresponding to alternative input definitions.[13] The estimated nonneutrality parameters for the index of technical change, i.e. the γ_j's in Eq. (3), for each input definition can then be compared with the description provided from Binswanger's decomposition indexes to evaluate the effects of the index used to measure the pace of technical change.

Table 1 defines the thirty-one inputs used in our design of solutions to each of the two process models. They have been structured to reflect the diversity of capital equipment, energy, and materials inputs to the steel-making technologies. The most disaggregate model used in our econometric analysis involved 19 inputs.[14] Inputs were also aggregated in steps to a four factor KLEM (capital, labor, energy and materials) framework. Table 2 defines the relationship between three of these definitions (the 19, 11 and 9 factor models) and the original 31 factor framework. The remaining two models bear the closest correspondence to current applications—a four factor KLEM and a five factor model that disaggregates the KLEM model's materials into ferrous and nonferrous components. The price indexes used for each input definition were measured using one form of the possible discrete approximations to the Divisia price index. Equation (4) provides a general definition of the price index relationship used for all five models.

& Jorgenson (1967). 1973 prices of investment goods have been collected from industry sources given in Russell & Vaughan (1976) and Vaughan, Russell & Cochrane (1976). For each class of assets a service life was also collected. In the version of the Russell–Vaughan model used in our analysis, we have assumed one-hoss-shay depreciation and have excluded analysis of income tax, investment tax credit and other influences, since our interest is in the effects of differing levels of capital's service price, not the source of these differences.

The service price for each type of capital was computed as:

$$CSP_i = q(r/(1-(1+r)^{-N}i))$$

where:
CSP$_i$ = service price of ith type of capital
   r = rate of return on capital assumed to be 0.10
   q = price of capital good
   N_i = service price of the ith type of capital.

[13] The cost functions are defined for homogeneous technologies of degree one (i.e., constant returns to scale) because the Russell–Vaughan (1976) models are linear programming, process analysis models. This implies the following parametric restrictions to Eq. (3): $\alpha_1=1$, $\alpha_2=0$, and $\Theta_j=0$ for $j=1, 2, \ldots, n$.

[14] The reasons for selecting this level of aggregation follow from two considerations: the prospect for "corner solutions" with zero usage of several inputs with further disaggregation and the computational limits (and costs) to estimating flexible neoclassical cost functions with greater than 19 inputs.

Table 2. *Definition of input aggregates for nineteen, eleven and nine factor models*

Input number	Composition of factor aggregates[a]		
	19 factor model	11 factor model	9 factor model
1	Maintenance 1	Maintenance 1	Nonferrous materials 1+2+3+9+10+11+12
2	Coal 2+3	Coal 2+3	Ferrous materials 6+7
3	Natural gas 4	Natural gas 4	Energy 4+5
4	Fuel oil 5	Fuel oil 5	Labor 8
5	Iron ore 6	Iron ore 6	BTG capacity 14
6	Purchased scrap 7	Purchased scrap 7	Hot metal capital capacity 13+15+16+17+18+19+20
7	Labor 8	Labor 8	Arc capacity 21+24+25+26+27
8	All other operating 9+10+12	All other operating 9+10+11+12	Finishing capital capacity 22+23
9	Lime 11	Steel capital 13+15+16+17+18 +19+20+21+22+23 +24+25+26+27	Pollution abatement capital capacity 28+29+30+31
10	Blast furnace capacity 13+15+16+17	BTG capacity capital 14	–
11	BTG capacity 14	Pollution abatement capital capacity 28+29+30+31	–
12	BOF capacity 18+19	–	–
13	OH capacity 20	–	–
14	ARC capacity 21+24+25+26+27	–	–
15	Finishing capacity 22+23	–	–
16	Air pollution treatment capacity 28	–	–
17	Air pollution recovery capacity 29	–	–
18	Water pollution treatment capacity 30	–	–
19	Water pollution recovery capacity 31	–	–

[a] The number associated with each aggregate indicate the input from the 31 factor definition that is used in these aggregates.

$$\ln P_{Aj} = \sum_{i=1}^{N_A} \overline{M}_{ij}(\ln P_{ij} - \ln P_{iB}) \tag{4}$$

where:

P_{Aj} = price index for the aggregated factor for the jth solution

P_{ij} = price for the ith component of the aggregate used to define factor A for the jth solution

P_{iB} = price for the ith component for the base solution

$\overline{M}_{ij}$ = share of the ith factor in the total expenditures on the N_A components of aggregate A for the jth solution

N_A = number of components for aggregate A.

III. Results

Table 3 reports the summary regression models for each of the Binswanger indexes of nonneutral changes in input usage due to technical change in the nineteen factor model.[15] The cost share elasticities required for these indexes were estimated using a sample composed of the solutions to the static, *ex ante* process model. The restricted Zellner (1962) seemingly unrelated regression estimator was used to estimate the cost share equations derived from a linear homogeneous translog cost function.[16] These estimated parameters exhibit nearly complete agreement in their description of the direction of nonneutral technical change with what would have been anticipated based on the engineering features of each of the three innovations. Accordingly, our evaluation of the performance of indexes of the pace of technical change can rely on a comparison of the signs of these estimated parameters (for the relevant input and innovation specific index) with the signs of the estimated nonneutrality parameters from the cost

---

[15] The specific model used for these results was:

$dR_{ij} = \beta_0 + \beta_1 \text{PREHEA}_j + \beta_2 \text{CONCAS}_j + \beta_3 \text{DIRRED}_j$

where:

dR_{ij} = Binswanger index estimated as defined in Eq. (2) for the 19 factor model with the ith factor and jth solution.

PREHEA_j, CONCAS_j, DIRRED_j = share of total capital expenditures associated with each of scrap preheating, continuous casting, direct reduction for the jth solution.

The numbers in parentheses are t-ratios for the null hypothesis of no association. They are not intended as formal test statistics, but rather as a gauge of the variability in the model's summary of movements in the Binswanger indexes.

[16] The restrictions imposed on these share equations are consistent with linear homogeneity in input prices and symmetry in cross price effects (i.e., the ε_{ij}'s). A more complete discussion of the properties of this neoclassical description of the static *ex ante* technology is given in Kopp & Smith (1981).

Table 3. *Binnwanger's Indexes of nonneutral technical change and specific innovations: The Nineteen Factor Model[a]*

| | Mat | | | | | | Energy | | |
| | Non-Fe Mat. | | | Fe Mat. | | | | | |
Variables	Maint	Coal	Oth.	Line	Ore	Scrap	NGAS	Oil	Lab
Intercept	0.004 (0.279)	0.020 (1.625)	−0.008 (−0.945)	0.004 (1.978)	0.065 (2.473)	−0.179 (−3.074)	0.002 (0.305)	−0.008 (−1.103)	−0.0 (−0.
Prehea	0.085 (1.281)	0.445 (7.968)	−0.017 (−0.455)	0.067 (8.163)	0.960 (8.113)	−1.532 (−5.826)	−0.052 (−2.176)	−0.145 (−4.643)	0.08 (1.40
Concas	−0.021 (−0.314)	−0.125 (−2.202)	0.039 (1.032)	−0.024 (−2.928)	−0.406 (−3.386)	1.078 (4.046)	−0.027 (−1.130)	0.045 (1.416)	−0.0 (−0.
Dirred	0.073 (1.034	−0.303 (−5.069)	0.070 (1.763)	−0.007 (−0.828)	0.126 (0.993)	−0.258 (−0.917)	0.279 (10.941)	0.033 (0.981)	−0.1 (−1.
R^2	0.021	0.717	0.089	0.608	0.561	0.451	0.709	0.354	0.12

[a] The numbers in parentheses below the estimated coefficients are t-ratios for the null hypothesis association.

functions derived using the solutions to the innovation augmented model. These comparisons are straightforward in the case of the innovation specific indexes—PREHEA (scrap preheating), CONCAS (continuous casting), and DIRRED (direct reduction). The analysis of the results using our overall index of the pace of technical change is somewhat more difficult.

Tables 4 thru 6 report our estimates of the nonneutrality parameters, i.e., the γ_j's in Eq. (3), for translog cost functions corresponding to each of the three innovation specific indexes of technological change under five different input definitions.[17] The brackets in each table indicate the relationships between inputs with progressive increases in aggregation moving from left to right in each table (i.e., the 19, 11, 9, 5 and 4 input definitions). Since we are evaluating the neoclassical model as an approximation to an underlying engineering description of this production process and its innovations, there are no "true" values for these estimated parameters. Rather, we have evaluated them by comparing the alternative descriptions of the innovations in the most disaggregated model—Binswanger indexes versus the

---

[17] The results using the Binswanger indexes are based on 98 of the 125 solutions. The solutions associated with variations in the prices of each of the six innovations' capital equipment and liquid nitrogen (an input exclusively associated with cryogenic shredding) were eliminated. The rationale for this omission follows from the objective of the Binswanger decomposition—to classify innovations associated with variation in the factor prices of inputs other than the innovations (or their equipment). By contrast, the cost function estimates are based on all 125 observations. In this case the methodology is attempting to "sort out" static input substitution and innovation related changes in the composition of input usage.

al	STL CAP								
	HM CAP					PA CAP			
	BL. FUR	BOF	OH	ARC	FCAP	AIRT	AIRR	WATT	WATR
6 10)	0.022 (2.175)	0.006 (1.658)	0.001 (0.508)	0.011 (2.077)	0.075 (11.134)	0.000 (0.291)	0.001 (2.978)	−0.001 (−1.050)	0.000 (1.971)
7 222)	0.298 (6.588)	0.212 (13.104)	−0.022 (−3.557)	−0.109 (−4.749)	−0.183 (−5.967)	0.003 (1.439)	0.014 (9.636)	0.000 (0.132)	0.067 (8.163)
)	−0.122 (−2.660)	−0.045 (−2.749)	0.003 (0.394)	−0.051 (−2.201)	−0.363 (−11.712)	−0.001 (−0.552)	−0.007 (−4.427)	0.001 (0.405)	−0.024 (−2.928)
5)	−0.232 (−4.811)	−0.073 (−4.226)	−0.020 (−2.944)	0.419 (17.125)	−0.082 (−2.523)	−0.004 (−1.841)	0.013 (8.413)	0.001 (0.471)	−0.007 (0.828)
	0.669	0.824	0.135	0.868	0.627	0.137	0.593	0.914	0.011

nonneutrality parameters for each of the specific indexes (i.e., comparing the signs of the estimated parameters in each row of Table 3 with those in the relevant columns of Tables 4 thru 6).

Our findings indicate that where *a priori* predictions for input usage effects (based on the engineering features of each innovation) were possible, there was complete agreement between the signs of the estimated parameters measuring nonneutral technical change in the two models. This conclusion was upheld for all three of the innovation specific indexes. It would seem to indicate that despite the adoption of all three innovations simultaneously in most of the model's solutions, a single innovation-specific index in a neoclassical cost function is nonetheless capable of discriminating its respective input effects. Indeed, even with inputs for which the engineering descriptions of these innovations could not be relied upon to unambiguously predict the input usage effects, the signs of the estimated parameters in both models (using the nineteen factor framework) generally agree.[18]

---

[18] When these estimated parameters were "screened" using the ratio of the estimated parameter to its estimated standard error as a gauge of "important" changes in input usage there were only three inconsistencies between the Binswanger results and those derived using the estimated cost functions. One arose for each ranking.

Ranking	*Input with Inconsistency*
PREHEA	Water Pollution Recover Equipment
CONCAS	Arc Capacity
DIRRED	Air Pollution Recovery Equipment

Table 4. *Estimated nonneutrality parameters using expenditures on scrap preheating capital*

Factor inputs	Models				
	19 factor	11 factor	9 factor	5 factor	4 factor
Maintenance	2.00×10^{-5} (0.619)	8.37×10^{-5} (0.266)			
Coal	1.91×10^{-4} (5.134)	2.04×10^{-4} (4.820)	2.82×10^{-4} (4.884)	$-^a$	
All other operating inputs	-1.63×10^{-5} (−0.947)	$-^a$			1.03×10^{-4} (1.928)
Iron ore	2.88×10^{-4} (4.180)	2.97×10^{-4} (3.952)	-2.14×10^{-4} (−2.770)	-2.22×10^{-4} (−2.868)	
Scrap	-4.08×10^{-4} (2.855)	-4.12×10^{-4} (−2.740)			
Fuel oil	-4.40×10^{-5} (−2.605)	-4.81×10^{-5} (−2.797)	-1.75×10^{-4} (−6.525)	-1.84×10^{-4} (−6.610)	-1.74×10^{-4} (−6.189)
Natural gas	-7.55×10^{-5} (−4.432)	-8.26×10^{-5} (−4.499)			
Labor	1.77×10^{-5} (0.649)	2.02×10^{-5} (0.747)	$-^a$	4.37×10^{-5} (1.671)	$-^a$
Blast furnace capital	1.19×10^{-4} (4.270)				
BOF capital	9.25×10^{-5} (7.009)		3.02×10^{-4} (5.877)		
OH capital	-2.85×10^{-6} (−2.996)	7.15×10^{-5} (1.978)			
ARC capital	-1.06×10^{-4} (−5.784)		-1.55×10^{-4} (−6.171)		
Finishing capital	-4.79×10^{-5} (−3.439)		-1.53×10^{-5} (−1.315)		
Air pollution treatment capital	6.90×10^{-7} (0.722)			7.52×10^{-5} (2.090)	4.36×10^{-5} (1.011)
Air pollution recovery capital	3.17×10^{-6} (3.926)				
Water pollution treatment capital	1.78×10^{-8} (0.016)	1.40×10^{-6} (0.745)	2.29×10^{-6} (1.163)		
Water pollution recovery capital	-1.27×10^{-6} (−2.256)				
BTG capital	-5.19×10^{-5} (−6.385)	-5.50×10^{-5} (−5.574)	-6.58×10^{-5} (−5.128)		
$\bar{R}^2$	0.842	0.826	0.854	0.745	0.655

^{a} The cost shares corresponding to these factors were omitted from the estimated system. The numbers in parentheses below the estimated coefficients are t-ratios for the null hypothesis of no association.

Table 5. *Estimated nonneutrality parameters using expenditures on continuous casting capital*

Factor inputs	Models				
	19 factor	11 factor	9 factor	5 factor	4 factor
Maintenance	-8.49×10^{-5} (−2.500)	-7.27×10^{-5} (−2.210)			
Coal	-1.96×10^{-4} (−4.729)	-2.40×10^{-4} (−4.827)	-3.50×10^{-4} (−6.412)	$-^a$ −	
All other operating inputs	1.10×10^{-5} (0.599)	$-^a$ −			1.48×10^{-4} (2.833)
Iron ore	4.57×10^{-4} (−6.416)	-4.77×10^{-4} (−6.496)	5.02×10^{-4} (7.546)	5.11×10^{-4} (7.731)	
Scrap	8.71×10^{-4} (6.012)	8.98×10^{-4} (6.160)			
Fuel oil	5.56×10^{-5} (3.110)	6.12×10^{-5} (3.443)	9.62×10^{-5} (3.299)	1.11×10^{-4} (3.674)	1.06×10^{-4} (3.498)
Natural gas	-1.17×10^{-6} (−0.062)	8.47×10^{-6} (0.415)			
Labor	-3.52×10^{-5} (−1.230)	-3.92×10^{-5} (−1.392)	$-^a$ −	-5.67×10^{-5} (−2.178)	$-^a$ −
Blast furnace capital	-1.43×10^{-4} (−4.707)				
BOF capital	-6.43×10^{-5} (−4.178)		-3.03×10^{-4} (−5.951)		
OH capital	-7.69×10^{-7} (−0.779)	-1.98×10^{-4} (−5.605)			
ARC capital	5.24×10^{-5} (2.436)		6.60×10^{-5} (2.394)		
Finishing capital	-1.47×10^{-5} (−0.954)		-2.09×10^{-6} (−0.175)	-2.14×10^{-4} (−6.727)	-2.02×10^{-4} (−5.183)
Air pollution treatment capital	-1.96×10^{-6} (−1.980)				
Air pollution recovery capital	-3.91×10^{-6} (−4.721)				
Water pollution treatment capital	-5.85×10^{-7} (−0.498)	-8.73×10^{-6} (−4.620)	1.30×10^{-5} (−5.928)		
Water pollution recovery capital	-6.71×10^{-7} (−1.139)				
BTG capital	4.00×10^{-4} (4.122)	4.62×10^{-5} (4.281)	5.58×10^{-5} (5.029)		
$\bar{R}^2$	0.839	0.825	0.852	0.756	0.658

[a] The cost shares corresponding to these factors were omitted from the estimated system. The numbers in parentheses below the estimated coefficients are *t*-ratios for the null hypothesis of no association.

Table 6. *Estimated nonneutrality parameters using expenditures on direct reductional capital*

Factor inputs	Models				
	19 factor	11 factor	9 factor	5 factor	4 factor
Maintenance	-9.04×10^{-5} (-2.726)	-6.81×10^{-5} (-2.144)			
Coal	-2.62×10^{-4} (-7.253)	-2.91×10^{-4} (-7.911)	-3.45×10^{-4} (-6.320)	$-^{a}$ —	
All other operating inputs	4.75×10^{-5} (2.645)	$-^{a}$ —			-3.48×10^{-5} (-0.656)
Iron ore	-3.16×10^{-4} (-4.569)	-3.55×10^{-4} (-5.061)	2.81×10^{-4} (3.810)	3.00×10^{-4} (4.056)	
Scrap	6.25×10^{-4} (4.553)	6.72×10^{-4} (4.910)			
Fuel oil	5.07×10^{-5} (2.871)	6.15×10^{-5} (3.625)	2.15×10^{-4} (8.592)	2.25×10^{-4} (8.841)	2.15×10^{-4} (8.474)
Natural gas	1.14×10^{-4} (6.601)	1.26×10^{-4} (7.540)			
Labor	-7.09×10^{-5} (-2.657)	-7.98×10^{-5} (-3.125)	$-^{a}$ —	-8.92×10^{-5} (-3.645)	$-^{a}$ —
Blast furnace capital	-1.71×10^{-4} (-6.257)				
BOF capital	-8.33×10^{-5} (-6.086)		-3.33×10^{-4} (-6.740)		
OH capital	-1.33×10^{-6} (-1.301)	-1.60×10^{-4} (-4.775)			
ARC capital	1.47×10^{-4} (8.088)		2.05×10^{-4} (9.085)		
Finishing capital	-2.20×10^{-5} (-1.429)		-1.62×10^{-5} (-1.350)		
Air pollution treatment capital	-2.28×10^{-6} (-2.296)			-9.35×10^{-5} (-2.656)	-9.35×10^{-5} (-2.284)
Air pollution recovery capital	-2.39×10^{-6} (-2.946)	-6.97×10^{-6} (-3.906)	-7.20×10^{-6} (-3.006)		
Water pollution treatment capital	7.87×10^{-8} (0.065)				
Water pollution recovery capital	-4.02×10^{-7} (-0.659)				
BTG capital	6.20×10^{-5} (7.243)	7.29×10^{-5} (8.186)	7.90×10^{-5} (7.827)		
$\bar{R}^2$	0.837	0.822	0.856	0.749	0.661

[a] The cost shares corresponding to these factors were omitted from the estimated system. The numbers in parentheses below the estimated coefficients are *t*-ratios for the null hypothesis of no association.

Table 7. *Estimated nonneutrality parameters using total expenditures on innovation related capital*

Factor inputs	Models				
	19 factor[a]	11 factor	9 factor	5 factor	4 factor
Maintenance	-2.98×10^{-5} (-0.894)	-1.87×10^{-5} (-0.581)			
Coal	5.38×10^{-5} (1.310)	2.14×10^{-5} (0.465)	-2.22×10^{-5} (-0.358)	$-^{a}$ $-$	
All other operating inputs	2.35×10^{-5} (1.333)	$-^{a}$			-7.47×10^{-5} (-1.344)
Iron ore	1.57×10^{-4} (2.176)	1.20×10^{-4} (1.510)	-6.68×10^{-5} (-0.839)	-5.79×10^{-5} (-0.705)	
Scrap	1.70×10^{-4} (-1.148)	-1.30×10^{-4} (-0.831)			
Fuel oil	-4.69×10^{-5} (-2.771)	-3.44×10^{-5} (-1.979)	2.35×10^{-4} (0.783)	3.61×10^{-5} (1.104)	3.39×10^{-5} (1.039)
Natural gas	8.28×10^{-7} (0.044)	1.63×10^{-5} (0.815)			
Labor	1.09×10^{-5} (0.391)	1.40×10^{-6} (0.051)	$-^{a}$ $-$	7.65×10^{-6} (0.282)	$-^{a}$ $-$
Blast furnace capital	3.59×10^{-5} (1.192)				
BOF capital	5.00×10^{-5} (3.424)		-3.17×10^{-6} (-0.056)		
OH capital	-1.87×10^{-6} (-1.957)	1.25×10^{-5} (0.336)			
ARC capital	-3.45×10^{-5} (-1.666)		4.13×10^{-5} (1.487)		
Finishing capital	-3.70×10^{-5} (-2.522)		8.45×10^{-6} (0.717)	4.37×10^{-5} (1.167)	3.71×10^{-5} (0.846)
Air pollution treatment capital	-3.83×10^{-7} (-0.397)				
Air pollution recovery capital	2.35×10^{-6} (2.856)	-7.75×10^{-7} (-0.408)	9.91×10^{-7} (0.394)		
Water pollution treatment capital	-4.29×10^{-7} (-0.378)				
Water pollution recovery capital	-1.08×10^{-6} (-1.913)				
BTG capital	-2.49×10^{-5} (-2.773)	-1.19×10^{-5} (-1.097)	1.96×10^{-6} (0.166)		
$\bar{R}^2$	0.835	0.819	0.850	0.738	0.636

[a] The cost shares corresponding to these factors were omitted from the estimated system. The numbers in parentheses below the estimated coefficients are t-ratios for the null hypothesis of no association.

As inputs are aggregated the estimated nonneutrality parameters provide a remarkably consistent description of the effects of each innovation. Our numerical findings indicate that, with input aggregation, the sign of the effect attributed to technical change seems to correspond to a simple average of the individual contributions (without apparent regard to the share of each component input in these aggregates). Moreover the input aggregation does not appear to confound the innovation specific indexes in "sorting out" the effects of conflicting innovations.

Turning to the overall index based on the total expenditures for the equipment associated with all three innovations relative to total capital expenditures, the record is much less desirable. First, a comparison of the estimates in Table 3 with those using the total index is itself more problematical. We must estimate the "net" effect of the three innovations using the Binswanger index description in order to have a consistent benchmark for evaluating the estimated nonneutrality parameters in Table 7. We have estimated the sign of these net effects as the sign of the weighted average of the coefficients for the summary equations given for each input in Table 3 across the capital shares for the three innovations. The weights used were based on the average proportion of total capital expenditures on all innovations that was associated with each innovation individually.[19]

A comparison of the signs of these weighted indexes with the signs of the nonneutrality parameters in the nineteen factor cost function using the index based on aggregate expenditures for all innovations indicated very little agreement. Thirteen of the eighteen estimated parameters in Table 7 do not agree in sign with the sign of the weighted average of the coefficients estimated using the Binswanger indexes. In addition the relationship appears to deteriorate with input aggregation.

IV. Implications

This paper has reported the first evaluation of the performance of alternative indexes of the pace of technological change. The analysis has focused on the agreement between the actual direction of nonneutral input effects and that estimated within a cost function framework using different indexes of the introduction of specific technical innovations.[20] Our evaluation was

---

[19] The specific shares of total expenditures on equipment associated with technical innovations were: CONCAS=0.77, PREHEA=0.09, and DIRRED=0.14.

[20] As we indicated earlier this evaluation is compared in a two-step analysis: (1) comparison of the indexes derived from the Binswanger decomposition with the changes in input usage implied by the engineering features of each innovation; and (2) use of the "validated" Binswanger indexes to evaluate the estimated non-neutrality parameters in estimated cost functions.

This approach was necessary because there were no "true" parameters that could be compared to the cost function estimates.

experimental and used an engineering, process analysis framework to describe the true state of both static production activities and the innovations to them.

Our findings unambiguously support the use of technologically explicit indicators of technolocal change. In the presence of multiple, conflicting (in their effects on some inputs) innovations, these specific indexes correctly identified the input effects for each individual innovation. By contrast, a general index of the pace of all innovations, akin to what an ideal time trend might measure, did not offer a consistent description of the direction of the innovations' net effects on input usage. While it should be acknowledged that our results are based on experimental analysis using process analysis models as the description of the "true" technology, they do seem to offer fairly unambiguous support for the methodological improvements to the measurement of nonneutral technical change recently proposed by both Denny et al. (1981) and Christensen et al. (forthcoming). This support is maintained over widely differing levels of aggregation and under conditions that are likely to resemble many of the attributes of real-world applications.

References

Berndt, E. R. & Khaled, M. S.: Parametric productivity measurement and choice among flexible function forms. *Journal of Political Economy 87*, December 1979.

Berndt, E. R. & Wood, D. O.: Technology, prices and the demand for energy. *Review of Economics and Statistics 57*, August 1975.

Berndt, E. R. & Wood, D. O.: Engineering and econometric interpretations of energy-capital complementarity. *American Economic Review 69*, June 1979.

Binswanger, H. P.: The measurement of technical change biases with many factors of production. *American Economic Review 64*, December 1974.

Binswanger, H. P. & Ruttan, V. M.: *Induced innovation: technology, institutions and development.* Johns Hopkins, Baltimore, 1978.

Christensen, L. R., Cummings, D. & Schoech, P. E.: Econometric estimation of scale economies in telecommunications. Working Paper No. 8201, Social Systems Research Institute, University of Wisconsin, Madison, forthcoming in L. Courville, A. R. Dobell and A. de Fontenay, editors, *Econometric analysis of telecommunications: Theory and applications*, Vol. I, North Holland.

Christensen, L. R., Jorgenson, D. W. & Lau, L. J.: Conjugate duality and the transcendental logarithmic production function. Unpublished paper presented at the Second World Congress of the Econometric Society, Cambridge, England, 1970.

Denny, M., Fuss, M., Everson, C. & Waverman, L.: Eastimating the effects of diffusion of technological innovations in telecommunications: the production structure of Bell Canada. *Canadian Journal of Economics 14*, February 1981.

Diewert, W. E.: A note on aggregation and elasticities of substitution. *Canadian Journal of Economics 7*, February 1974.

Hall, R. & Jorgenson, D. W.: Tax policy and investment behavior. *American Economic Review 61*, March 1967.

Jorgenson, D. W. & Fraumeni, B. M.: Relative prices and technical change. In *Modeling and measuring natural resource substitution* (ed. E. R. Berndt & B. C. Field). MIT Press, Cambridge, 1981.

Kamien, M. I. & Schwartz, N. L.: Optimal 'induced technical change'. *Econometrica 36*, January 1968.

Kopp, R. J. & Smith, V. K.: Input substitution, aggregation, and engineering descriptions of production activities. *Economic Letters 5,* 1980 *a.*

Kopp, R. J. & Smith, V. K.: Measuring factor substitution with neoclassical models: an experimental evaluation. *Bell Journal of Economics 11,* Autumn 1980 *b.*

Kopp, R. J. & Smith, V. K.: The measurement of nonneutral technological change. Working Paper 81-4, University of North Carolina at Chapel Hill, January 1981.

Lopez, R. E.: The structure of production and the derived demand for inputs in Canadian manufacturing. *American Journal of Agricultural Economics 62,* February 1980.

Marsden, J., Pingry, D. & Whinston, A.: Engineering foundations of production functions. *Journal of Economic Theory 9,* October 1974.

Russell, C. S. & Vaughan, W. J.: *Steel production: processes, products, and residuals.* Johns Hopkins, Baltimore, 1976.

Salter, W. E. G.: *Productivity and technical change.* Cambridge University Press, Cambridge, 1960.

Samuelson, P. A.: Relative shares and elasticities simplified: comment. *American Economic Review 63,* September 1973.

Shephard, R. W.: *Theory of cost and production functions.* Princeton University Press, Princeton, 1970.

Smith, V. K. & Vaughan, W. J.: Strategic detail and process analysis models for environmental management: an econometric analysis. *Resources and Energy 3,* January 1981.

Stigler, G.: Economic problems in measuring changes in productivity. In *Output, input and productivity.* Princeton University Press, Princeton (NBER Income & Wealth Series), 1961.

Vaughan, W. J., Russell, C. S. & Cochrane, H. C.: *Government policies and the adoption of innovations in the integrated iron and steel industry.* Report prepared for the National Science Foundation, National Rand D Assessment Program under Grant No. RDA74-18148-A01. NTIS, Springfield, May 1976.

Wills, J.: Technical change in the U.S. primary metals industry. *Journal of Econometrics 10,* April 1979.

Zellner, A.: An efficient method of estimating seemingly unrelated regressions and tests for aggregation bias. *Journal of the American Statistical Association 58.* June 1962.

Feedback from Productivity Growth to R & D*

William J. Baumol

Princeton University, Princeton, NJ and New York University, NY, USA

Edward N. Wolff

New York University, NY, USA

Abstract

It is shown that while the scale of R & D activity affects the rate of growth of productivity in manufacturing, that rate of growth, in turn, affects the relative cost of R & D and, hence, its demand. For relative productivity of manufactures and R & D services are crucial in determining their relative prices. Thus, success in R & D and the consequent increase in manufacturing productivity may raise the relative price of R & D, reducing the quantity demanded. Formal models of this feedback process are provided and show how it can lead to oscillatory behavior and to a slowdown of the economy's long-run productivity growth.

I. Introduction

It has long been recognized that R & D makes a vital contribution to the rate of the growth of economy's productivity, however defined and measured. But we have been unable to find previous theoretical analyses which take simultaneous account of the likelihood that there is also a connection going the other way—from productivity to the magnitude of R & D activity. Yet it is clear that such a relationship is likely. Productivity affects the quantity of resources available for investment generally and for investment in R & D in particular. It also influences the price of output and, hence, the cost of R & D relative to output price. In both these ways, investment in R & D is apt to be affected.

This paper outlines a preliminary model which encompasses the feedback process emerging from the two-way relationship between productivity growth and the scale of R & D activity. It thereby constitutes an early attempt to provide a formal analysis of the productivity growth process.[1] It also provides some initial results which are, perhaps, rather surprising. For

---

* The authors are deeply grateful to the Division of Information Science and Technology of the National Science Foundation for its support of the research reported here.

[1] In this presentation, we deliberately avoid many of the complex and difficult problems involved in measurement of the pertinent variables and empirical estimation of the model. Where appropriate, some of the relevant issues will be discussed briefly in footnotes.

it reveals a mechanism which may threaten to price commercial R & D activity out of the market in the long run. Moreover, it shows, paradoxically, that the more successful the record of R & D in stimulating productivity growth the more powerful this mechanism may prove. Finally, the intertemporal path described by this model turns out not necessarily to be monotonic, with outlays on R & D steadily approaching some long run equilibrium level; rather it is apt to be oscillatory with expenditure on R & D alternately exceeding and falling short of its long run equilibrium.

II. R & D as Asymptotically Stagnant Activity

There is no need to discuss the ways in which R & D contributes to productivity growth. They are apparent and have been discussed extensively in the literature.[2] However, the relationship in the other direction is rather less obvious. Assuming that one can define a per unit cost of R & D, we will show now that in the short run a rise in the rate of overall productivity growth through technological progress is likely to reduce that unit cost.[3] On the other hand, in the long run the relationship may well go

---

[2] See National Science Foundation (1977), Nadiri (1977), Griliches (1979), and Schankerman (1979) for reviews of the literature. We are here deliberately skirting many of the complex issues involved in the definition of R & D. These involve the difference between basic and applied R & D, see e.g. Mansfield (1980); the distinction between process and product R & D, see, e.g. Scherer (1981 a) the difference between the effects of privately-financed and government-financed R & D, see e.g. Levy & Terlyckyj (1981); and whether there is growing specialization in the focus of R & D in areas such as defense, the environment, pollution control, and health. Also, the analysis of the effects of R & D on productivity growth has been carried out at three different levels—that of the firm, see, e.g., Nadiri & Bitros (1980); the industry, see, e.g., Griliches & Lichtenberg (1981); and the aggregate level, see, e.g., Griliches (1980). The appropriate measures of R & D and the level of analysis will, of course, both have to be determined before empirical work on our model begins. For now, it is helpful to recognize that both basic and applied, process and product, and privately-financed and total (though not government-financed) R & D have all generally been found to have a significant stimulative effect on both labor productivity growth and some form of total factor productivity growth. Moreover, the relation has generally been found to be statistically significant and positive at the firm, industry, and aggregate levels.
[3] Again, complex issues arise in measurement of the "output" of the R & D activity, the "unit cost" of R & D, and the "price" of R & D. This, of course, is a problem which plagues the measurement of output in many service activities, such as health, education, and the government. Ideally, the measure of R & D output would indicate the improvements in products or processes that are actually utilized in production. The R & D activity does at least permit some "countable" measure of this type of output—namely, patents and research papers. Patents have, in fact, been used recently to measure R & D activity; see, e.g. Scherer (1981 b). This is not to argue, of course, that patents (or research papers), are ideal or even particularly good measures of R & D output, since patents may correspond to very heterogenous improvements in technology (for example, the patent for the transistor versus a patent for a new toothpaste flavor).
  Inability to provide an adequate measure of R & D output makes it difficult to offer a reliable measure of unit cost or price (in our model, price and unit cost are assumed equal). But, assuming we had an adequate measure of output (and assuming R & D current expenditure

the other way, with relative cost per unit of R & D output rising more rapidly the faster the rate of growth of the economy's productivity.

To explain this it is necessary to summarize briefly and extend the unbalanced growth model constructed by one of us more than a decade ago; see Baumol (1967). In that model the economy was divided into two parts: a progressive sector (manufacturing) in which productivity per unit of input grows rapidly and cumulatively, and a stagnant sector (services such as education, auto repair and live performing arts) in which productivity growth is inherently negligible. Because in the long run inputs can move from either of these sectors to the other, wages and other input prices will tend to stay abreast of one another in the two sectors. It then follows rigorously that the unit cost of a product of the stagnant sector must rise higher and higher relative to that of the progressive sector. Moreover, the more rapid the growth of productivity the faster the relative cost (and presumably the relative price) of the stagnant sector output will mount. This has been called the *cost disease* of the services.

Returning now to óur main topic, it is clear that R & D activity fits neither the mold of a stagnant sector nor that of a progressive one. It can be thought of as having two primary components: sophisticated equipment and human labor. The human thought process, at least so far, constitutes an indispensible part of successful R & D. The equipment is subject to rapid technological change bringing increased power and sophistication and constantly serving to reduce its cost. This is not obviously true of the human input component.

An analogy can bring out what can happen in such a case. Computation is an activity which has a similar two-part structure corresponding, roughly speaking, to its hardware and software components. Computer hardware provides what is the most spectacular story of success in achieving great and persistent technological advance, one which has, for the better part of several decades, reduced the cost of the equipment needed for a given set of calculations by something on the order of 25 per cent per year compounded. It is hard to imagine anything which fits more clearly the specifications of a progressive sector.

On the other hand, while the techniques of software creation have improved, they have done so only slowly. It is estimated that *in real terms* using general price deflators, cost per unit of software has been rising at about 6 per cent per year. This is precisely what one would expect of a

---

data are reliable), we would still have difficulty in measuring the unit cost of R & D "in real terms." This stems from the difficulty of constructing a reliable price index for R & D expenditure. The National Science Foundation uses a weighted average of an hourly compensation index and an implicit price deflator with *fixed* weights to construct its measure of R & D "in constant prices"; see Jaffe (1972). This index is not appropriate for our purposes, since we have found that the input mix in the R & D activity has changed significantly over time.

stagnant activity from the unbalanced growth model, and it is the cost behavior experience which has been shown to characterize many of the personal services.

We come now to a second crucial feature of such an activity which also follows rigorously from the arithmetic relationships. In computation the very nature of the cost performance of its two components has automatically lead to a steady change in their share of total cost. With hardware cost decreasing 25 percent and software cost rising 6 percent per year it was predictable that the share of software in the total cost of a given set of computations must inevitably rise precipitately. One estimate indicates that the share of labor rose from 5 percent of the total in 1973 to about 80 percent in 1978.

The preceding pattern clearly must apply whenever an activity is composed of a stagnant and a progressive component, in more or less given proportions. Inevitably, with the passage of time the former must constitute more and more of the activity's total cost.

A third relationship also follows necessarily from these premises. In the early days of such an activity, when the progressive component dominates total cost, the unit cost of the activity is apt to fall, perhaps even very rapidly. But as the stagnant component accounts for more and more of total outlay, that cost decline must decelerate, ultimately coming to a halt and finally reversing itself. When hardware constitutes 90 percent or more of the cost of computation its 25 percent increase in productivity must swamp the 6 percent annual rise in its labor cost which is a mere 10 percent of the total. But when labor's cost share rises to 80 percent, even if all of the remainder falls at a 25 percent rate, the decline in unit cost will virtually have come to a halt.

The cost trends of such an activity will then approach asymptotically those of the stagnant sector as the share of the progressive inputs in total cost approaches zero asymptotically. That is why we refer to such activities as *asymptotically stagnant*. It is easy to provide a formal model manifesting the pattern of behavior just described, but the logic of the verbal argument seems sufficiently clear and is clearly compelling.

Cost and, consequently, price behavior for such an activity is also clear. The more rapid the rate of growth in productivity in the asymptotically stagnant activity, the more rapidly its behavior will approach that of one in the stagnant sector. And the more rapid the rate of growth of productivity in the progressive sector the more quickly relative costs and prices in the other sectors will increase.

The basic hypothesis in the following analysis is that R & D lies in the asymptotically stagnant sector, that most of it will eventually be vulnerable to the cost disease, and that at least some of it already is.

III. The Simplest Model

We are now in a position to begin our formal analysis whose character we will illustrate with the aid of two simple models. We begin with one that is completely elementary and which pays for its lack of complexity with some clear misrepresentations. Using linear relationships let us describe the stimulating effect of R & D upon the rate of growth of productivity in the progressive sector via the equation

$$r_{t+1} = a + bZ_t \quad (a, b > 0) \tag{1}$$

where r_t = rate of growth of progressive-sector productivity in period t, and Z_t = expenditure on commercial R & D in period t.

The reason for the distinction between what we refer to as "commercial R & D", and the remaining activity in this field, which we will call "autonomous R & D", will become clear later.

To produce a closed model we must now introduce a second relationship describing the determination of Z_t. Here we assume that we have passed the date, t^*, up to which the costs of the R & D activity in question have been decreasing (relatively) with time so that it has entered the stagnant phase of its history. Thus, using the progressive sector output as the numeraire, both unit cost and price of this R & D activity will be an increasing function of r_t, the rate of growth of productivity in the progressive sector. Indeed, for simplicity we take the price of R & D and r_t to be proportionate. Then, if the demand curve for R & D is negatively sloping, we may write the demand function as[4]

$$Z_t = u - vr_t \quad (u, v > 0). \tag{2}$$

Combining (1) and (2) we obtain immediately

$$r_{t+1} = (a + bu) - bvr_t \tag{3}$$

---

[4] Here we have been very brief in our discussion of the reverse relation between the demand for R & D and the productivity growth it induces in the progressive sector. Our basic assumption is that the real price of the product of the progressive sector moves inversely to its rate of productivity growth. This, in turn, can be derived from the assumption that the economy is in competitive equilibrium, with firms making zero profits. This assumption is more or less helpful when analyzing the long-run secular movements of the economy. In the short-run, of course, profits—actually, rents—are likely to be earned by the firms providing the innovations (for why else would they engage in R & D?). In the medium-run, the rents are likely to be dissipated as the innovations are diffused throughout the economy. This process will also, in reality, be influenced by many other factors, such as market structure, changes in demand and output levels, and changes in input prices. Our model essentially considers the long-run movement of the economy through positions of short-run equilibrium after rents from innovation have been dissipated.

which is a first-order linear difference equation with the constant coefficient $(-bv)$. Setting $r_{t+1}=r_t=r_e$ in (3) and solving for r_e we immediately obtain the equilibrium value

$$r_e = (a+bu)/(1+bv) > 0. \tag{4}$$

Then, provided $0<bv<1$, r_t will exhibit a stable time path which converges in the limit to the equilibrium value (4). This level will be higher the larger the autonomous component of growth rate, a, and the larger the quantity intercept, u, of the demand curve. It will be decreased by a larger absolute value of the response rate, v, of the demand for R & D to an increase in its price.

All of this is obvious enough. What is perhaps less likely to have been expected is the oscillatory character of the time path of r_t which follows as one of the most basic attributes of linear difference equations from the sign of the coefficient, $-bv$. Indeed, the solution of the difference equation (3) can readily be show to be

$$r_t = (-bv)^t (r_0-r_e)+r_e. \tag{5}$$

Thus, if in one period $r_t>r_e$, then in the next period the inequality will be reversed, i.e., r_t will alternate between values above and below its equilibrium level, approaching r_e gradually by oscillatory steps of declining amplitude.

Even if this characteristic of the time path of r_t is somewhat unexpected it is not difficult to explain. For this model shows us that a burst of R & D activity soon stimulates rapid growth of productivity in the progressive sector. But that in turn raises the price of R & D and reduces the quantity demanded. As a result, in the following period productivity growth is slowed, permitting a reduction in R & D price which stimulates demand for it once again. We have here a set of relationships formally identical with those of the cobweb model and so both the consequences and the explanations are perfectly analogous.

IV. A Somewhat More Sophisticated Model

The model which has just been described is obviously a gross oversimplification. Its simple linear form, its disregard of other influences and its rudimentary lag structure all render it suspect. Yet, even this crudest of models does succeed in encompassing the two-way relationship between R & D and productivity growth and shows that the feedback process which is involved does constitute the basis for an operational construct with interesting properties that lend themselves readily to analysis.

It is also not difficult to take preliminary steps that impart some degree of increased sophistication to the model. One of its more obvious shortcomings, as has just been mentioned, is its lag structure. As formulated up to this point it implies that the system, as it were, has no memory, that current cost depends on productivity growth in the immediately preceding period, and that the cost-saving effects of earlier growth evaporate after an instant of influence. This is, of course, nonsense. Once R & D has taught us a more efficient productive technique there need be no reversion to its predecessor, and further increases in productivity can be expected to be cumulative in their effects.

We deal with this issue here in such detail not because we believe it to be the vital ingredient missing from our first model, but because it permits an effective illustration of the way in which the sophistication of the model can be increased. More important, as we will see, the modified model to which this consideration leads brings out an important qualitative observation—the possibility that the relationships we are discussing will progressively reduce the amount of R & D that is induced by ordinary commercial considerations, and gradually push this activity toward extinction.

Our revised model employs our linear growth stimulation function (1) as before. Now, however, it is convenient to rewrite our demand function explicitly introducing p_t, the "unit price" of R & D, by writing

$$Z_t = u - wp_t \quad (u, w > 0). \tag{2'}$$

This enables us to assume that current productivity growth determines not p_t itself, but its rate of growth so that

$$p_{t+1} - p_t = hr_t. \tag{6}$$

From (2') we obtain immediately

$$Z_{t+1} - Z_t = -w(p_{t+1} - p_t) \tag{7}$$

so that, substituting this into (6) we have together with (1) the simultaneous difference equation system

$$\left.\begin{array}{l} Z_{t+1} - Z_t = -whr_t. \\ r_{t+1} \quad\ = a + bZ_t. \end{array}\right\} \tag{8}$$

As is well known, the time path of this system is determined by the roots x_1, x_2 of the characteristic equation

$$\begin{vmatrix} x-1 & wh \\ -b & x \end{vmatrix} = x^2 - x + bwh = 0. \tag{9}$$

Clearly the roots of this quadratic equiation must satisfy

$$x_1+x_2=1 \quad \text{and} \quad x_1x_2=bwh. \tag{10}$$

It follows immediately that if these roots are real they must both be positive. For if just one of them were nonpositive their product could not equal the positive number *bwh,* while if both were nonpositive their sum could not be equal to unity.

We see also from the first equation in (10) that if both roots are positive each of them must have a value less than unity.

Thus in this positive roots case the system *must* have a time path which is both monotonic and stable, converging gradually toward its equilibrium value.

However, there is a second possibility. By (9) and the standard formula for the roots of a quadratic equation, if $bwh>\frac{1}{4}$ then the roots will assume the complex values

$$x_i = \frac{1}{2} \pm (\sqrt{1-4bwh})/2.$$

In that case, as any standard discussion of difference equations indicates, the time paths of Z_t and r_t will involve fluctuations whose frequency and amplitude depend on the magnitude of *bwh.*

Moreover, as is well known, the absolute value of each of the complex roots is equal to *bwh,* so that the system will exhibit fluctuations if $bwh>\frac{1}{4}$ and it will be stable if $bwh<1$.

This is as far as we can go in describing qualitatively the nature of the time path which (if $bwh<1$) must take the system toward its equilibrium values, r_e and Z_e. But what are those equilibrium values? These can be obtained readily from (8) by setting $Z_{t+1}=Z_t=Z_e$ and $r_{t+1}=r_t=r_e$. This immediately yields the rather unpleasant result

$$r_e = 0, \quad Z_e = -a/b<0.$$

In other words, growth in this system converges toward zero, and output of commercial R & D approaches the negative limit $-a/b$. This result is, of course, unpleasant not only because of its unfortunate economic implications but because of the inherent impossibility of a negative R & D output.

It is not difficult to show what has gone wrong, and to remedy the problem with the aid of a bit of *ad hoc* adjustment. If we reexamine (1), that is, the second equation in (8) then we see that the constant term can be interpreted as the growth effect of autonomous R & D—that is, it relates to R & D activities such as those carried out by amateur inventors which are not constrained by a budget for outlays on labor, and perhaps some types of governmentally financed R & D such as that included in military expenditure, which are readily sheltered from financial impediments within the relevant range. Granting that some such R & D will always take place and that, it too, can be expected to contribute to productivity growth, it follows that r_t will not converge to zero.

In formal terms, our problem is ascribable to the strict linearity assumptions which have been employed so far. But if to our basic equations (8) we adjoin the necessary nonnegativity requirement, $Z_t \geqslant 0$, it is clear that the system becomes nonlinear, or, rather, piecewise linear. That is, the demand function (2') is replaced by

$$Z_t = \begin{cases} u - w p_t & \text{for } p_t \leqslant u/w \\ 0 & \text{otherwise.} \end{cases} \qquad (2'')$$

It is then easy to show graphically that the nonlinear system will converge to the intuitively plausible values: $r = a$; $Z_e = 0$. In other words, in this case the limiting values of the variables involve complete cessation of economically induced R & D, while productivity growth is fed only by exogenous R & D activity.

V. On the Significance of Dynamic Models

Given the extreme unreality of the two constructs which have just been described, it is tempting simply to dismiss their policy implications. Yet, while one must be careful not to go too far in urging upon policymakers the significance of implications derived from abstract and preliminary constructs, one must also avoid going too far in the other direction.

The practical value of difference equation models of the sort offered here lies in their ability to provide noteworthy warnings of pitfalls which may plausibly beset the real state of affairs but which are likely to be overlooked by intuition and routine observation. Difference equation models can, for example, show how even automatic policies which common sense would judge to be contracyclical may in fact backfire and exacerbate the fluctuations they are designed to reduce. Similarly, in our case here, we have seen that the role of R & D in productivity growth may be more complex and may lead to more unhappy consequences than might otherwise have been suspected.

In other words, while dynamic models are likely to be most unreliable as instruments for the actual design of practical policies, the hidden dangers which they call to our attention should not be disregarded lightly. This is particularly so when, as is often possible in retrospect, one can provide an argument which is logically defensible and intuitively plausible showing how the possible pitfalls revealed by the dynamic models can arise in practice. Because such an argument is independent of the simplifications and rigidities inherent in the equations of the formal model it can impart substantial additional weight to its implications.

VI. Heuristics of the Dynamic Disincentives for R & D

In the case with which we are dealing such a persuasive scenario can, indeed, be provided. For this purpose we need merely note that by our assumptions, when R & D succeeds in increasing the productivity of manufacturing, it automatically increases its own relative cost in comparison with that of manufactures and thereby reduces its own financial attractiveness to business. Thus the very success of R & D activity serves to undermine its own demand. Paradoxically, then, the more spectacular the record of past success of R & D activity the more strongly it will tend, if not to price itself out of the market, at least to inhibit business demand for it.

This is not a felicitous story. It suggests that a slowing down of productivity growth may be a predictable consequence of the workings of the innovation mechanism that feeds it. Nor is there any obvious policy program well suited to deal with such a structural problem. One can, of course, use this analysis as the basis for recommendation of an increased assumption of responsibility by the public sector for the financing of the nation's R & D activity. But, as we know, such a recommendation may well run into problems in terms of costs and benefits. Only if it can be shown that the process that has been described here involves significant externalities does this become unlikely. That is one of the issues that remains to be explored in this arena.

One may well ask, finally, whether there is any empirical evidence suggesting the presence of the problems whose possibility has been raised here. The answer is that no systematic evidence of this sort seems to be available so far, though the data will be examined carefully in our future research. But there are various straws in the wind. For example, some casual inquiries confirm the impression that agencies which provide financial support for research seem to find that rising costs increasingly inhibit the number of projects they can finance, even though there has been no decline in real terms in the agency's overall budget. There are also data indicating that in industry, even though outlays on R & D have been rising relative to value of output, the number of scientists and engineers has fallen relative to output. This is just the sort of behavior our model predicts. Such data are hardly conclusive, indeed they can hardly be treated as substantial evidence. Yet they do lend some support to an analysis which seeks to throw new light on the determinants of productivity growth and which suggests some sources of concern which seem previously not to have been considered.

References

Baumol, William J.: Macroeconomics of unbalanced growth: The anatomy of urban crisis. *American Economic Review 57*, 415–426, June 1967.

Griliches, Zvi: Issues in assessing the contribution of research and development to productivity growth. *Bell Journal of Economics 10* (1), 92–116, Spring 1979.

Griliches, Zvi: R & D and the productivity slowdown. *American Economic Review 70* (2), 343–48, May 1980.

Griliches, Zvi & Lichtenberg, Frank: R & D and productivity growth at the industry level: Is there still a relationship. Mimeo, 1981.

Jaffe, S. A.: A Price index for deflation of academic R & D expenditures. National Science Foundation Publication 72–310, 1972.

Levy, David & Terlyckyj, Nestor: Government-financed R & D and productivity growth: Macroeconomic evidence. Mimeo, 1981.

Mansfield, Edwin: Basic research and productivity increase in manufacturing. *American Economic Review 70* (5), 863–73, December 1980.

Nadiri, M. Ishaq: The contribution of research and development to economic growth. Mimeo, October 1977.

Nadiri, M. Ishaq & Bitros, George: Research and development expenditures and labor productivity at the firm level. In *New developments in productivity measurement and analysis* (ed. John Kendrick and Bea Vaccara). NBER, New York, 1980.

National Science Foundation. *Relationships between R & D and economic growth/productivity*. Washington, November 1977.

Scherer, F. M.: Inter-industry technology flows and productivity growth. Mimeo. 1981 *a*.

Scherer, F. M.: Using linked patent and R & D data to measure inter-industry technology flows. Mimeo, 1981 *b*.

Schankerman, Mark: Essays on the economics of technical change: The determinants, rate of return, and productivity impact of research and development. Ph.D. Thesis, Harvard University, 1979.

PART II EFFICIENCY

The Measurement of Waste within the Production Sector of an Open Economy

W. Erwin Diewert*

University of British Columbia, Vancouver, BC, Canada

Abstract

A methodology for measuring the loss of output that can be attributed to distortions within the production sector of an open economy is proposed. Examples of distortions are: tariffs on imported intermediate inputs, taxes or subsidies on exports, specific taxes on an output that is used as an input by another industry, (nonneutral) corporate income taxes, interindustry monopolistic markup pricing, and union induced wage differentials. The methodology generalizes the earlier work of Allais and Debreu.

I. Introduction

The general equilibrium study of deadweight loss due to inefficient schemes of taxation has a long history in economics, beginning perhaps with Pareto,[1] continuing with Hotelling (1938), Allais (1943, 1973, 1977). Boiteux (1951), Debreu (1951, 1954) and Harberger (1964), and it is still an active area of research at present.[2]

In this paper, we propose a methodology for measuring *only* the waste that may be present in the production sector of an open economy, as opposed to measuring the general equilibrium loss (which evaluates the waste that may be present in both the consumption and production sectors). However, in the concluding section, we indicate how our methodology can be extended to the general equilibrium case.

There are at least two advantages that a production loss measure has compared to a more complete general equilibrium loss measure: (i) production loss measures require information only on the technology of the country and the size of the distortions within the production sector, whereas the general equilibrium measures require additional information on the tastes of consumers (information that is very difficult to obtain in practice), and (ii) there is less scope for disagreement as to what the reference

---

* Financial support from the SSHRC of Canada is gratefully acknowledged.
[1] The contributions of the early pioneers in the subject (including Cournot, Dupuit and especially Pareto) are very ably reviewed by Allais (1973, 1977). See also Auerbach (1982).
[2] For example, see Auerbach (1982), Diewert (1981) and King (1982).

undistorted equilibrium should be in the production context compared to the general equilibrium context (where the welfares of different households may have to be traded off).

Before outlining the contents of the paper, it may be appropriate to delineate more precisely what types of waste that we shall attempt to measure. Debreu (1951; p. 285) distinguishes three sources of waste in the allocation of resources: (i) waste due to the underemployment of available physical resources (e.g. unemployed workers), (ii) waste due to technical inefficiency in production (e.g., some production unit does not obtain a maximal amount of good one that is technically feasible, given that it is producing a given vector of other outputs and utilizing a given vector of inputs), and (iii) waste due to the imperfection of economic organization (e.g., different production units, while technically efficient, face different prices for the same input or output, and this causes net outputs aggregated across production units to fall below what is attainable if the economic organization were efficient). We do not measure the first type of waste in the present paper; in order to do so, a general equilibrium approach would be required. Our general production loss measure that appears below in Section II measures both the second and third kind of waste. However, in subsequent sections when we develop quadratic approximations to the production loss, we assume technical efficiency, and hence we measure only the third type of loss in those sections. However, as Debreu (1951; p. 286) notes, the third type of loss is the most interesting (and the hardest for the layman to understand) and hence the one where a numerical evaluation is most useful.

The kinds of imperfection in economic organization or more briefly, the kinds of *distortion* that our methodology can handle include the following: (i) tariffs on imports of intermediate inputs (quotas can also be modelled if we can calculate their tariff equivalents), (ii) export subsidies or taxes, (iii) industry specific taxes or subsidies that vary across industries (e.g., a tax on the output of one industry where this output is used as an input in other industries), (iv) any corporate or business income tax where the tax base is not equivalent to cash flow, (v) interindustry markup monopolistic or monopsonistic behavior on the part of producers, and (vi) union induced wage differentials for the same type of labour service. All of these distortions imply that firms (or industries) face different effective price vectors for their inputs and outputs.

In Section II, we present our first loss measure in a rather abstract form. It is an adaptation of the general equilibrium loss measure of Allais (1943, 1977) to the production context. In Section III, we assume that the individual production sectors either exhibit constant returns to scale or convexity. These extra hypotheses allow us to derive a dual expression for the loss. In Section IV, we add to the hypotheses of Section III, certain differentiability hypotheses. The dual loss measure developed in Section III is then approximated to the second order, and our approximate Allais loss measure is obtained. In Section V, we consider a new loss measure that is a variant of Debreu's (1951, 1954) general equilibrium loss measure adapted to the production context. Our treatment of the Debreu loss is briefer than our treatment of the Allais loss, since the underlying foundations are similar. Section V concludes.

II. An Adaptation of the Allais Loss to the Production Sector

We distinguish M commodities that are traded internationally at constant prices $(p_1^*, p_2^*, \ldots, p_M^*)^T \equiv p^* \gg 0_M$.[3] In addition, we assume that there are N domestic commodities (e.g., primary inputs, domestic services, etc.) that are traded only within the borders of the country or region under consideration. Finally, we assume that there are K distinct production units (e.g., plants, firms or industries in the constant returns to scale case) in the region, where the kth production unit has access to a technologically feasible set of net outputs[4] of internationally traded and domestic goods, S^k, $k=1, 2, \ldots, K$.

We assume that we can observe an initial equilibrium of this economy's production sector; i.e., we have $(u^{k*}, v^{k*}) \in S^k$ for $k=1, 2, \ldots, K$. Define the economy's net amount of foreign exchange b^* and net output vector of domestic commodities v^* for this initial equilibrium by:

$$b^* \equiv \sum_{k=1}^{K} p^* \cdot u^{k*} \tag{1}$$

$$v^* \equiv \sum_{k=1}^{K} v^{k*}. \tag{2}$$

Consider the following (primal) *central planning problem* where we attempt to maximize the total amount of foreign exchange produced by the entire production sector, subject to producing at least the vector v^* of domestic commodities:

$$\underset{\substack{(u^k, v^k) \in S^k \\ k=1, \ldots, K}}{\text{maximize}} \left\{ \sum_{k=1}^{K} p^* \cdot u^k : \sum_{k=1}^{K} v^k \geq v^* \right\} \equiv b^o \tag{3}$$

---

[3] Thus we are assuming the region in question is small and cannot affect world prices p^*. Notation: $p^* \gg 0_M$ means each component of the (column) vector p^* is positive, $p^* \geq 0_M$ means each component is nonnegative, and $p \cdot x \equiv p^T x \equiv \sum_{m=1}^{M} p_m x_m$ denotes the inner product of the vectors p and x.

[4] Let $(u_1, \ldots, u_M, v_1, \ldots, v_N) \in S^k$. If $u_m > 0$ and $v_n > 0$ ($u_m < 0, v_n < 0$) then the mth internationally traded good and the nth domestic good are being produced as outputs (inputs) in sector k. We assume throughout that the S^k are closed, nonempty subsets of R^{M+N}.

where we have assumed that the maximum exists and the optimal amount of foreign exchange produced is $b^o \equiv \Sigma_{k=1}^{K} p^* \cdot u^{ko}$ where (u^{ko}, v^{ko}), $k=1, 2, \ldots, K$ is a solution to (3).

The *Allais production loss*[5] pertaining to the initial equilibrium is now defined as

$$A_L \equiv b^o - b^* \geqslant 0, \tag{4}$$

where the inequality in (4) follows from the fact that our initial equilibrium production vectors (u^{k*}, v^{k*}) $k=1, \ldots, K$, are feasible for the maximization problem (3) (but "usually" they will not be optimal so the inequality in (4) will "usually" be strict).

Thus the Allais loss is simply the extra amount of foreign exchange we could extract out of the production sector (without reducing domestic production) by having an optimal internal rearrangement of production.

The problem with the abstract loss formula (4) is that it dies not give us any indication of how big the difference between b^o and b^* is. A natural way to proceed is to form a second order approximation to the loss and this is what we shall do in Section IV. However, in order to provide our second-order approximation, it proves to be convenient to find a dual expression for the maximization problem (3).

III. A Dual Expression for the Allais Production Loss

In order to obtain a dual expression for (3), we require that the sectoral production possibility sets S^k satisfy some addition assumptions; namely either constant returns to scale or convexity. Thus we now assume:

$$S^k \equiv \{(u, v) = z_k(y, x) \quad \text{where} \quad z_k \geqslant 0 \quad \text{and} \quad (y, x) \in C^k\}$$
$$\text{for} \quad k = 1, 2, \ldots, K_1; \tag{5}$$

$$S^k \text{ is a convex set}[6] \quad \text{for} \quad k = K_1 + 1, K_1 + 2, \ldots, K. \tag{6}$$

Assumption (5) means that the first K_1 production units are subject to constant returns to scale; i.e., S^k is a cone, z^k represents a nonnegative scale variable for sector k and C^k represents a feasible set of input–output coefficients for sector k.

If production is subject to constant returns to scale in some sector k, then if $(y^i, x^i) \in C^k$ for $i=1, 2, \ldots, I$, we shall assume that the composite produc-

---

[5] The Allais (1943, 1973, 1977) loss is a general equilibrium loss measure that involves consumer preferences (and a closed economy). However, the loss measure defined by (4) is a straightforward adaptation of his basic idea. Allais also stressed that his loss measure was free of unnecessary convexity assumptions, a feature that extends to our suggested measure (4).
[6] A set S is convex if $x^1 \in S$, $x^2 \in S$, $0 \leqslant \lambda \leqslant 1$ implies $\lambda x^1 + (1-\lambda) x^2 \in S$.

tion plan $\Sigma_{i=1}^{I} z_i(y^i, x^i)$ is also feasible for any nonnegative scales $z_i \geq 0$. This is the usual assumption made in activity analysis.[7] This freedom of choice assumption means that the convex hull[8] of S^k, denoted by con S^k, is actually available to the production manager in sector k. Hence we may replace the sets S^k and C^k in (5) by con S^k and con C^k whenever we find it convenient to do so.

Using assumptions (5) and (6), we may rewrite the primal maximization problem (3) as:

$$b^o = \underset{u^k, v^k, x^k, y^k, z^k}{\text{maximize}} \left\{ \sum_{k=1}^{K_1} p^* \cdot y^k z_k + \sum_{k=K_1+1}^{K} p^* \cdot u^k : \sum_{k=1}^{K_1} x^k z_k + \sum_{k=K_1+1}^{K} v^k \geq v^*; \right.$$

$$(y^k, x^k) \in \text{con } C^k \quad \text{and} \quad z_k \geq 0 \quad \text{for } k = 1, 2, \ldots, K_1$$

$$\left. \text{and} \quad (u^k, v^k) \in S^k \quad \text{for } k = K_1+1, \ldots, K \right\}$$

$$= \underset{x^k, y^k, z^k, u^k, v^k}{\text{max}} \left\{ \underset{w \geq 0_N}{\text{min}} \left\{ \sum_{k=1}^{K_1} p^* \cdot y^k z_k + \sum_{k=K_1+1}^{K} p^* \cdot u^k + w \right. \right.$$

$$\times \left(\sum_{k=1}^{K_1} x^k z_k + \sum_{k=K_1+1}^{K} v^k - v^* \right);$$

$$(y^k, x^k) \in \text{con } C^k \quad \text{and} \quad z_k \geq 0 \quad \text{for } k = 1, \ldots, K_1$$

$$\left. \left. \text{and} \quad (u^k, v^k) \in S^k \quad \text{for } k = K_1+1, \ldots, K \right\} \right\} \tag{7}$$

where $w \equiv (w_1, \ldots, w_N)^T \geq 0_N$ is a nonnegative vector of Kuhn-Tucker-Lagrange multipliers (or shadow prices) for the N domestic resource contraints in the primal problem (3). The equality (7) follows by applying the Uzawa (1958; p. 34)—Karlin (1959; p. 201) Saddle Point Theorem.[9] This theorem also implies that the order in which we maximize or minimize is immaterial.

---

[7] See Koopmans (1951).

[8] If S is a subset in R^{M+N}, con $S \equiv \{ \Sigma_{i=1}^{M+N+1} \lambda_i x^i : x^i \in S$ and $\lambda_i \geq 0$ for $i = 1 \ldots, M+N+1$ and $\Sigma_{i=1}^{M+N+1} \lambda_i = 1 \}$. See Karlin (1959; p. 400).

[9] Karlin's version of the Theorem requires that: (i) the primal problem have a finite maximum, (ii) the objective and the (inequality) constraint functions in the primal be concave functions in the vector of decision variables (which is true in our case because these functions are linear), (iii) the sets S^k be convex and (iv) the Slater constraint qualification condition hold: there exist $(\bar{u}^k, \bar{v}^k \in S^k$ such that $\Sigma_{k=1}^{K} \bar{v}^k \gg v^*$, an assumption which we now make.

In order to make further progress, we define the *unit* (scale) *profit functions*[10] π^k for the constant returns to scale sectors by (8) and the *profit functions* π^k for the convex sectors by (9): for $p \geqslant 0_M$ and $w \geqslant 0_N$, define

$$\pi^k(p, w) \equiv \max_{x, y} \{p \cdot y + w \cdot x : (y, x) \in C^k\}, \quad k = 1, \ldots, K_1; \tag{8}$$

$$\pi^k(p, w) \equiv \max_{u, v} \{p \cdot u + w \cdot v : (u, v) \in S^k\}, \quad k = K_1 + 1, \ldots, K. \tag{9}$$

If we denote a solution to (7) by w^o; x^{ko}, y^{ko} and z_k^o for $k = 1, \ldots, K$; and u^{ko}, v^{ko} for $k = K_1 + 1, \ldots, K$, then by rearranging terms in (7) and making use of definitions (8) and (9), it is clear that we have $\pi^k(p^*, w^o) = p^* \cdot y^{ko} + w^o \cdot x^{ko}$ for $k = 1, \ldots, K_1$ and $\pi^k(p^*, w^o) = p^* \cdot u^{ko} + w^o \cdot v^{ko}$ for $k = K_1 + 1, \ldots, K$. Hence (7) may be rewritten as (define $z^o \equiv (z_1^o, \ldots, z_{K_1}^o)^T \geqslant 0_{K_1}$):

$$b^o = \max_{z \geqslant 0_{K_1}} \min_{w \geqslant 0_N} \left\{ \sum_{k=1}^{K_1} \pi^k(p^*, w) z_k + \sum_{k=K_1+1}^{K} \pi^k(p^*, w) - w \cdot v^* \right\}$$

$$= \sum_{k=1}^{K_1} \pi^k(p^*, w^o) z_k^o + \sum_{k=K_1+1}^{K} \pi^k(p^*, w^o) - w^o \cdot v^*. \tag{10}$$

Thus $z^o \geqslant 0_{K_1}$ and $w^o \geqslant 0_N$ solves the max–min problem in (10) and the resulting optimal value equals b^o, the optimal value of the primal objective function in (3). Note that problem (10) is an unconstrained problem involving only $K_1 + N$ variables (the k_1 sectoral scale variables for the constant returns to scale sectors and the N equilibrium domestic prices), whereas the primal problem involved $K(M+N)$ variables and many constraints.

The saddle point problem in (10) will be our starting point for the derivation of a quadratic approximation to the Allais loss (4). Before proceeding to this derivation, we note that the Karlin-Uzawa Saddle Point Theorem may be applied to (10) in order to obtain a constrained minimization problem involving only the domestic price variables w. The resulting "pure" price dual to (3) is:

$$b^o = \min_{w \geqslant 0_N} \left\{ \sum_{k=K_1+1}^{K} \pi^k(p^*, w) - w \cdot v^* : \pi^k(p^*, w) \leqslant 0, \quad k = 1, \ldots, K_1 \right\}. \tag{11}$$

Note that the z_k^o are the optimal Lagrange multipliers for the K_1 nonpositive profit constraints in (11).

Additional material on profit functions of the form (9) may be found in

---

[10] For additional material on unit profit functions, see Diewert and Woodland (1977). We note that C^k in (9) may be replaced by con C^k and the same π^k results.

Diewert (1973). In order to obtain a clearer picture of the concept of a unit profit function of the form (8), suppose that sector 1 can produce only output y_1. Then the technology may be represented by an ordinary production function f^1, where $y_1 = f^1(-y_2, \ldots, -y_M, -z_1, \ldots, -x_N)$ (remembering that inputs are indexed negatively). In this case, the corresponding unit cost function is defined as

$$c^1(p_2, \ldots, p_M, w_1, \ldots, w_N)$$
$$\equiv \min \{-\Sigma_{m=2}^M p_m y_m - \Sigma_{n=1}^N w_n x_n : f^1(-y_2, \ldots, -y_M, -x_1, \ldots, -x_N)$$
$$\geqslant 1, -y_2 \geqslant 0, \ldots, -y_M \geqslant 0, -x_1 \geqslant 0, \ldots, -x_N \geqslant 0\}.$$

In this case, π^1 may be defined in terms of c^1 by

$$\pi^1(p_1, p_2, \ldots, p_M, w_1, \ldots, w_N) = p_1 - c^1(p_2, \ldots, p_M, w_1, \ldots, w_N).$$

Moreover, in this case, the set C^1 may be defined in terms of the production function f^1 as follows: $C^1 \equiv \{(1, y_2, \ldots, y_M, x_1, \ldots, x_N): f^1(-y_2, \ldots, -y_M, -x_1, \ldots, -x_N) \geqslant 1, -y_2 \geqslant 0, \ldots, -y_m \geqslant 0, -x_1 \geqslant 0, \ldots, -x_N \geqslant 0\}$.

Similarly, if each of the constant returns to scale industries can produce only one output, we may rewrite the unit profit functions in (8) in terms of unit cost functions, and the sets C^k in (8) are essentially the negatives of the usual unit output production possibility sets.

IV. A Second-Order Approximation to the Allais Loss

The max–min problem (10) that is dual to the economy's primal foreign exchange maximization problem (3) is our starting point in this section. In order to simplify the notation, we assume that all sectors are subject to constant returns to scale so that $K_1 = K$.[11]

In order to derive our second-order approximation to the Allais loss (4), we shall be forced to make a number of additional assumptions: (i) the solution z^o and w^o to (10) is unique and positive (i.e., $z^o \gg 0_K$ and $w^o \gg 0_N$); (ii) the unit profit functions π^k, $k = 1, \ldots, K$ are twice continuously differentiable at p^*, w^o; (iii) Samuelson's (1947) strong second-order conditions hold for the constrained minimization problem (11),[12] and (iv) the econo-

---

[11] This does not represent a loss of generality. For sectors that have a convex technology but do not exhibit constant returns to scale, we may follow the approach of McKenzie (1959; p. 66) and introduce a sector specific fixed factor to which the pure profits of the sector will be imputed. This entails the addition of an extra sector specific good to the list of domestic goods.

[12] From the Appendix in Diewert and Woodland (1977), it can be shown that this assumption is equivalent to: (i) the N by K matrix $X^o \equiv [\nabla_w \pi^1(p^*, w^o), \ldots, \nabla_w \pi^k(p^*, w^o)]$ is of rank K (so the number of sectors is equal to or less than the number of domestic goods) and (ii) the N by N matrix $\Sigma_{k=1}^K \nabla_{ww}^2 \pi^k(p^*, w^o) z_k^o + X^o X^{oT}$ is positive definite. These assumptions are also necessary and sufficient for the matrix on the l.h.s. of (25) to have an inverse.

my's distorted equilibrium production vectors $(y^{k^*} z_k^*, x^{k^*} z_k^*) \in S^k$ for $k=1,\ldots,K$ are technically efficient in the sense that for $k=1,\ldots,K$,

(y^{k^*}, x^{k^*}) is a solution to the unit scale profit maximization problem
$$\max_{y,x} \{(p^*+\tau^k)\cdot y+(w^*+t^k)\cdot x: (y,x)\in C^k\} \equiv \pi^k(p^*+\tau^k, w^*+t^k). \tag{12}$$

In (12), $z_k^* \geq 0$ is the observed sector k scale (let us identify the distorted * equilibrium with an observed equilibrium); p^* is the observed vector of foreign prices for internationally traded goods; $p^*+\tau^k \gg 0_M$ is the corresponding price vector faced by sector k (so τ^k is the sector k traded goods distortions vector) for $k=1,\ldots,K$; $w^* \geq 0_N$ is the "general" vector of domestic commodity prices,[13] and $w^*+t^k \gg 0_N$ is the observed vector of domestic prices faced by sector k (so t^k is the sector k domestic goods distortions vector) for $k=1,\ldots,K$.

We are now in a position to study Debreu's third type of efficiency loss, the waste due to imperfect economic organization. Even though each sector individually is not wasting resources—this follows from (12)—there will usually be an overall waste of resources when we aggregate over production sectors, *if the relative prices that each sector faces are different*. This conclusion will eventually emerge from the algebra below.

Before we do the algebra, let us determine whether our present framework can model the six types of distortion that we mentioned in the introduction. It is clear how the existence of industry specific tariffs, subsidies or taxes on internationally traded goods would lead to unequal τ^k vectors. If the tariffs, etc. were uniform across all industries, then $\tau^k=\tau$ for all k. (This is the usual case treated in international trade theory.) It is also reasonably clear how the existence of taxes on the output of one industry which is used as an input into other industries leads to unequal t^k vectors. If an industry supplying an output to other industries behaves like a markup monopolist, this too will lead to unequal t^k vectors. It is also the case that differential taxes or subsidies on sectors will lead to unequal t^k (e.g., consider the different corporate and noncorporate income tax treatments that are common in most Western countries, the corresponding farm and nonfarm distinctions, the special tax allowances given to manufacturing industries, and the special tax incentives that are often given to export oriented industries). Unionized and nonunionized industries usually compete in the same labour markets; if the compensation packages are different (and they frequently are), this too will lead to unequal domestic distortion vectors t^k. Thus our rather abstract assumption (12) is consistent with an immense variety of specific distortions present in the production sectors of

---

[13] There is some freedom of choice in choosing w^* and the t^k. The simplest way of resolving this ambiguity would be to choose $t^k=0_N$ for some sector k and then w^* may be interpreted as the observed vector of domestic goods prices for sector k.

most economies. These distortions are induced either by governments, unions or by non price-taking behavior on the part of firms.

Some additional implications can be drawn from our assumption (12). First, it is well known that when there are constant returns to scale in a production sector, then profits are either zero or infinite in that sector. If we assume that the observed sector be production vector $z_k^*(y^{k*}, x^{k*})$ is consistent with profit maximizing behavior and $z_k > 0$, then we must have

$$\pi^k(p^*+\tau^k, w^*+t^*) = (p^*+\tau^k)\cdot y^{k*}+(w^*+t^k)\cdot x^{k*} = 0; \quad k = 1,\ldots, K. \tag{13}$$

Second, if the unit profit functions π^k is differentiable with respect to its price arguments at the point $(p^*+\tau^k, w^*+t^k)$, then by a result due originally to Hotelling (1932; p. 594), the solution (y^{k*}, x^{k*}) to (12) is unique and may be computed by partially differentiating π^k with respect to its price arguments: i.e., we have:

$$y^{k*} = \nabla_p\pi^k(p^*+\tau^k, w^*+t^k); x^{k*} = \nabla_w\pi^k(p^*+\tau^k, w^*+t^k) \tag{14}$$

where $\nabla_p\pi^k \equiv (\partial\pi^k/\partial p_1,\ldots,\partial\pi^k/\partial p_M)^T$ and $\nabla_w\pi^k \equiv (\partial\pi^k/\partial w_1,\ldots,\partial\pi^k/\partial w_N)^T$. Thus if each π^k is differentiable, we may rewrite (2) as follows:

$$\sum_{k=1}^{K} x^{k*} z_k^* = \sum_{k=1}^{K} \nabla_w\pi^k(p^*+\tau^k, w^*+t^k) z_k^* = v^*. \tag{15}$$

Let us now look at the implications of assumptions (i) and (ii). Since $z^o \gg 0_K$ and $w^o \gg 0_N$ solve the Saddle Point maximization problem (10) and the unit profit functions π^k are all assumed to be differentiable at (p^*, w^o), the following first-order necessary conditions for (10) will be satisfied:

$$\sum_{k=1}^{K} \nabla_w\pi^k(p^*, w^o) z_k^o = v^*; \tag{16}$$

$$\pi^k(p^*, w^o) = 0; k = 1, \ldots, K. \tag{17}$$

We wish to map the optimal equilibrium (w^o, z^o) that satisfies (16) and (17) into the distorted equilibrium (w^*, z^*) that satisfies (15) and (13). Hence let ξ be a scalar which goes from 0 to 1 and define $w(\xi) \equiv [w_1(\xi),\ldots,w_N(\xi)]^T$ and $z(\xi) \equiv [z_1(\xi),\ldots,z_K(\xi)]^T$ as the solution to the following system of $N+K$ equations:[14]

---

[14] Our differentiability assumptions on the π^k and our assumption that the strong second order conditions hold for (11) are sufficient to imply (using the Implicit Function Theorem) that a unique once differentiable solution $w(\xi)$, $z(\xi)$ to (18) and (19) exists for ξ sufficiently close to 0. This is all that we require for our second-order approximation.

$$\sum_{k=1}^{K} \nabla_w \pi^k(p^* + \tau^k \xi, w(\xi) + t^k \xi) z_k(\xi) = v^*; \tag{18}$$

$$\pi^k(p^* + \tau^k \xi, w(\xi) + t^k \xi) = 0, \quad k = 1, 2, \ldots, K. \tag{19}$$

Note that by using (16) and (17), we see that $w^o = w(0)$ and $z^o = z(0)$ satisfy (18) and (19) when $\xi = 0$, and using (15) and (13), $w^* = w(1)$ and $z^* = z(1)$ satisfy (18) and (19) when $\xi = 1$.

Before we differentiate (18) and (19), it is convenient to make a few definitions. Define the sector k substitution matrix $S^k(\xi)$ $k = 1, 2, \ldots, K$ by

$$S_k(\xi) \equiv \begin{bmatrix} S^k_{pp}, S^k_{pw} \\ S^k_{wp}, S^k_{ww} \end{bmatrix} \equiv \begin{bmatrix} \nabla^2_{pp} \pi^k(\xi) z_k(\xi), \nabla^2_{pw} \pi^k(\xi) z_k(\xi) \\ \nabla^2_{wp} \pi^k(\xi) z_k(\xi), \nabla^2_{ww} \pi^k(\xi) z_k(\xi) \end{bmatrix} \tag{20}$$

where $\pi^k(\xi)$ means $\pi^k(p^* + \tau^k \xi, w(\xi) + t^k \xi)$, $\nabla^2_{pp} \pi^k$ denotes the M by M matrix of second-order partial derivatives of π^k with respect to its first M arguments, $\nabla^2_{pw} \pi$ denotes the M by N matrix of second-order partial derivatives of π^k with respect to its first M arguments and then with respect to its last N arguments, etc. Note that by using Hotelling's Lemma (14), $\nabla^2_{pp} \pi^k z_k = (\nabla_p y^k) z_k$, the matrix of marginal responses of outputs of traded goods to marginal increases in the price of traded goods, holding the sectorial scale constant, while $\nabla^2_{pw} \pi^k z_k = (\nabla_w y^k) z_k$, the matrix of marginal responses of outputs of traded goods to marginal increases in the prices of domestic goods, holding the sectoral scale constant.

From the definition of the unit profit function (8), we deduce that π^k is a convex positively linearly homogeneous function in its price arguments and hence the substitution matrix $S^k(\xi)$ defined by (2) is positive semidefinite, and satisfies the following restrictions:

$$\begin{bmatrix} S^k_{pp}(\xi), S^k_{pw}(\xi) \\ S^k_{wp}(\xi), S^k_{ww}(\xi) \end{bmatrix} \begin{bmatrix} p^* + \tau^k \xi \\ w(\xi) + t^k \xi \end{bmatrix} = \begin{bmatrix} 0_M \\ 0_N \end{bmatrix}, \quad k = 1, \ldots, K. \tag{21}$$

Define the ξ equilibrium matrix of input–output coefficients for traded goods by $Y(\xi)$ and for domestic goods by $X(\xi)$:

$$Y(\xi) \equiv [y^1(\xi), \ldots, y^k(\xi)] \equiv [\nabla_p \pi^1(\xi), \ldots, \nabla_p \pi^k(\xi)]; \tag{22}$$

$$X(\xi) \equiv [x^1(\xi), \ldots, x^K(\xi)] \equiv [\nabla_w \pi^1(\xi), \ldots, {}_w\pi^K(\xi)]. \tag{23}$$

Using Euler's Theorem on linearly homogeneous functions and definitions (22) and (23), the zero profit restrictions (19) may be rewritten as

$$[p^* + \tau^k \xi]^T y^k(\xi) + [w(\xi) + t^k \xi]^T x^k(\xi) = 0, \quad k = 1, \ldots, K. \tag{24}$$

Differentiate equations (18) and (19) with respect to ξ and evaluate the resulting derivatives when $\xi=0$. Using definitions (20), (22) and (23), the resulting system of equations may be written as

$$\begin{bmatrix} \sum_{k=1}^{K} S_{ww}^{ko}, X^o \\ X^{oT}, 0_{KxK} \end{bmatrix} \begin{bmatrix} w'(0) \\ z'(0) \end{bmatrix} = -\begin{bmatrix} \sum_{k=1}^{K}(S_{wp}^{ko}\tau^k + S_{ww}^{ko}t^k) \\ (\tau^{lT}y^{lo}+t^{lT}x^{lo}, \ldots, \tau^{KT}y^{Ko}+t^{KT}x^{Ko})^T \end{bmatrix}$$

(25)

where $S_{ww}^{ko} \equiv S_{ww}^{k}(0)$, $S_{wp}^{ko} \equiv S_{wp}^{k}(0)$, $X^o \equiv X(0)$, $x^{ko} \equiv x^k(0)$ and $y^{ko} \equiv y^k(0)$. Note that $w'(0) \equiv [dw_1(0)/d\xi, \ldots, dw_N(0)/d\xi]^T$ and $z'(0) \equiv [dz_1(0)/d\xi, \ldots, dz_K(0)/d\xi]^T$.

For each equilibrium of the economy indexed by ξ for $0 \leqslant \xi \leqslant 1$, define the *Allais* objective function $A(\xi)$ for the economy as the net amount of foreign exchange that the production sector produces at the equilibrium indexed by ξ, or alternatively, define $A(\xi)$ as the net value of internationally traded goods produced by the entire production sector, where the goods are valued at the international prices p^*; i.e.,

$$A(\xi) \equiv \sum_{k=1}^{K} p^* \cdot \nabla_p \pi^k(p^* + \tau^k \xi, w(\xi) + t^k) \, z_k(\xi) \tag{26}$$

where $w(\xi)$ and $z(\xi)$ are defined as the solution to (18) and (19).

Using (26), we may rewrite our Allais loss A_L defined by (4) as:

$$A_l = A(0) - A(1) \tag{27}$$

Our approximating strategy is to approximate $A(1)$ by the second-order Taylor Series expansion of A around $\xi=0$, $A(0)+A'(0)(1-0) +1/2\,A''(0)(1-0)^2$. Thus we need to calculate the first and second derivatives, $A'(0)$ and $A''(0)$.

Upon differentiating (26) with respect to ξ, we obtain

$$A'(\xi) = \sum_k p^{*T} \nabla_{pp}^2 \pi^k(p^* + \tau^k\xi, w(\xi) + t^k\xi)\, \tau^k z_k(\xi) +$$

$$\sum_k p^{*T} \nabla_{pw}^2 \pi^k(p^* + \tau^k\xi, w(\xi) + t^k\xi)\, [w'(\xi) + t^k]\, z_k(\xi) +$$

$$\sum_k p^{*T} \nabla_p \pi^k(p^* + \tau^k\xi, w(\xi) + t^k\xi)\, z_k'(\xi)$$

---

[15] For references to the literature on all this, see Diewert (1974).

$$= -\xi \sum_{k=1}^{K} \left[\tau^{kT} S_{pp}^{k}(\xi) \, \tau^{k} + t^{kT} S_{wp}^{k}(\xi) \, \tau^{k} + \tau^{kT} S_{pw}^{k}(\xi) \, w'(\xi) \right.$$

$$+ \tau^{kT} S_{pw}^{k}(\xi) \, t^{k} + t^{kT} S_{ww}^{k}(\xi) \, w'(\xi) + t^{kT} S_{ww}^{k}(\xi) \, t^{k}$$

$$\left. + t^{kT} y^{k}(\xi) \, z_{k}'(\xi) + t^{kT} x^{k}(\xi) \, z_{k}'(\xi) \right] \tag{28}$$

where to derive (28) we have used definitions (20), the symmetry of the matrices $S^{k}(\xi)$, the homogeneity relations (21), the zero profit relations (24), the definitions (22) and (23), and the identity which results when we differentiate equations (18) with respect to ξ, and then premultiply the resulting equations by $w(\xi)^{T}$. Thus using (28) when $\xi = 0$, we find that

$$A'(0) = 0. \tag{29}$$

Premultiply the first N equations in (25) by $w'(0)^{T}$ and premultiply the last K equations in (25) by $z'(0)^{T}$. If we eliminate the common term $w'(0)^{T} X^{o} z'(0) = z'(0)^{T} X^{oT} w'(0)$ from the resulting equations, we obtain the following equation:

$$\sum_{k=1}^{K} \left[\tau^{kT} y^{ko} z_{k}'(0) + t^{kT} x^{ko} z_{k}'(0) \right]$$

$$= \sum_{k=1}^{K} \left[w'(0)^{T} S_{ww}^{ko} w'(0) + w'(0)^{T} S_{wp}^{ko} \tau^{k} + w'(0)^{T} S_{ww}^{ko} t^{k} \right]. \tag{30}$$

Now differentiate (28) with respect to ξ, evaluate the resulting derivatives at $\xi = 0$ and use the identity (30). We find that

$$-A''(0) = \sum_{k=1}^{K} \left[\tau^{kT}, w'(0)^{T} + t^{kT} \right] \begin{bmatrix} S_{pp}^{ko}, S_{pw}^{ko} \\ S_{wp}^{ko}, S_{ww}^{ko} \end{bmatrix} \begin{bmatrix} \tau^{k} \\ w'(0) + t^{k} \end{bmatrix} \geq 0 \tag{31}$$

where the inequality follows from the positive semidefiniteness of the sectoral substitution matrices $S^{ko} \equiv S^{k}(0)$ defined by (20). Note that the vector of domestic price derivatives $w'(0)$ evaluated at the optimal equilibrium is defined by (25) in terms of the sectoral substitution matrices S^{ko}, the input–output matrices X^{o}, Y^{o}, and the distortion vectors $\tau^{1}, \ldots, \tau^{K}$ and $t^{1}, \ldots, t^{K}$.

Using (29) and (31), our quadratic approximation to the Allais loss (27) is

$$\bar{A}_{L} \equiv A(0) - [A(0) + A'(0) + 1/2 A''(0)] = -A''(0)/2, \tag{32}$$

where $A''(0)$ is defined by (31).

Thus in order to calculate the approximate amount of foreign exchange $\bar{A}_{L}$ that is being wasted due to distortions within the production sector of an economy, we need to know the distortion vectors in each sector τ^{k}, t^{k}, the input–output matrices for the economy X^o, evaluated at the optimal solution to the maximization problem (3), and the optimal sectoral substitution matrices S^{ko}. We can make a further approximation to the approximate loss (32) by replacing the optimal matrices X^o, Y^o and the S^{ko} by the observed distorted equilibrium matrices X^*, Y^* and $S^{k*} \equiv S^k(1)$ respectively. This final approximate loss measure[16] has the advantage that it depends only upon local information about the production sector around an observed distorted equilibrium; this approximate loss measure will at least provide us with order of magnitude estimates of the potential gain from removing the distortions within the production sector of an economy.

One may be tempted to think that the approximate loss defined by (32) is additive across sectors. This is not quite the case, since $w'(0)$ appears in each of the terms in the summation in (31). Hence if the distortions τ^1, t^1 increase in sector 1, we cannot conclude that the overall approximate loss will also increase, since the change in τ^1 and t^1 will generally change $w'(0)$ as well, via (25).[17] However, we can say that the approximate loss increases quadratically as *all* distortions increase linearly. This follows from (32), (31) and (25): note that if τ^k and t^k are replaced by $\lambda\tau^k$ and λt^k for some $\lambda > 0$ for $k = 1, \ldots, K$, then from (25), the initial $w'(0)$ is replaced by $\lambda w'(0)$. Conversely, the approximate loss decreases as all distortions are reduced proportionately.[18]

There is one interesting special case of the above that is worth noting. If $N = K$ so that the number of domestic goods equals the number of constant returns to scale sectors, then even in a distorted equilibrium, foreign prices essentially determine the structure of domestic prices.[19] In this case, $w'(0)$ is determined by the last K equations of (25):

$$w'(0)^T = [\tau^{1T} y^{lo} + t^{1T} x^{lo}, \ldots, \tau^{KT} y^{Ko} + t^{KT} x^{Ko}] [X^o]^{-1} \tag{33}$$

In this case, $w'(0)$ may be computed from a knowledge of the distortions and the input output coefficient matrices X^o and Y^o alone.

V. An Adaptation of the Debreu Loss to the Production Sector

Recall (1) and (2), the definitions of b^* and v^*, the amounts of foreign exchange and domestic goods respectively being produced in a distorted

---

[16] This kind of aproximation is not unusual in the applied welfare economics literature; e.g., see Harberger (1974).

[17] This kind of negative result is a standard one in the theory of the second best. For references to the piecemeal policy literature (and some positive results), see Hatta (1977).

[18] A somewhat similar piecemeal result has been obtained by Smith (1980) in the context of a complete general equilibrium model.

[19] In the undistorted case (or the case where $\tau^k = \tau$ and $t^k = 0_N$ for every k), this observation reduces to McKenzie's (1955) Domestic Price Equalization Theorem, which generalizes Samuelson's (1953–4) Factor Price Equalization Theorem.

equilibrium of the production sector of an economy. In the previous sections, we have measured the inefficiency of the distorted equilibrium by calculating the extra amount of foreign exchange that could be produced in an undistorted equilibrium while still producing the vector v^* of domestic goods. Thus we have measured the loss in terms of a numeraire "good", foreign exchange. We may want to consider measuring the loss in terms of an alternative good or combination of goods. Thus define the $N+1$ dimensional, nonnegative, nonzero "basket" vector by $(\beta_0, \beta_1, \ldots, \beta_N)$ $\equiv (\beta_0, \beta) > 0_{1+N}^T$. We now attempt to measure the loss of output due to distortions within the production sector in terms of a nonnegative multiple $r \geq 0$ of this numeraire basket of goods (β_0, β). Thus r^o is the solution to the following constrained maximization problem (where for simplicity, we have assumed that all sectors are subject to constant returns to scale):

$$\max_{r, z \geq 0_K, (y^k, x^k) \in C^k} \left\{ r : \sum_{k=1}^{K} p^{*T} y^k z_k \geq b^* + \beta_0 r; \sum_{k=1}^{K} x^k z_k \geq v^* + \beta r \right\} = r^o. \tag{34}$$

Note that $r^o \geq 0$ since if we set $r=0$, the observed distorted equilibrium satisfies the constraints in (34) and hence $r=0$ is feasible for (34). It is clear that if we set $\beta_0 = 1$ and $\beta = 0_N$, then the optimal value r^o to the Debreu maximization problem equals $b^o - b^*$, where b^o was the optimal value for the old Allais maximization problem (3). Hence the Debreu framework contains the Allais model as a special case. Let r^o, $z^o \geq 0_K$ and $(y^{ko},$ $x^{ko}) \in C^k$ for $k = 1, \ldots, K$ solve (34).

Defining the unit profit functions π^k as in section 3 and applying the Uzawa-Karlin Saddle Point Theorem, we find that the max–min dual to (34) is (35) below:

$$r^o = \max_{r, z \geq 0_K}, \min_{\lambda \geq 0, w \geq 0_N} \left\{ r(1 - \lambda \beta_0 - w^T \beta) + \sum_{k=1}^{K} \pi^k(\lambda p^*, w) z_k - \lambda b^* - w^T v^* \right\}. \tag{35}$$

Since we want to derive a quadratic approximation to the loss, we shall assume that the solution to (35) is $r^o \geq 0$, $z^o \geq 0_K$, $\lambda^o > 0$, $w^o \geq 0_N$ and the unit profit functions π^k are twice continuously differentiable at $(\lambda^o p^*, w^o)$. Differentiation of the objective function in (35) with respect to r yields the following first order necessary condition for (35):

$$\lambda^o \beta_0 + w^{oT} \beta = 1. \tag{36}$$

λ^o and w^o have the standard Lagrange multiplier interpretations; i.e., $\lambda^o(w^o_i)$ tells us the marginal increase that would occur in r if the undistorted economy received an exogenous gift of one unit of foreign exchange (of the first domestic good), etc. This is consistent with (36), which tells us if the economy received an exogenous gift of the entire basket of goods (β_0, β) then r would increase by one unit.

The r^o which occurs in (34) or (35) is a variant of Debreu's (1951) [1954] *coefficient of resource utilization.*[20]

Let ξ be a scalar that varies between 0 and 1 and maps the efficient equilibrium—the solution to (34) or (35)—into an observed distorted equilibrium, where producer prices in sector k are given by $\lambda^* p^* + \tau^k$ for traded goods and $w^* + t^k$ for domestic goods, for $k = 1, \ldots, K$. The τ^k retain their interpretations as distortion vectors as in the previous section. The scaling factor for international prices $\lambda^* > 0$ is chosen so that λ^* and w^* satisfy the following equation (which involves the numeraire basket coefficients β_0 and β):

$$\lambda^* \beta_0 + w^{*T}\beta = 1. \tag{37}$$

Consider the following system of $1+N+K+1$ equations in the $1+N+K+1$ unknowns λ, w, z and r (regarded as functions of ξ for $0 \leqslant \xi \leqslant 1$):

$$\sum_{k=1}^{K} p^{*T}\nabla_p \pi^k(\lambda(\xi)p^* + \tau^k\xi, w(\xi) + t^k\xi) z_k(\xi) - \beta_0 r(\xi) = b^* \tag{38}$$

$$\sum_{k=1}^{K} \nabla_w \pi^k(\lambda(\xi)p^* + \tau^k\xi, w(\xi) + t^k\xi) z_k(\xi) - \beta r(\xi) = v^* \tag{39}$$

$$\pi^k(\lambda(\xi)p^* + \tau^k\xi, w(\xi) + t^k\xi) = 0, \quad k = 1, \ldots, K. \tag{40}$$

$$1 - \beta_0 \lambda(\xi) + \beta^T w(\xi) = 0. \tag{41}$$

We note that when $\xi = 0$, (38)–(41) reduce to the first-order necessary conditions for the max–min problem (35). When $\xi = 1$, (38) to (41) are the equations that characterize an observed distorted equilibrium, if we note (1) and (2), $r(1) \equiv 0$, and if we normalize prices in the distorted equilibrium so that (37) is satisfied.

Differentiate (38)–(41) with respect to ξ, and evaluate the resulting derivatives at $\xi = 0$:

---

[20] The main differences are: (i) Debreu's economy is closed, (ii) Debreu chooses (β_0, β) to be proportional to the economy's endowment of fixed factors, and (iii) Debreu also measures the waste that occurs in the consumer sector (if all consumers had Leontief type preferences with no substitution, this difference vanishes). However, our present model (34) is clearly a straightforward adaptation of Debreu's basic idea to the production sector.

$$\begin{bmatrix} \displaystyle\sum_{k=1}^{K} p^{*T} S_{pp}^{ko} p^{*}, & \displaystyle\sum_{k} p^{*T} S_{pw}^{ko}, & p^{*T} Y^{o}, & -\beta_{0} \\ \displaystyle\sum_{k=1}^{K} S_{wp}^{ko} p^{*}, & \displaystyle\sum_{k} S_{ww}^{ko}, & X^{o}, & -\beta \\ Y^{oT} p^{*}, & X^{oT}, & 0_{K \times K}, & 0_{K} \\ -\beta_{0}, & -\beta^{T}, & 0_{K}^{T}, & 0 \end{bmatrix} \begin{bmatrix} \lambda'(0) \\ w'(0) \\ z'(0) \\ r'(0) \end{bmatrix} =$$

$$- \begin{bmatrix} \displaystyle\sum_{k} (p^{*T} S_{pp}^{ko} \tau^{k} + p^{*T} S_{pw}^{ko} t^{k}) \\ \displaystyle\sum_{k} (S_{wp}^{ko} \tau^{k} + S_{ww}^{ko} t^{k}) \\ (\tau^{lT} y^{lo} + t^{lT} x^{lo}, \ldots, \tau^{KT} y^{K0} + t^{KT} x^{K0})^{T} \\ 0 \end{bmatrix} \tag{42}$$

where S_{pp}^{ko}, S_{pw}^{ko}, S_{ww}^{ko}, X^{o} and Y^{o} are defined as in the previous section below (25), except that $\lambda^{o} p^{*}$ replaces p^{*} as the vector of optimal traded goods prices. We may proceed in a manner analogous to that of the previous section (assume the coefficient matrix on the left hand side of (42) is nonsingular etc.) and we may calculate the following derivatives of the coefficient of resource utilization:

$$r'(0) = 0; \tag{43}$$

$$-r''(0) = \sum_{k=1}^{K} [(\lambda'(0) p^{*} + \tau^{k})^{T}, (w'(0) + t^{k})^{T}] \begin{bmatrix} S_{pp}^{ko}, S_{pw}^{ko} \\ S_{wp}^{ko}, S_{ww}^{ko} \end{bmatrix} \begin{bmatrix} \lambda'(0) p^{*} + \tau^{k} \\ w'(0) + t^{k} \end{bmatrix} \geq 0$$

$$\tag{44}$$

where the inequality in (44) follows from the positive semidefiniteness of the sectoral substitution matrices S^{ko}. Note that $\lambda'(0)$ and $w'(0)$ are defined by (42).

Recall that $r(0) \equiv r^{o}$ and $r(1) = 0$. We wish to obtain a quadratic approximation to $r(0) = r(0) - r(1)$, since $r(1) = 0$. Approximate $r(1)$ by $r(0) + r'(0) + r''(0)/2$. Hence

$$r(0) = r^{o} \cong -r''(0)/2 \tag{45}$$

where $r''(0)$ is defined by (44). If we wish to value the approximate loss in units of foreign exchange, valuing the "waste" basket of goods (β_{0}, β) at the undistorted equilibrium prices (λ^o, w^o), we find using (36) that our quadratic approximation to the monetary value of the Debreu loss is

$$D_L = (\lambda^o \beta_0 + w^{oT} \beta)(-r''(0))/2\lambda^o = -r''(0)/2\lambda^o \geq 0, \qquad (46)$$

where $r''(0)$ is defined by (44).[21] It can be verified that if $\beta_0 \equiv 1$ and $\beta \equiv 0_N$, then the approximate Debreu Loss defined by (46) reduces to the approximate Allais loss defined by (32).[22]

Our discussion of the Allais loss is relevant also to the Debreu loss and will not be repreated here.

In summary, the Debreu approximate loss is somewhat more complex than the corresponding Allais loss, due to the extra terms involving $\lambda'(0)$, but it is quite similar otherwise. Hence since simplicity is a virtue, for most empirical applications, we would recommend the use of the Allais loss concept.

VI. Alternative Interpretations, Extensions and Limitations

We conclude with some alternative interpretations, some extensions, and some limitations of our models.

The first point to note is that we do not require the assumption that the economy under consideration be open. If the economy is closed, simply take $M=1$ and regard the single "internationally traded good" as a numeraire domestic good and set $p^*=1$.

We have not mentioned "reference price" measures of output loss due to distortions such as Farrell's (1957; p. 255) *price efficiency* measure or equivalently, the producer analogue of Hicks (1941–2; p. 128) *Paasche variation* adopted from the consumer context to the producer context.[23] However, our Allais loss measure (4) does contain these Hicks-Farrell loss measures as a special case: we need only assume that $N=0$ so that there are no "domestic" goods (or we could allow for a sector specific fixed factor for each sector) and assume that all goods appear as "internationally traded goods" with p^* being the appropriate "optimal" reference price vector.

---

[21] Since $\lambda(1) \equiv \lambda^*$ is observable and $\lambda^o \equiv \lambda(0)$, we may linearly approximate λ^o by $\lambda^* - \lambda'(0)$ where $\lambda'(0)$ is defined by (42).

[22] If $\beta_0 \equiv 1$ and $\beta \equiv 0_N$, then the last equation in (42) implies that $\lambda'(0)=0$. Thus we have $\lambda^o \equiv \lambda(0) = \lambda(1) \equiv \lambda^* = 1$ under these conditions.

[23] Refer to the diagram on page 127 of Hicks :1941–2) and think of the I_1 indifference curve as being the negative of the economy's efficient production possibility set. Let the price line tangent to this efficient surface at A represent "optimal" producer prices. Move this price line in a parallel fashion until it passes through an observed inefficient equilibrium point B. The distance BB_2 in the Hicks diagram represents the loss of output valued at the base prices, and this is what Hicks calls the Paasche variation on the following page. Much of this appeared explicitly in the producer context in Figure 3.2 of Hicks (1940).

Hence there is no need for us to undertake a separate analysis for these reference price measures of productive inefficiency; we need only reinterpret our existing Allais model.

Thus far, we have held the number of production sectors fixed throughout the analysis. However, we may be interested in calculating the waste generated by a subset of our original K sectors, say sectors $1, 2, \ldots, R$. Obviously, we may apply the same methodology as outlined above to this task, with R replacing K and $v^R \equiv \Sigma_{k=1}^R v^{k*}$ replacing our old vector $v^* \equiv \Sigma_{k=1}^K v^{k*}$. Denote the resulting Allais loss as $A_L (1, 2, \ldots, R)$. We may also calculate the waste generated by the remaining sectors, where v^* is replaced by $\Sigma_{k=R+1}^K v^{k*}$, etc. Denote the resulting Allais loss as $A_L(R+1, \ldots, K)$. If we denote our original Allais loss by $A_L(1, \ldots, K)$, a comparison of feasible solutions for the corresponding maximization problems of the form (3) yields the following result:

$$A_L^\cdot(1, \ldots, K) \geqslant A_L(1, \ldots, R) + A_L(R+1, \ldots, K); \tag{47}$$

i.e., the overall gain that would result from the removal of *all* of the distortions within the production sector will generally exceed the partial gains that result from the removal of distortions within non overlapping subsets of the sectors. A similar result holds for the Debreu loss. If we interpret sectors $1, \ldots; K$ as the production sectors of separate countries, the (47) may be interpreted as saying that the world gains from having complete multilateral free trade will generally exceed the gains that occur then the countries have free trade within bloc 1 (consisting of countries $1, 2, \ldots, R$) and within bloc 2 (consisting of countries $R+1, \ldots, K$) but restricted trade between the blocs.

We may readily extend our analysis to encompass consumers. The "production possibility set" S^k of household k becomes the negative of a consumption possibility set; i.e., if f^k is the utility function of household k (with goods consumed indexed positively and goods supplied indexed negatively), then $S^k \equiv \{(-u^k, -v^k): u^k = -\bar{u}^k + u; v^k = -\bar{v}^k + v; f^k(u, v) \geqslant f^k(u^{k*}, v^{k*})\}$ where $\bar{u}^k$ and $\bar{v}^k$ are nonnegative vectors of fixed factors supplied inelastically by household k and (u^{k*}, v^{k*}) is household k's vector of commodity demands and (the negative of) variable factor supplies chosen in the distorted equilibrium. The corresponding profit function of the form (9) becomes $\pi^k(p, w) = p \cdot \bar{u}^k + w \cdot \bar{v}^k - m^k(f^k(u^{k*}, v^{k*}), p, w)$ where m^k is the household k expenditure function defined by $m^k(\alpha, p, w) \equiv \min_{u, v} \{p \cdot u + w \cdot v: f^k(u, v) \geqslant \alpha\}$. Now add household k to the list of nonconstant returns to scale "industries" (or define an artificial household k fixed factor and add household k to the list of constant returns to scale sectors) and apply the analysis above. The vector v^* that occurs in (2) may now be interpreted as a vector of net demands for domestic goods by the government in the distorted equilibrium. With this extended interpretation of our model, we have now captured the essence of the original models of Allais and Debreu.[24] Note however, since all consumers and producers will be facing the same prices in an optimal state, it may be necessary for the government to have access to household specific tax and transfer instruments in order to attain the optimal state.

The reader will recall that we raised the piecemeal policy problem in Section IV. The problem may be restated as follows. Suppose we reduce in magnitude one of the distortions (i.e., one of the components of τ^k or t^k for some k). Then can we conclude that the Allais loss will decrease? Unfortunately, the answer is no in general. However, it is true that there will always exist at least one distortion that can be reduced such that this reduction leads to a reduced Allais loss.[25] Thus, in theory, we could reduce distortions sequentially in such a way so as to travel to the zero distortion level in all sectors, and the Allais loss would decrease monotonically along this path of distortion reduction. However, this result is not as useful as we would like: we would prefer to know if reducing a *particular* set of distortions would lead to less overall loss.

Turning now to some limitations of our models, we note that our analysis assumed that there were no externalities between production sectors. This is an important omission.[26]

Another limitation is that our quadratic approximations were unable to deal with production sectors that exhibit increasing returns to scale (although our general loss measure (4) could deal with this complication).

Our methodology is not very well suited to the evaluation of production waste that may occur in a dynamic setting where investment is taking place. The problem is that at any point in time, we cannot observe the "distorted" production decisions that will occur in the future, and hence it is difficult to determine what the observed "distorted" reference equilibrium is in an intertemporal context. Our present methodology may be applied holding capital accumulation decisions fixed at their observed ("distorted") level, but the resulting loss estimates will tend to *understate* the actual losses, because we have not taken into account the fact that the current distortions will tend to induce inefficient capital accumulation decisions; e.g., consider the growth of "hot house" industries induced by prohibitive tariffs.

---

[24] Some differences remain. In particular, I cannot find a precise counterpart to the approximation formulae (32) and (45), although some formulae due to Boiteux (1951; p. 132) and Debreu (1954; pp. 19–21) appear to be quite close.

[25] Space limitations prevent us from proving this assertion here. It is also true that a proportional reduction in all distortions will reduce the Allais loss (and not only the approximate Allais loss as we showed in Section IV).

[26] For a method of modelling externalities and references to the literature see Archibald (1980).

Another apparant limitation of our methodology is that it is unable to evaluate the losses in efficiency that may occur *between* the producer and consumer sectors. However, in theory, we have already indicated how this limitation maý be overcome: we need only introduce additional sectors corresponding to various household classes, and move to the general equilibrium loss measures of Allais and Debreu.

A final qualification with respect to our methodology for measuring inefficiency within the production sector of an economy must be noted. If all of the distortions are removed, then usually domestic prices will change (recall the vector of price derivatives $w'(0)$ in (25) and (42)). Hence, usually some consumers will be hurt by these induced price changes and it may be necessary (or desirable) to compensate some (or all) of these consumers for their losses.[27]

We conclude on a speculative note. During the 1950s and 1960s, most Western economies experienced rapid growth while international trade grew even more rapidly, stimulated perhaps by the large reductions in barriers to trade that took place on a multilateral basis during that period. On the other hand, during the seventies and eighties, we have experience much lower rates of growth and a dramatic decline in total factor productivity (which is the ratio of output growth to input growth).[28] Could the large unexplained portion of this productivity decline be explained by the rapid growth in government programs, discriminating tax policies, hidden barriers to trade and regulatory activities that had the effect of increasing distortions within the world economy? Perhaps not, but it seems clear if the current trend to increase both hidden and overt barriers to international trade continues, then world total factor productivity will continue to decline. We hope that the methodology outlined above will lead to empirical attempts to estimate the waste that is now present both within and between the production sectors of various countries.

References

Allais, M.: *A la recherche d'une discipline économique*, Tome I. Imprimerie Nationale, Paris, 1943.

Allais, M.: La theorie générale des surplus et l'apport fondamental de Vilfredo Pareto. *Revue d'Economie Politique 83*, 1044–1097, 1973.

Allais, M.: Theories of general economic equilibrium and maximum efficiency. In *Equilibrium and disequilibrium in economic theory* (ed. E. Schwodiauer), pp. 129–201. D. Reidel Publishing Co., Dordrecht, Holland, 1977.

---

[27] However, if the government can change commodity taxes, then it will always be possible for the government to translate an increase in productive efficiency into a welfare increase for each household; see Diewert (1982).

[28] See Norsworthy, Harper and Kunze (1979) for an attempt to explain the decline in total factor productivity in the U.S.

Archibald, G. C.: Adaptive control of some producer-producer externalities. *Journal of Economic Behavior and Organization 1*, 81–96, 1980.

Auerbach, A.: The theory of excess burden and optimal taxation. Forthcoming in the *Handbook of Public Economics*, 1982.

Boiteux, M.: Le 'revenu distruable' et les pertes économiques. *Econometrica 19*, 112–133, 1951.

Debreu, G.: The coefficient of resource utilization. *Econometrica 19*, 273–292, 1951.

Debreu, G.: A classical tax-subsidy problem. *Econometrica 22*, 14–22, 1954.

Diewert, W. E.: Functional forms for profit and transformation functions. *Journal of Economic Theory 6*, 284–316, 1973.

Diewert, W. E.: Applications of duality theory. In *Frontiers of quantitative economics* (ed. M. D. Intriligator and D. A. Kendrick), Vol II, pp. 106–171. North-Holland, Amstersdam, 1974.

Diewert, W. E.: The measurement of deadweight loss revisited. *Econometrica 49*, 1225–1224, 1981.

Diewert, W. E.: Cost benefit analysis and project evaluation: A comparison of alternative approaches. Discussion Paper 82–25, Department of Economics, University of British Columbia, Vancouver, September, 1982.

Diewert, W. E. & Woodland, A. D.: Frank Knight's theorem in linear programming revisited. *Econometrica 45*, 375–398, 1977.

Farrell, M. J.: The measurement of productive efficiency. *Journal of the Royal Statistical Society, Series A 120*, 253–281, 1957.

Harberger, A. C.: The measurement of waste. *American Economic Review 54*, 58–76, 1964.

Harberger, A. C.: *Taxation and welfare*. Little, Brown and Company, Boston, 1974.

Hatta, T.: A theory of piecemeal policy recommendations. *Review of Economic Studies 44*, 1–21, 1977.

Hicks, J. R.: The valuation of the social income. *Economica 7*, 105–124, 1940.

Hicks, J. R.: Consumers' surplus and index numbers. *The Review of Economic Studies 9*, 126–137, 1941–2.

Hotelling, H.: Edgeworth's taxation paradox and the nature of demand and supply functions. *Journal of Political Economy 40*, 577–616, 1932.

Hotelling, H.: The general welfare in relation to problems of taxation and of railway and utility rates. *Econometrica 6*, 242–269, 1938.

Karlin, S.: *Mathematical methods and theory in games, programming and economics*, Vol. 1. Addison-Wesley Publishing Co., Reading, Massachusetts, 1959.

King, M. A.: Welfare analysis of tax reforms using household data. Discussion Paper, Department of Economics, The University of Birmingham, Birmingham, England, 1982.

Koopmans, T. C. (ed.): *Activity analysis of production and allocation*. Cowles Commission Monograph No. 13. Wiley, New York, 1951.

McKenzie, L. W.: Equality of factor prices in world trade. *Econometrica 23*, 239–257, 1955.

McKenzie, L. W.: On the existence of general equilibrium for a competitive market. *Econometrica 27*, 54–71, 1959.

Norsworthy, J. R., Harper, M. J. & Kunze, K.: The slowdown in productivity growth: Analysis of some contributing factors. *Brookings Papers on Economic Activity 10*, 387–421, 1979.

Samuelson, P. A.: *Foundations of economic analysis*. Harvard University Press, Cambridge, Massachussetts, 1947.

Samuelson, P. A. Prices of factors and goods in general equilibrium. *The Review of Economic Studies 21*, 1–20, 1953–4.

Smith, Alasdair: Optimal public policy in open economies. Discussion Paper, London School of Economics, August 1980.

Uzawa, H.: The Kuhn-Tucker theorem in concave programming. In *Studies in linear and nonlinear programming* (ed. K. H. Arrow, L. Hurwicz and H. Uzawa), pp. 32–37. Stanford University Press, Stanford, California, 1958.

The Structure of Technical Efficiency*

Rolf Färe

Southern Illinois University, Carbondale, IL, USA

Shawna Grosskopf

Southern Illinois University, Carbondale, IL, USA

C. A. Knox Lovell

University of North Carolina, Chapel Hill, NC, USA

Abstract

It is common practice to decompose measures of efficiency into component measures of technical and allocative efficiency. In this paper we show how, and why, to decompose a general measure of technical efficiency into component measures of purely technical efficiency, congestion, and scale efficiency, and we investigate the properties of each measure. We do so for a multiple-output technology which satisfies a weak axiom system that does not include either constant returns to scale or strong input disposability.

I. Introduction

In a pathbreaking and belatedly influential paper, Farrell (1957) investigated the structure of productive efficiency. He showed that productive (or overall) efficiency could be decomposed into the product of technical efficiency and allocative (or price) efficiency. He also showed how to measure productive efficiency and its two components, and provided a cost interpretation for each. This structure devised by Farrell eventually provided the impetus for a rich variety of empirical research on the magnitude and the sources of productive inefficiency.[1]

By investigating the structure of productive efficiency Farrell was able to provide an answer to the question: What is productive inefficiency, and where does it come from? However to the best of our knowledge nobody has addressed the logical subsequent question: What is technical inefficien-

---

* We are indebted to the Editor and two referees for their helpful comments on an earlier draft of this paper.

[1] For an econometric survey of this work see Førsund, Lovell & Schmidt (1980), and for a topical survey see Färe, Grosskopf & Lovell (1982, Chapter 1).

cy, and where does it come from? In this paper we address this question by investigating the structure of technical efficiency. In the interest of brevity, we only sketch an outline of the logic of this structure, omitting proofs of results that are contained in Färe, Grosskopf & Lovell (1982).

The production technology we use is described in Section II. Our assumptions on the structure of technology are less restrictive than those employed by Farrell in two respects. We do not impose constant returns to scale and strong input disposability, and, more significantly we allow for the production of multiple outputs. Consequently our measure of technical efficiency is also less restrictive than that developed by Farrell. We then show in Section III that our measure of technical efficiency decomposes into the product of three terms: a Farrell measure of technical efficiency, a measure of input congestion, and a measure of scale efficiency. Thus our investigation of the structure of technical efficiency reveals that a firm can be technically inefficient if it operates on the interior of its production set, if it operates in a congested region of its technology, or if it operates at too large or too small scale.

II. The Production Technology

A production technology transforming inputs $x \in R^n_+$ into outputs $u \in R^m_+$ is modelled by an input correspondence $L: R^m_+ \rightarrow P(R^m_+)$ mapping each output vector $u \in R^m_+$ to the set $L(u) \subseteq R^n_+$ consisting of all input vectors $x \in R^n_+$ capable of producing at least the output vector u. ($P(R^n_+)$ is the set of all subsets of R^n_+.) L is assumed to satisfy the following axioms:

$L.1^2$ $0 \notin L(u)$, $u \geq 0$,   and $L(0) = R^n_+$,

$L.2$ $\|u^l\| \rightarrow +\infty$ as $l \rightarrow +\infty \Rightarrow \bigcap\limits_{l=1}^{+\infty} L(u^l)$ is empty,

$L.3$ $x \in L(u) \Rightarrow \lambda x \in L(u)$, $\lambda \geq 1$,

$L.4$ L is a closed correspondence,

$L.5$ $L(\theta u) \subseteq L(u)$, $\theta \geq 1$.

L is not assumed to satisfy strong disposability of inputs

$L.3.S$ $y \geq x \in L(u) \Rightarrow y \in L(u)$,

or constant returns to scale

CRS $L(\theta u) = \theta L(u)$, $\theta > 0$,

---

[2] $y \leq x$ means $y \leq x$ but $y \neq x$.

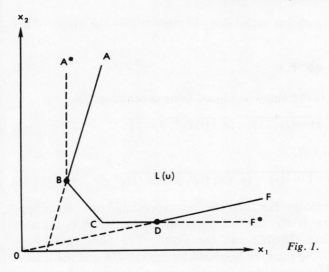

Fig. 1.

both of which were employed by Farrell (1957; 254–56) in the single-output context. It is the relaxation of these two assumptions that enables us to investigate the structure of technical efficiency.

A part of our investigation of the structure of technical efficiency is based on a distinction among three different subsets of $L(u)$. These three subsets, namely the isoquant, the weak efficient subset, and the efficient subset, are defined by

$$\text{Isoq } L(u) := \begin{cases} \{x : x \in L(u), \lambda x \notin L(u) & \text{for } \lambda < 1\}, & u \geq 0, \\ \{0\}, u = 0. \end{cases} \tag{1}$$

$$\text{WEff } L(u) := \begin{cases} \{x : x \in L(u), y \overset{*}{<} x \Rightarrow y \notin L(u)\}, & u \geq 0, \\ \{0\}, u = 0. \end{cases} \tag{2}^3$$

$$\text{Eff } L(u) := \begin{cases} \{x : x \in L(u), y \leq x \Rightarrow y \notin L(u)\}, & u \geq 0, \\ \{0\}, u = 0. \end{cases} \tag{3}$$

To clarify the distinctions among the three subsets of $L(u)$, consider the technology depicted in Figure 1.

$L(u)$ consists of the set of input vectors on or inside $ABCDF$. Isoq$L(u)$ consists of the set of input vectors on $ABCD$, WEff$L(u)$ consists of the set of input vectors in BCD, and Eff$L(u)$ consists of the set of input vectors on BC. These distinctions arise whenever L satisfies $\{L.1–L.5\}$ but not $L.3.S$. The expanded input set bounded by A^*BCDF^* does satisfy $L.3.S$. An

---

[3] $y \overset{*}{<} x$ means $y \leq x$ and either $y_i < x_i$ or $y_i = x_i = 0$ for $i = 1, \ldots, n$.

equivalent way of representing technology is provided by the graph of the technology, namely

$$GR: = \{(u, x): x \in L(u), u \in R_+^m\}. \tag{4}$$

Corresponding to GR is the smallest closed cone containing GR,

$$\overline{K(GR):} = \overline{\{(u, x): (u, x) = (\lambda v, \lambda y), \quad (v, y) \in GR, \lambda \geqq 0\}}, \tag{5}$$

and the star-closure of GR,

$$\overline{(GR)^*:} = \overline{\{(u, x): (u, x) = (\lambda v, \lambda y), \quad (v, y) \in GR, \lambda \in [0, 1]\}}. \tag{6}$$

The graph of the technology GR, and the corresponding cone technology $\overline{K(GR)}$ and star-closure $\overline{(GR)^*}$ are illustrated in Figure 2. GR is the area bounded by the surface $OPCRB$ and the x-axis. The cone technology $\overline{K(GR)}$ generated by GR is the area bounded by the ray OA and the x-axis. The star-closure $\overline{(GR)^*}$ generated by GR is the area bounded by the surface $OQCRB$ and the x-axis. It is apparent from (5) and (6) and Figure 2 that $\overline{K(GR)}$ satisfies CRS, while $\overline{(GR)^*}$ exhibits nonincreasing returns to scale. A part of our investigation of the structure of technical efficiency is based on a distinction among GR, $\overline{K(GR)}$ and $\overline{(GR)^*}$, a distinction which arises if and only if L does not satisfy CRS.[4] Finally, associated with $\overline{K(GR)}$ is an input correspondence $L^K(u)$, and associated with $\overline{(GR)^*}$ is an input correspondence $L^*(u)$.[5]

III. The Structure of Technical Efficiency

In this section we analyze the structure of technical efficiency defined on a technology satisfying $\{L.1–L.5\}$ but not necessarily $L.3.S$ or CRS. We obtain four primary and two derived measures of technical efficiency, and we show how Farrell's measure, generalized to a multiple-output context, fits into the structure.

Since our primary interest is in the role of the Farrell measure in this structure, we begin by introducing the effective domain of the Farrell measure as

$$D(F): = \{(u, x): \exists \lambda \geqq 0 \quad \text{such that } \lambda x \in L(u)\}. \tag{7}$$

The Farrell measure can now be defined as

---

[4] The implications for efficiency measurement of the scale-related distinctions among GR, $\overline{(GR)^*}$ and $\overline{K(GR)}$ for a single-output technology satisfying $\{L.1–L.5, L.3.S\}$ have been noted by Afriat (1972).

[5] It is possible that neither $\overline{K(GR)}$ nor $\overline{(GR)^*}$ is the graph of a technology, in which case neither $L^K(u)$ nor $L^*(u)$ can be defined. The possibility of this phenomenon of forever-increasing returns to scale is remote, and we ignore it.

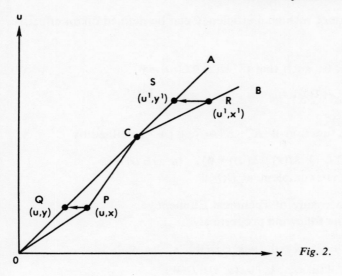

Fig. 2.

Definition (8). The function F: $R_+^m \times R_+^n \to R_+ \cup \{+\infty\}$ defined by

$$F(u, x):= \begin{cases} \min \{\lambda \geqq 0: \lambda x \in L(u)\}, (u, x) \in D(F), \\ +\infty, (u, x) \in \text{complement } D(F), \end{cases}$$

is called the Farrell Measure of Technical Efficiency.[6]

For $x \in L(u)$, $(F(u, x) \cdot x)$ is the smallest radial displacement of x that can produce u. $F(u, x)$ satisfies the following properties:

$F.1 \quad 0 < F(u, x) < +\infty, \quad u \geqslant 0, (u, x) \in D(F)$,

$F.2 \quad F(u, \lambda x) = \lambda^{-1} F(u, x), \quad \lambda > 0, (u, x) \in D(F)$,

$F.3 \quad L(u) = \{x: 0 < F(u, x) \leqq 1\}, \quad u \geqslant 0$,

$F.4 \quad \text{Isoq } L(u) = \{x: F(u, x) = 1\}, \quad u \geqslant 0$.

$F.1$ and $F.2$ are self-explantory. $F.3$ states that $F(u, x)$ provides a complete characterization of a technology satisfying $\{L.1–L.5\}$. $F.4$ states that $F(u, x) = 1$ if and only if $x \in \text{Isoq } L(u)$, and so the Farrell measure uses the isoquant as its reference set for efficiency measurement.

---

[6] Axioms $\{L.1–L.5\}$ suffice to guarantee that the minima in Definitions (8), (10), (14) and (17) exist. Moreover, each of the efficiency measures developed in this section is an input-based measure describing the efficiency of input vector x in the production of output vector u. It is of course possible to use the dual output correspondence to define output-based measures of the efficiency of output vector u produced from input vector x.

A second measure of technical efficiency can be defined on an effective domain

$$D(W): = \{(u, x): \exists \lambda \geqq 0 \quad \text{such that } (\lambda \cdot M(x) \cap L(u)) \neq \emptyset\}, \tag{9}$$

where $M(x): = \{y: 0 \leqq y \leqq x\}$, as

Definition (10). The function $W: R_+^m \times R_+^n \rightarrow R_+ \cup \{+\infty\}$ defined by

$$W(u, x): = \begin{cases} \min\{\lambda \geqq 0: (\lambda \cdot M(x) \cap L(u)) \neq \emptyset\}, & (u, x) \in D(W), \\ +\infty, (u, x) \in \text{complement } D(F), \end{cases}$$

is called the Weak Measure of Technical Efficiency.

$W(u, x)$ satisfies the following properties:

W.1 $0 < W(u, x) < +\infty, \quad u \geqq 0, (u, x) \in D(W),$

W.2 $W(u, \lambda x) = \lambda^{-1} W(u, x), \quad \lambda > 0, (u, x) \in D(W),$

W.3 $L(u) \subseteq \{x: 0 < W(u, x) \leqq 1\}, \quad u \geqq 0,$

W.4 $\text{WEff}\, L(u) = \{x: x \in L(u), W(u, x) = 1\}, \quad u \geqq 0.$

W.1 and W.2 are self-explantory. W.3 states that the input set $L(u)$ is no larger than, and may be smaller than, the set of input vectors for which $0 < W(u, x) \leqq 1$.[7] W.4 states that $W(u, x) = 1$ if and only if $x \in \text{WEff}\, L(u)$, and so the weak measure uses the weak efficient subset as its reference set for efficiency measurement.

To illustrate $W(u, x)$ and its relationship to $F(u, x)$, consider the weakly disposable technology depicted in Figure 3.

For $x \in L(u)$ at point P, $F(u, x)$ contracts x as far as possible down the ray OP provided $(F(u, x) \cdot x)$ can produce u. Thus $F(u, x) = OQ/OP$. $W(u, x)$ pushes the nonpositive orthant $M(x)$ as far as possible down the same ray OP under the condition that $(W(u, x) \cdot M(X))$ has a nonempty intersection with $L(u)$. The origin of $(W(u, x) \cdot M(x))$ is located at point R, and the intersection of $(W(u, x) \cdot M(x))$ with $L(u)$ occurs at point $T \in L(u)$. Thus $W(u, x) = OR/OP < OQ/OP = F(u, x)$. However if the technology had satisfied $L.3.S$, Isoq $L(u)$ would have become vertical at point T, including point R, and we would have had $W(u, x) = OR/OP = F(u, x)$. This suggests

Proposition (11). *Let L satisfy $\{L.1–L.5\}$. Then $W(u, x) \leqq F(u, x)$. Moreover, $W(u, x) = F(u, x)$ for all $(u, x) \in R_+^m \times R_+^n$ if and only if L also satisfies $L.3.S$.*

---

[7] W.3 becomes and equality, and $W(u, x)$ completely characterizes technology, if, and only if, $L.3.S$ holds, in which case Isoq $L(u) = \text{WEff}\, L(u)$ and $F(u, x) = W(u, x)$.

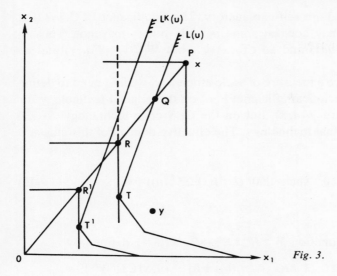

Fig. 3.

Suppose now that technology satisfies $\{L.1–L.5\}$ but not $L.3.S$, so that there exists (u, x) such that $W(u, x) < F(u, x)$. The difference between the two (RQ in Figure 3) is a radial measure of a nonradial phenomenon: the excessive usage of a subset of inputs attributable to a lack of strong input disposability, commonly called congestion. Congestion occurs when reducing usage of a subset of inputs, holding constant the usage of all remaining inputs, generates an increase in some outputs and a reduction in none. In Figure 3 input x_2 congests technology at points such as P, Q and R since a reduction in x_2, holding x_1 constant, allows for the production of some output vector $v \geqslant u$.[8] We are thus led to the following definition of input congestion, which we interpret as a component of technical efficiency.

Definition (12). For $x \in L(u)$, $u \geqslant 0$, the Congestion Measure is $C(u, x): = W(u, x)/F(u, x)$.

The properties satisfied by $C(u, x)$ are derived from those of $W(u, x)$ and $F(u, x)$, and include

$C.1$ $0 < C(u, x) \leqq 1$,

$C.2$ $C(u, x) = 1$ if and only if x does not congest u,

$C.3$ $C(u, \lambda x) = C(u, x), \quad \lambda > 0$.

---

[8] The phenomenon of congestion and its relationship to a lack of strong disposability are examined by Färe & Svensson (1980). Examples include traffic congestion in the production of transportation, reduced grain yield due to excessive fertilization, and output loss due to featherbedding and other union work rules. Note also that the practice of radial measurement of an essentially nonradial phenomenon is not new; Farrell (1957) did so with allocative inefficiency.

Properties $C.1$ and $C.3$ are self-explanatory. The significance of C.2 is that some input vectors may congest some u while others may not. Thus in Figure 3 $W(u, x) < F(u, x)$ and so $C(u, x) < 1$, but $W(u, y) = F(u, y)$ and so $C(u, y) = 1$.

In order to introduce a measure of scale efficiency, we first need to define a weak measure of technical efficiency, not on the original technology for which we already have $W(u, x)$, but on the CRS cone technology $\overline{K(GR)}$ generated by the original technology. The effective domain of this measure is

$$D(W^K): = \{(u, x): \exists \lambda \geqq 0 \quad \text{such that} \quad (\lambda \cdot M(x) \cap L^K(u)) \neq \emptyset\}, \tag{13}$$

and we have

Definition (14). The function $W^K: R_+^m \times R_+^n \to R_+ \cup \{+\infty\}$ defined by

$$W^K(u, x): = \begin{cases} \min \{\lambda \geqq 0: (\lambda \cdot M(x) \cap L^K(u)) \neq \emptyset\}, & (u, x) \in D(W^K), \\ +\infty, (u, x) \in \text{complement } D(W^K), \end{cases}$$

is called the Weak Cone Measure of Technical Efficiency.

$W^K(u, x)$ satisfies properties similar to $\{W.1-W.4\}$ of $W(u, x)$ and, by virtue of the CRS property of the cone technology, $W^K(\theta u, x) = \theta \cdot W^K(u, x)$, $\theta > 0$.

$W^K(u, x)$ is illustrated in Figure 3. For $x \in L(u)$ at point P, $W^K(u, x)$ pushes the nonpositive orthant $M(x)$ as far as possible down the ray OP provided that $(W^K(u, x) \cdot M(x))$ has a nonempty intersection with $L^K(u)$. The origin of $(W^K(u, x) \cdot M(x))$ occurs at point R', and the intersection of $(W^K(u, x) \cdot M(x))$ with $L^K(u)$ occurs at point $T' \in L^K(u)$. Thus $W^K(u, x) = OR'/OP < OR/OP = W(u, x)$. Had technology exhibited CRS, then $L^K(u) = L(u)$ and $W^K(u, x) = W(u, x)$. The role of returns to scale in the relationship between $W^K(u, x)$ and $W(u, x)$ is further clarified by Figure 2.

At point P, $(u, x) \in GR$ and so $x \in L(u)$. If technology had exhibited CRS with point C remaining feasible, then output u could have been produced with a smaller input vector, so that $y \in L^K(u)$. This suggests that the distance QP can serve as a measure of the excessive input usage attributable to deviations from CRS.[9] Formally,

---

[9] Our scale efficiency measure $S(u, x)$ is basically the same as one (of several) proposed by Førsund & Hjalmarsson (1979), who interpret the distance QP in Figure 2 as measuring how close the production unit is to operating at technically optimal scale, defined as that (u, x) for which output per unit of input is maximized. It is in this sense that $S(u, x)$ constitutes a component of technical efficiency. Note that we, and Førsund & Hjalmarsson, use technically optimal scale as the benchmark. Other writers use the price-dependent notion of profit-maximizing scale as the benchmark, and these two benchmarks do not necessarily coincide.

Definition (15). For $x \in L(u)$, $u \geq 0$, the Scale Efficiency Measure is $S(u, x) := W^K(u, x)/W(u, x)$.

The properties of $S(u, x)$ are derived from those of $W^K(u, x)$ and $W(u, x)$ and from the fact that $W^K(u, x) = W(u, x)$ if and only if technology exhibits CRS, and include

S.1 $0 < S(u, x) \leq 1$,

S.2 $S(u, x) = 1$ if and only if $S(u, x)$ is scale efficient,

S.3 $S(u, \lambda x) = S(u, x)$, $\lambda > 0$.

Suppose $S(u, x) < 1$. We do not yet know whether scale inefficiency results from increasing returns to scale (as at point P in Figure 2) or from decreasing returns to scale (as at point R in Figure 2). However a determination can be made on the basis of the relationship of $\overline{(GR)^*}$ to $\overline{K(GR)}$. In order to do so we introduce another weak measure of technical efficiency, this one on the non-increasing returns to scale star technology $\overline{(GR)^*}$ generated by the original technology. The effective domain of this measure is

$$D(W^*) := \{(u, x): \exists \lambda \geq 0 \quad \text{such that } (\lambda \cdot M(x) \cap L^*(u)) \neq \emptyset\}, \tag{16}$$

and we have

Definition (17). The function $W^*: R_+^m \times R_+^n \to R_+ \cup \{+\infty\}$ defined by

$$W^*(u, x) := \begin{cases} \min \{\lambda \geq 0: (\lambda \cdot M(x) \cap L^*(u)) \neq \emptyset\}, & (u, x) \in D(W^*), \\ +\infty, (u, x) \in \text{complement } D(W^*), \end{cases}$$

is called the Weak Star Measure of Technical Efficiency.

$W^*(u, x)$ satisfies properties similar to $\{W.1–W.4\}$ of $W(u, x)$. More importantly, a comparison of $W^*(u, x)$ with $W^K(u, x)$ enables us to determine wheter $S(u, x) < 1$ is due to increasing or decreasing returns to scale. Referring to Figure 2, for all points on OPC (excluding C) we have $W^K(u, x) = W^*(u, x) < 1$, while for all points on CRB (excluding C) we have $W^K(u, x) < W^*(u, x) = 1$. It follows that if $W^K(u, x) = W^*(u, x)$ as at point P, $S(u, x) < 1$ is due to increasing returns to scale while, if $W^K(u, x) < W^*(u, x)$ as at point R, $S(u, x) < 1$ is due to decreasing returns to scale. At point C we have $W^*(u, x) = W^*(u, x) = 1$, and $S(u, x) = 1$.

Using Definitions (8), (12), (14) and (15), we arrive at the following decomposition of the Weak Cone Measure of Technical Efficiency:

$$W^K(u, x) = F(u, x) \cdot C(u, x) \cdot S(u, x). \tag{18}$$

Equation (18) describes the structure of technical efficiency. It states that a production unit is technically inefficient if x is on the interior of $L(u)$ $(F(u, x) < 1)$, if x congests u $(C(u, x) < 1)$, or if (u, x) is not scale efficient

$(S(u, x) < 1)$. Moreover, by comparing $W^K(u, x)$ with $W^*(u, x)$ we can tell whether $S(u, x) < 1$ is due to increasing or decreasing returns to scale. We note in closing that Farrell (1957) assumed that the technology satisfied $\{L.1-L.5\}$ and $L.3.S$, CRS. These two additional assumptions imply that $C(u, x) = 1$ and $S(u, x) = 1$, and so in his work $W^K(u, x) = F(u, x)$.

References

Afriat, S.: Efficiency estimation of production functions. *International Economic Review 13* (3) (October), 568–98, 1972.

Färe, R., Grosskopf, S. & Lovell, C. A. K.: *The measurement of efficiency of production.* 1982.

Färe, R. & Svensson, L.: Congestion of production factors. *Econometrica 48* (7) (November), 1745–53, 1980.

Farrell, M.: The measurement of productive efficiency. *Journal of the Royal Statistical Society,* Series A, General, *120* (3), 253–81, 1957.

Førsund, F. & Hjalmarsson, L.: Generalized Farrell measures of efficiency: An application to milk processing in Swedish dairy plants. *Economic Journal 89* (354) (June), 294–315, 1979.

Førsund, F., Lovell, C A. K. & Schmidt, P.: A survey of frontier production functions and of their relationship to efficiency measurement. *Journal of Econometrics 13* (1) (May), 5–26, 1980.

Shephard, R. W.: *The theory of cost and production functions.* Princeton University Press, Princeton, 1970.

PART III AGGREGATION, QUASI-FIXED FACTORS AND COST OF ADJUSTMENT

Aggregating Quasi-fixed Factors

*Larry G. Epstein**

University of Toronto, Ontario, Canada

Abstract

The problem of aggregating quasi-fixed factors within the context of the adjustment-cost model is addressed. Two alternative theoretical justifications are considered, one based on a form of Hicks' aggregation and the other on weak separability. It is argued that the latter is not relevant to practical situations. On the other hand, the former can be used to justify empirical dynamic factor demand studies which employ aggregated input categories. Some implications for data construction procedures are discussed.

I. Introduction

The great majority of factor demand studies are based on the assumption of instantaneous adjustment by firms to prevailing prices. Specification and testing in these studies are guided by the well-developed theory of static profit maximization (or cost minimization). Recently there has emerged a growing body of empirical dynamic factor demand studies that go beyond the above static framework and focus on the nature of adjustment paths adopted by firms; see Schramm (1970), Sargent (1978), Berndt, Fuss & Waverman (1979), Meese (1980), Berndt & Morrison (1981), Epstein & Denny (1983), Hansen & Sargent (1981), Pindyck & Rotemberg (1982). While the adjustment-cost model provides a broad theoretical framework for these studies, some gaps remain between the empirical specifications and the theoretical model.

One such gap is addressed in this paper—the problem of the aggregation of inputs in the context of the adjustment-cost model. The empirical studies cited invariably use highly aggregated input categories. We will investigate the theoretical justification for such aggregation. (No justification has yet been provided in the literature.[1]) As a by-product of the investigation some

---

* The author gratefully acknowledges the comments of two referees and the financial support of the University of Toronto and the Social Sciences and Humanities Research Council of Canada.
[1] A related analysis of aggregation is carried out by Blackorby & Schworm (1980) who discuss the aggregation of multiple grades of an exhaustible resource. They do not produce any results that are useful for our context.

guidance will be provided to the empirical analyst regarding the "proper" procedure for constructing aggregate data.

In the context of standard consumer and producer models the two most general justifications for aggregating over goods or factors are (1) Hicks' Aggregation Theorem, and (2) homogeneous weak separability. Hicks (1946, pp. 312–3) showed that if the prices of goods move proportionately, that group may be viewed as defining a single commodity. In the producer context the theorem has been proven and discussed by Diewert (1978, 1980). The method of homogeneous weak separability is due to Leontief (1947); see also the references cited in Diewert (1980). In addition to providing a theoretical justification for factor demand studies that use aggregate factor inputs, both of these methods provide guidance for the empirical analyst in constructing data. In the case of (1) the quantity of the composite factor is given by the expenditure (at fixed prices) on the factors to be aggregated, while in the case of method (2) exact index numbers may be used in data construction; see Diewert (1976).

Turn now to the problem of aggregation in the adjustment-cost model. Perfectly variable factors may be aggregated as in the standard producer model and thus are ignored here. However, the aggregation of quasi-fixed inputs is more problematical. Two alternative aggregation procedures are investigated. A Hicksian aggregation procedure is formulated and analyzed in Section III. Unlike the case in the standard producer model, the procedure is not valid for all "micro" or disaggregate technologies. This is easy to see since even if all market rental prices for quasi-fixed factors vary proportionately, that is not necessarily the case for the corresponding vector of shadow prices. The class of "micro" technologies which permit Hicks' aggregation is characterized below. Given a "micro" technology from this class one can define a "macro" or aggregate technology that employs composite factors as inputs and which may serve as the basis for empirical analysis. The validity of Hicks' aggregation imposes no restrictions on the "macro" technology. Thus broad justification is provided for the use of aggregate inputs if (i) market rental prices are expected to vary proportionately, and (ii) if one is willing to maintain the hypothesis of a "suitable micro" technology. (These points are examined in some detail for the class of technologies which generate the popular accelerator adjustment rule.) Implications for data construction are pointed out.

A straightforward application to our model of the method of weak separability is analyzed in Section IV. While in theory it may provide a basis for aggregation, it is argued that this method does not provide a satisfactory basis for aggregation in practical situations. Thus the use of exact index numbers would seem to be inappropriate for the construction of aggregates of quasi-fixed factors.

Section II defines the model and briefly outlines the duality between production functions and value functions which is extremely useful for the formulation and derivation of the results below; see Epstein (1981 a). (The usefulness of duality should not be surprising in light of its widespread applications in production theory in general and in problems of factor aggregation in particular.) Section V concludes. Proofs are relegated to an appendix.

The following notation is adopted: E^k is k-dimensional Euclidean space, Ω^k and $\bar{\Omega}^k$ are the open and closed positive orthants, respectively. For $x \in E^k$, $x>0$ means that $x \in \Omega^k$. All vectors are column vectors unless transposed by the superscript τ. A dot over a function denotes differentiation with respect to time. If $h(x)=h(x_1, \ldots, x_k)$ is real-valued, h_{xx} is the Hessian $(h_{x_i x_j})$. If $h(x)=(h^1(x), \ldots, h^l(x))$ then h_x is the matrix $(h^i_{x_j})_{ij}$. If $P:[0, \infty) \to E^k$ then P_{+T} denotes the function from $[0, \infty)$ into E^k that maps t into $P(t+T)$.

II. The Model

Consider the following disaggregated or micro profit maximization problem:

$$J(K_0, L_0, P, W) \equiv \max \int_0^{\infty,} e^{-rt} [F(K, L, \dot{K}, \dot{L}) - P^\tau(t) K - W^\tau(t) L] \, dt \qquad (1)$$

$$\text{subject to } K(0) = K_0, \ L(0) = L_0,$$

where $F(K, L, \dot{K}, \dot{L})$ is a production function defining the maximum amount of output y that can be produced given the stocks of quasi-fixed factors $K \in \Omega^n$, $L \in \Omega^m$ and given the vector of net investment $(\dot{K}, \dot{L})$. (For ease of exposition refer to K and L as capital and labor respectively.) $P:[0, \infty) \to \Omega^m$ and $W:[0, \infty) \to \Omega^m$ describe expectations concerning future rental prices for K and L respectively. The output price is normalized to unity. $r>0$ is the (constant) real rate of discount. J defines the value of the firm given (K_0, L_0, P, W). Denote the micro optimization problem (1) by $O_F(K_0, L_0, P, W)$.

We will frequently consider optimization problems where price expectations are static, i.e. $P(t)=p$ and $W(t)=w \, \forall t$. In that case we abuse notation somewhat and write $(P, W) = (p, w)$, $J(K_0, L_0, p, w)$ and $O_F(K_0, L_0, p, w)$. Denote by $\dot{K}^*(K_0, L_0, p, w)$, $\dot{L}^*(K_0, L_0, p, w)$ and $y^*(K_0, L_0, p, w)$ the policy functions that describe optimal decisions at $t=0$ in $O_F(K_0, L_0, p, w)$.

The following standard regularity conditions are imposed on production functions:

T.1. $F:\Phi \to \bar{\Omega}^1$ where $\Phi = \Phi_1 \times \Phi_2 \subset \Omega^{n+m} \times E^{n+m}$ is bounded and open; F is twice continuously differentiable.

T.2. $F_K, F_L > 0$ and for each i and j, $F_{\dot{K}_i} \gtrless 0$ as $\dot{K}_i \lessgtr 0$ and $F_{\dot{L}_j} \gtrless 0$ as $\dot{L}_j \lessgtr 0$.

T.3. For each $(K, L) \in \Phi_1$, $(F(K, L, \cdot, \cdot)$ is strongly concave on Φ_2.

The analysis of factor aggregation is facilitated by resorting to the value function J which provides a complete representation of the technology equivalent to that provided by F, i.e., for every F there is a unique J and conversely. (For this duality, F must satisfy a set of regularity conditions, Conditions (T), which include T.1–T.3 above. Then J satisfies a "dual" set of regularity conditions. For details the reader is asked to refer to Epstein (1981 a), where it is shown that Conditions (T) are not overly restrictive from an empirical point of view.)[2]

Occasionally, one may derive from F a macro production function f whose arguments are $(z, L, \dot{z}, \dot{L})$, where $z \in \Omega^1$ represents the stock of aggregate capital. Corresponding to f we may consider the aggregate or macro optimization problem

$$\max_{\dot{z}, \dot{L}} \int_0^\infty e^{-rt} [f(z, L, \dot{z}, \dot{L}) - Q(t) z - W^\tau(t) L] \, dt \qquad (2)$$

$$\text{subject to } z(0) = z_0 \text{ and } L(0) = L_0.$$

(Q is a profile of expected rental prices for aggregate capital.) Denote the macro problem by $O_f(z_0, L_0, Q, W)$.

III. Hicks' Aggregation

Suppose that capital rental prices are expected to vary in proportion, i.e.

$$P(t) = \Theta(t) \bar{p}, \quad t \geq 0, \qquad (3)$$

for some $\bar{p} \in \Omega^n$ and scalar-valued function Θ. (Write $P = \Theta \bar{p}$.) Hicks' aggregation in standard models suggests the use of $\bar{p}^\tau K$ as a measure of aggregate capital. The use of such a measure is valid under the conditions we now specify.

Definition 1. The (micro) production function F satisfying T.1–T.3 is said to permit Hicks' aggregation of capital stocks, for a given $\bar{p}$, if it is the case that:

---

[2] Two modifications of the Epstein (1981 a) analysis are adopted. For simplicity, adjustment costs are taken to depend on net rather than gross investment. Also, investment is not restricted to be non-negative. These changes have straightforward implications for the duality between production functions and value functions.

(a) There exists a macro production function f satisfying the appropriate versions of T.2–T.3 on its domain, a bounded open subset of $\Omega^{n+1} \times E^{n+1}$.

(b) If $O_F(K_0, L_0, \Theta\bar{p}, w)$ has a solution then so does $O_f(\bar{p}^{\tau}K_0, L_0, \Theta, W)$. Moreover, the solutions of the two problems are consistent in the sense that optimal time profiles of output and labor are identical in the two problems and the optimal capital profiles are $\{K^*(t)\}_0^\infty$ and $\{\bar{p}^{\tau}K^*(t)\}_0^\infty$ for the micro and macro problems, respectively.

Our formulation of Hicks' aggregation is natural and self-explanatory. If the conditions in the definition are met the formula $z = \bar{p}^{\tau}K$ describes a simple procedure for data construction whereby the aggregate stock is a rental price ($\bar{p}$) weighted sum of the individual capital stocks.

The micro technologies which permit Hicks' aggregation are now characterized, primarily in terms of the corresponding value functions.

Theorem 1. Let F satisfy T.1–T.3 and let $\bar{p}$ be fixed. Let $J(K_0, L_0, \Theta\bar{p}, W)$ denote the value of problem $O_F(K_0, L_0, \Theta\bar{p}, W)$. Then F permits Hicks' aggregation of capital stocks if and only if either of the following equivalent statements is valid.

$$J_{k_i}(K, L, \Theta\bar{p}, W) = J_{K_j}(K, L, \Theta\bar{p}, W) \cdot \bar{p}_i/\bar{p}_j \quad \forall i,j, \quad \text{or} \tag{4}$$

$$J(K, L, \Theta\bar{p}, W) = H(\bar{p}^{\tau}K, L, \Theta, W) \quad \text{for some function } H. \tag{5}$$

Hicks' aggregation is not valid for all micro technologies. Rather, it is legitimate precisely when proportional variation of capital rental prices implies, equation (4), that the corresponding shadow prices of capital vary in the same proportion. This is the case only if the value function has the functional representation in (5). By the duality between value functions and production functions (5) completely characterizes the micro technologies which admit Hicks' aggregation for $\bar{p}$.

The practical application of the aggregation procedure requires some clarification. Imagine a temporary equilibrium framework in which the firm continually revises its expectations and plans as the base period ($t=0$) changes. Theorem 1 is valid as long as in each base period future rental prices are expected to move proportionately. There is no explicit requirement that actual rental prices vary (even approximately) proportionately. However, if that is not the case and the firm revises its estimate of $\bar{p}$, there are two consequences for the empirical practitioner: (a) the macro adjustment-cost problem is not an ordinary one since the macro production function f depends on $\bar{p}$, and (b) aggregate capital stock data, derived from the formula $z = \bar{p}^{\tau}K$, must be continually recalculated as $\bar{p}$ changes. Thus aggregation to a standard macro adjustment-cost problem is justified by

Theorem 1 only if expectations in *any* base period are described by $P=\Theta\bar{p}$, where Θ but not $\bar{p}$ may subsequently be revised.

The constraint this imposes on actual rental prices depends on the empirical analyst's view of the firm's expectations formation process. To illustrate, suppose a "rational expectations" view is adopted and that actual prices follow a stochastic process of the form $p(t)=\Lambda(t)\bar{p}+u(t)$ for all t, where $\Lambda(\cdot)$ defines a real-valued stochastic process and where the $u(t)$'s are white noise. A firm that is aware of this process will predict future rental prices according to (3), with $\Phi(t)$ equal to the expected value of $\Lambda(t)$ conditional on the information available at the base period $t=0$. Note that observed rental prices, in contrast to expected rental prices, need not be exactly proportional to $\bar{p}$.[3]

Some insight into the circumstances under which Hicks' aggregation is valid is readily derived. First, an immediate implication of (4) is that $J_{K_i}J_{K_j}\geqslant 0$ $\forall i,j$. Thus Hicks' aggregation is not possible if prices and stocks are such that it is optimal to invest in one capital good ($\Rightarrow J_{k_i}>0$) and disinvest in another ($\Rightarrow J_{K_j}<0$).

Second, though an explicit representation of the micro production functions dual to the value functions having the form (5) has not been obtained, we can deduce some restrictions imposed by (5) on the micro production functions. Say that a point $(K,L,\dot{K},\dot{L})$ is *supported* by the price profile (P, W) if $(\dot{K},\dot{L})$ is optimal initial investment in $O_F(K,L,P,W)$. It is shown in the proof of Theorem 1 that if F admits Hicks' aggregation of capital stocks given $\bar{p}$, then

$$F_{\dot{K}_i}/F_{K_i}=F_{\dot{K}_j}/F_{K_j}\quad \forall i,j, \tag{6}$$

and for all points $(K,L,\dot{K},\dot{L})$ that may be supported by some profile $(P, W)=(\Theta\bar{p}, W)$. Consider a point where $\dot{K}_j\neq 0$ and rewrite (6) in the form

$$F_{\dot{K}_i}/F_{\dot{K}_j}=F_{K_i}/F_{K_j}. \tag{7}$$

The l.h.s. is the marginal rate of transformation between "outputs" $\dot{K}_i$ and $\dot{K}_j$, while the r.h.s. gives the marginal rate of substitution between the inputs K_i and K_j. Thus (7) states that factors i and j may be substituted one for the other at the same rate whether the factors are viewed as inputs into the production process or whether adjustments in their stocks are the prime

---

[3] One could argue that $P(0)=\Theta(0)\bar{p}$ equals the realized rental price at $t=0$ so that realized rental prices must vary exactly in proportion. But in fact $\Theta(0)\bar{p}$ is the firm's $t=0$ expectation of the rental price and includes a capital gains term which is not observable to the firm at $t=0$. Thus $\Theta(0)\bar{p}$ need not equal the rental price which is eventually realized. This point is perhaps clearer in a discrete-time framework.

concern. This is an intuitively plausible precondition for the aggregation of the ith and jth factors.[4]

As the preceding discussion has shown, Theorem 1 provides some information about the validity of a macro analysis that employs an aggregate capital measure. Nevertheless, Theorem 1 is not totally satisfactory. For one thing, it leaves open the question of whether micro technologies consistent with (4) or (5) exist at all! More particularly, we would like examples of micro and corresponding macro technologies which are suitable for empirical work.

An explicit micro production function that admits Hicks' aggregation for $\bar{p}$ is

$$F(K, L, \dot{K}, \dot{L}) = G(\alpha^\tau K, L, \dot{L}) - D(\alpha^\tau \dot{K}, L, \dot{L}),$$

where α is a scalar multiple of $\bar{p}$. (Both (5) and (6) are readily established.) But F is not strongly concave in $\dot{K}$ thus violating Condition T.3. As a consequence and as discussed in the next section, such a specification is not a satisfactory basis for aggregation in practical situations.

To describe a more useful class of micro technologies which admit Hicks' aggregation we proceed by specifying value functions consistent with (5). The corresponding F's are only implicit but they are well-behaved; in particular, they satisfy Conditions (T) which include T.1–T.3 and other desirable properties. This procedure via value functions is natural in view of the characterization in Theorem 1 and the existence of a duality. It is also appealing in light of the state of the art in generating functional forms for dynamic factor demands for empirical analysis.

In connection with the latter point let us identify in the literature two approaches to the problem of functional form specification. The most common approach is to postulate that the production function is quadratic, i.e., a polynomial of degree 2. In that case the Euler-Lagrange equations for the corresponding optimization problem may be solved explicitly and yield an accelerator adjustment rule for quasi-fixed factors. The second approach is based on the duality between production functions and value functions developed in Epstein (1981 a). A functional form is hypothesized for the value function rather than the production function. Then a generalized Hotelling's Lemma may be applied to the value function to generate a much broader class of solutions than is possible with the first approach. As initially formulated the dual approach maintains static expectations. It is readily extended to expectations processes which are defined by first order

---

[4] In general (6) is necessary for Hicks' aggregation. One might suspect that it is also sufficient for the validity of Hicks' aggregation, but we have been able to prove this only for micro problems where optimal net investment in each capital stock is negative, see Epstein (1981 b). In the latter reference several examples are provided of functions F satisfying (6).

differential equations. (Epstein and Denny illustrate such an extension.) Finally Epstein (1983) has extended the dual approach to general nonstatic expectations for the class of technologies which generate accelerator adjustment rules.

Thus the following two applications of Theorem 1 are sufficient for all current and potential empirical work in light of the state of the art in generating functional forms for dynamic factors demands.[5] First we look at Hicks' aggregation in the context of accelerator adjustment rules and general expectations. Then we consider more general technologies and adjustment rules but with restricted (static or first-order) expectations processes.

Example 1. Suppose first that expectations are static. Consider the following functional form for the value function:

$$J(K, L, p, w) = \alpha(p, w) + \beta(c^\tau K, L) + [p^\tau w^\tau] A \begin{bmatrix} K \\ L \end{bmatrix}, \tag{8}$$

where $c^\tau = (c_1, ..., c_n)$, A is a constant $(n+m) \times (n+m)$ matrix with the block partitioned form $A = (A_{ij})_{i,j=1,2}$. For appropriate choices of α, β, c and A, J will be a well-behaved value function that defines implicitly a unique production function F satisfying (T) over a suitable domain. Moreover, the optimal adjustment of K and L takes the form of an accelerator rule with constant adjustment matrix M,[6]

$$M = \hat{r} + A^{-1}, \tag{9}$$

where here and below $\hat{r}$ denotes the identity matrix multiplied by the scalar r. In the special case where α and β are both quadratic J is dual to the commonly specified quadratic production function.

Fix $\bar{p}$. Since for now expectations are restricted to be static, consider Definition 1 and Theorem 1 when $\Theta(t) = \theta \, \forall t$, i.e. $\Theta = \theta$. Hicks' aggregation is valid if and only if $J_K(K, L, \Theta \bar{p}, w)$ is a scalar multiple of $\bar{p}$. That will be the case if the following additional assumptions are made:

(a) $c_i/c_j = \bar{p}_i/\bar{p}_j$ $\forall i$ and j,

(b) $A_{11}^\tau \bar{p} = d\bar{p}$ for some scalar d, and

(c) $A_{21} = g\bar{p}^\tau$ for some $m \times 1$ vector g. (10)

---

[5] That is not quite correct: Our examples do not cover studies that are based on the inefficient empirical strategy of estimating the Euler equations while disregarding the information contained in the transversality conditions; see Pindyck & Rotemberg (1982). In such an approach the firm's control problem is not solved. Thus any of a large number of functional forms for the production function may be adopted, but at a cost in terms of efficiency as noted.

[6] For details on this and other points made below, see Epstein (1981 a). Note that the discussion could be extended to accelerators where M depends on p and w.

(By redefining β we may replace (a) by (a') $\bar{p}=c$. Parts (b) and (c) may be reformulated in terms of the adjustment matrix M. Partition the latter into $(M_{ij})_{i,j=1,2}$. Then (b) and (c) are equivalent (because of (9)) to (b') $\bar{p}$ is an eigenvector of M_{11}^τ, and (c') M_{21}^τ equals a scalar multiple of the $n \times m$ matrix $\bar{p}v^\tau$ where v is an $m \times 1$ vector. Both restrictions are satisfied if M_{11} is a scalar multiple of the identity and if $M_{21}=0$, i.e., if all capital stocks are adjusted at the same speed and independently of one another and if labor is adjusted independently of the level of capital stocks. However, the restrictions are conceivably satisfied in much more general situations as well.)

If we adopt the assumptions (10) then

$$J(K, L, \theta\bar{p}, w) = H(\bar{p}^\tau K, L, \theta, w), \tag{11}$$

where

$$H(z, L, \theta, w) = a(\theta, w) + b(z, L) + [\theta \; w^\tau] B \begin{bmatrix} z \\ L \end{bmatrix}, \tag{12}$$

and

$a(\theta, w) \equiv \alpha(\theta\bar{p}, w),$
$b(z, L) \equiv \beta(z, L),$
$B \equiv (B_{ij})_{i,j=1,2}, \quad B_{11} \equiv d, \quad B_{12} \equiv \bar{p}^\tau A_{12},$
$B_{21} = g, \quad \text{and} \quad B_{22} = A_{22}.$

By Theorem 1, H is a well-behaved macro value function. Note that it generates a perfectly general accelerator adjustment rule for the stocks (z, L), with adjustment matrix $\hat{r} + B^{-1}$. In fact we could reverse the direction of the argument to prove that any given macro value function that generates an accelerator rule in (z, L) can be derived as above from a suitable micro value function. Thus empirical analysis of *any* accelerator adjustment mechanism involving aggregate inputs is justified given the required proportionality of rental prices if one is willing to maintain assumptions corresponding to (10) at the micro level.

It remains only to extend the discussion to the case of nonstatic expectations. Epstein (1983) has shown that for all technologies F that generate accelerator adjustment rules, nonstatic rental price paths may be aggregated into index numbers $(I^1(P, W), I^2(P, W))$ such that $t=0$ decisions in $O_F(K, L, P, W)$ are precisely the same as those in the static expectations problem $O_F(K, L, p, w)$, where $p = I^1(P, W)$ and $w = I^2(P, W)$. In fact, I^1 and I^2 are given by[7]

---

[7] This proposition is well known for quadratic production functions but is actually valid more generally.

$$\begin{bmatrix} I^1(P, W) \\ I^2(P, W) \end{bmatrix} = (\hat{r} - M^\tau) \int_0^\infty e^{-(\hat{r} - M^\tau)t} \begin{bmatrix} P(t) \\ W(t) \end{bmatrix} dt. \tag{13}$$

The extension of the above discussion to general expectations is now straightforward: Let F be the production function dual to the J in (8). Denote by $V(K, L, P, W)$ the value of $O_F(K, L, P, W)$, i.e., V is the extension of J to nonstatic expectations. Because of the noted existence of the intertemporal indices I^1 and I^2, $V_K(K, L, \Theta\bar{p}, W) = J_K(K, L, I^1(\Theta\bar{p}, W), I^2(\Theta\bar{p}, W))$. But assumptions (10) and (13) can be shown to imply that $I^1(\Theta\bar{p}, W)$ is a scalar multiple of $\bar{p}$. Thus we are back in the static expectations framework analyzed above and we may conclude that $J_K(K, L, I^1(\Theta\bar{p}, W), I^2(\bar{p}, W))$ is a scalar multiple of $\bar{p}$. By Theorem 1 this means that capital stocks may be aggregated even in the context of general price expectations.

To summarize, we have provided a theoretical justification for aggregate dynamic factor demand studies in the accelerator framework. The only restriction on expectations is the proportionality condition (3). The macro technology is unrestricted beyond the requirement that it generate an accelerator adjustment rule.

Example 2. Restrict expectations to be static so that (3) is replaced by (3')
$P(t) = \theta\bar{p} \, \forall t$, for some constant θ. Technologies may be specified indirectly by specifying a functional form for the value function $J(K, L, p, w)$. Epstein (1981 a) provides some examples of functional forms for J that are well-behaved for suitable parameter values and domains, and which do not generate accelerator adjustment rules. In the same way one may specify suitable functional forms for J which have the property that $J(K, L, \theta\bar{p}, w) = H(\bar{p}^\tau K, L, \theta, w)$ for some function H, and which thus permit Hicks' aggregation of capital stocks for the given $\bar{p}$. (The underlying micro production function F is well-behaved.) The macro value function $H(z, L, \theta, w)$ is unrestricted (beyond its basic regularity conditions). Thus a theoretical justification is provided for aggregate dynamic factor demand studies in a static expectations framework. (This justification may be extended to a framework where expectations are generated by arbitrary first order differential equations by applying the extended duality noted prior to Example 1.)

IV. Weak Separability

A natural way to impose separability is to postulate that the micro production function F can be written in the form

$$F(K, L, \dot{K}, \dot{L}) = f(\varphi(K), L, \dot{\varphi}(K), \dot{L}), \tag{14}$$

where $f(z, L, \dot{z}, \dot{L})$ is a macro production function satisfying the appropriate versions of T.1–T.3.

But the functional structure in (14) is not a satisfactory basis for aggregation in practical situations. Observe that $\dot{\varphi}(K) = \varphi_K(K)\dot{K}$. $\dot{K}$ and $\dot{L}$ are chosen to maximize the Hamiltonian $f(\varphi(K), L, \varphi_K\dot{K}, \dot{L}) + J_K\dot{K} + J_L\dot{L}$. Since $\dot{K}$ and $\dot{L}$ are unconstrained a solution would have to be interior and satisfy the first-order conditions $\varphi_i(K)/\varphi_j(K) = J_{K_i}/J_{K_j} \forall i, j$. These equations must be satisfied for all (K, p) in the domain of J. Thus J_K is a scalar multiple of φ_K and the net investment vector $(\dot{K}_1, ..., \dot{K}_n)$ appears in the Hamiltonian only in the form $\Sigma \varphi_i \dot{K}_i$. Thus optimal levels for $\dot{K}_i$'s are not uniquely determined even though there is a unique optimal value for $\Sigma \varphi_i \dot{K}_i$. If firms were to choose amongst indifferent plans on a random basis, (a better selection rule is not provided by the model), observed investment in disaggregated capital stocks would exhibit more erratic behaviour than is usually observed.

It is natural to wonder whether separability imposed on the dual value function would prove more useful. For simplicity let $m = 0$ and restrict attention to constant price profiles, denoted by lower case letters. Let

$$J(K, p) = G(\varphi(K), \theta(p)) \quad \forall(K, p) \in S \subset \Omega^{2n}, \tag{15}$$

for some real-valued functions φ, θ and G. $\varphi(K)$, $\theta(p)$ and G are natural candidates for aggregate capital, the corresponding rental price and the macro value function respectively. Unfortunately, the functional structure in (15) is inconsistent with the minimal assumptions that F is concave and that the micro optimization problem $O_F(K, p)$ has a solution for each $(K, p) \in S_1 \times S_2 \subset S$, for some closed balls S_1 and S_2 in Ω^n. The inconsistency is proven in the appendix under the innocuous assumption that θ is nondecreasing and continuous. (In fact it is shown that these assumptions are inconsistent with the weak separability of rental prices in J, whether or not K is also weakly separable.) The clear implication of this result is that the functional structure (15) does not provide a useful basis for aggregating inputs.

V. Concluding Comments

It has been demonstrated that the use of aggregate input categories is more difficult to justify in the adjustment-cost framework than in static models of the firm. For example, it was argued that weak separability does not provide a satisfactory basis for aggregation in practical situations while Hicks' aggregation is valid only for some micro technologies. These results suggest the need, even more urgent than in the context of static factor demand analysis, to develop and employ data having disaggregated input categories. On a more positive note, a theoretical justification, based on a form of Hicks' aggregation, has been provided for the large majority of empirical dynamic factor demand studies that employ aggregate input categories. The justification requires that rental prices always be expected to be proportional to a given vector $\bar{p}$ and that the micro technology satisfy suitable restrictions. The latter could be tested empirically given a suitably disaggregated data set.

Two extensions of the analysis which are straightforward but important for empirical work should be noted. Perfectly variable factors of production could be included. Moreover, the analysis may be adapted to models of cost minimization.

Appendix

Proof of Theorem 1. The equivalence of (4) and (5) is clear. Let F permit Hicks' aggregation and denote by $H(z_0, L_0, Q, W)$ the value of problem (2). Then (5) is a direct consequence of Definition 1.

Conversely, assume (4) or (5). Denote by $D_t J$ the total derivative $dJ(K, L, \Theta_{+t}\bar{p}, W_{+t})/dt$ and similarly for $D_t H$. The Hamilton-Jacobi equation corresponding to (1)—cf. Dreyfus (1965)—is

$$rJ(K, L, \Theta\bar{p}, W) - D_t J = \max_{\dot{K}, \dot{L}} \left\{ F(K, L, \dot{K}, \dot{L}) + J_K \dot{K} + J_L \dot{L} \right\} \tag{16}$$
$$- \Theta(0) \bar{p}^\tau K - W^\tau(0) L.$$

Differentiate with respect to K, apply the envelope theorem and (5). One obtains that $F_K^\tau(K, L, \dot{K}^*(K, L, \Theta\bar{p}, W), \dot{L}^*(K, L, \Theta\bar{p}, W))$ is a scalar multiple of $\bar{p}$. $\dot{K}^*$ and $\dot{L}^*$ denote solutions to (16). But $F_{\dot{K}}^\tau(K, L, \dot{K}^*, \dot{L}^*)$ is a scalar multiple of $\bar{p}$ since $F_{\dot{K}}^\tau(K, L, \dot{K}^*, \dot{L}^*) = -J_K^\tau(K, L, \Theta\bar{p}, W) = -H_z\bar{p}$. Thus

$$F_{\dot{K}_i}/F_{K_i} = F_{\dot{K}_j}/F_{K_j} \quad \forall i, j. \tag{6}$$

We need another preliminary result. Given F, define the variable indirect production function π by

$$\pi(K, I, p, L, \dot{L}) \equiv \max_{\dot{K}} \left\{ F(K, L, \dot{K}, \dot{L}) : p^\tau \dot{K} \geq I \right\}. \tag{17}$$

Such a construct has been analyzed in the context of consumer theory; see Diewert (1978). Use the first-order conditions for problem (17) and apply the envelope theorem and (6) to deduce that

$$\pi_{K_i}(K, I, \bar{p}, L, \dot{L})/\pi_{K_j}(K, I, \bar{p}, L, \dot{L}) = \bar{p}_i/\bar{p}_j \quad \forall i, j, \tag{18}$$

and therefore, that π can be expressed in the form

$$\pi(K, I, \bar{p}, L, \dot{L}) = \hat{\pi}(\bar{p}^\tau K, I, \bar{p}, L, \dot{L}). \tag{19}$$

We are now ready to prove that Hicks' aggregation is valid. Define f by

$$f(z, L, \dot{z}, \dot{L}) \equiv \hat{\pi}(z, \dot{z}, \bar{p}, L, \dot{L}). \tag{20}$$

Standard duality arguments show that f inherits properties T.2–T.3 (suitably modified).

$\dot{K}$ and $\dot{L}$ are chosen to maximize the Hamiltonian; see (16). Break the maximization into two stages and rewrite it in the form

$$\max_{\dot{z}, \dot{L}} \left\{ \max_{\dot{K}} \left\{ F(K, L, \dot{K}, \dot{L}) + H_z \bar{p}^\tau \dot{K} + H_L \dot{L} : \bar{p}^\tau \dot{K} = \dot{z} \right\} \right\}, \text{ or}$$

$$\max_{\dot{z}, \dot{L}} \left\{ f(z, L, \dot{z}, \dot{L}) + H_z \dot{z} + H_L \dot{L} \right\}. \tag{21}$$

Consider again $O_F(K_0, L_0, \Theta\bar{p}, W)$. It follows that the following two-stage decomposition is valid:

$$\max_{K, L} \int_0^\infty [F(K, L, \dot{K}, \dot{L}) - \Theta\bar{p}^\tau K - W^\tau L] \, dt$$

$$= \max_{z, L} \int_0^\infty e^{-rt} \left[\max_{\dot{K}} \{ F(K, L, \dot{K}, \dot{L}) : \bar{p}^\tau \dot{K} = \dot{z} \} - \Theta z - W^\tau L \right] dt$$

$$= \max_{z, L} \int_0^\infty e^{-rt} [f(z, L, \dot{z}, \dot{L}) - \Theta z - W^\tau L] \, dt.$$

The remainder of the proof is now evident. $\qquad\square$

It remains to prove the inconsistency asserted at the conclusion of Section IV. By assumption $(J(K, p)$ is well-defined on $S_1 \times S_2$. It is also concave in K since F is concave. Thus J is subdifferentiable in K. Purely for the sake of simplicity assume that J is actually differentiable in K. Then the Hamilton-Jacobi equation for the micro problem $O_F(K, p)$ implies that

$$rJ(K, p) = \max_{\dot{K}} \left\{ F(K, \dot{K}) - p^\tau K + J_K(K, p) \dot{K} \right\}. \tag{22}$$

Let ξ be an optimal value of $\dot{K}$ given $(K, \hat{p}) \in S_1 \times S_2$. From (22) it follows that $\forall p \in S_2$,

$$rJ(K, p) + p^\tau K - J_K(K, p) \xi \geq F(K, \xi),$$

with equality if $p = \hat{p}$. Thus the minimum in

$$\min_{p} \left\{ rJ(K,p)+p^{\tau}K-J_{K}(K,p)\,\xi : p \in S_2 \right\} \tag{23}$$

is attained at $p=\hat{p}$.

Suppose that rental prices are weakly separable in J, *i.e.*

$$J(K,p) = G(K, \theta(p)) \quad \forall(K,p) \in S \subset \Omega^{2n}. \tag{15'}$$

Then the minimization problem (23) takes the form

$$\min_{p} \left\{ rG[K, \theta(p)]+p^{\tau}K-G_{K}(K, \theta(p))\,\xi : p \in S_2 \right\}. \tag{24}$$

It is evident from the structure of the objective function in (24), that the minimizing value $\hat{p}$ must satisfy

$$p^{\tau}K \geqslant \hat{p}^{\tau}K \quad \forall p \in S_2 \text{ such that } \theta(p) = \theta(\hat{p}). \tag{25}$$

But $\hat{p}$ and K were chosen arbitrarily. Since (25) applies also when $\hat{p}$ is replaced by any other $\tilde{p} \in S_2$; it follows that

$$\hat{p}, \tilde{p} \in S_2 \quad \text{and} \quad \theta(\hat{p}) = \theta(\tilde{p}) \Rightarrow \hat{p}^{\tau}K = \tilde{p}^{\tau}K \quad \forall K \in S_1. \tag{26}$$

The conclusion in (26) is possible only if $\hat{p}$ and $\tilde{p}$ are equal. But since θ is nondecreasing and continuous there exist distinct price vectors in S_2 which imply the same values for θ. Thus (26) is impossible given the remaining assumptions. This proves that the functional structure (15') is inconsistent with the stated assumptions. (Note that the proof of inconsistency does *not* require that conditions T.1–T.3 be maintained.)

References

Berndt, E., Fuss, M. & Waverman, L.: A dynamic model of cost of adjustment and interrelated factor demands. Working Paper 7925, Institute for Policy Analysis, University of Toronto, Toronto, 1979.

Berndt, E. & Morrison, C.: Short-run labour productivity in a dynamic model. *Journal of Econometrics 16*, 339–365, 1981.

Blackorby, C. & Schworm, W. Multiple-grade models in the theory of exhaustible resources: Alternative characterizations and interpretations. Working Paper 80-31, University of British Columbia, Vancouver, 1980.

Diewert, W. E.: Exact and superlative index numbers. *Journal of Econometrics 4*, 115–145, 1976.

— Hicks' aggregation theorem and the existence of a real value-added function. In *Production economics: A dual approach to theory and applications* (ed. M. Fuss and D. McFadden). North-Holland, Amsterdam, 1978.

— Aggregation problems in the measurement of capital. In *The measurement of capital* (ed. D. Usher). University of Chicago Press, Chicago, 1980.

Dreyfus, S.: *Dynamic programming and the calculus of variations. Academic Press, New York*, 1965.

Epstein, L. G.: Duality theory and functional forms for dynamic factor demands. *Review of Economic Studies 48*, 81–95, 1981 *a*.
— Aggregating quasi-fixed factors, Working Paper 8122, Institute for Policy Analysis. University of Toronto, Toronto, 1981 *b*.
Epstein, L G.: Intertemporal price indices for the firm. *Journal of Economic Dynamics and Control*, 1983, forthcoming.
Epstein, L. & Denny, M.: The multivariate flexible accelerator model: Its empirical restrictions and an application to U.S. manufacturing, *Econometrica*, 1983, forthcoming.
Hansen, L. & Sargent, T.: Formulating and estimating dynamic linear rational expectations models. *Journal of Economic Dynamics and Control 2*, 7–46, 1980.
Hicks, J.: *Value and capital,* 2nd ed. Clarendon Press, Oxford, 1946.
Leontief, W.: Introduction to a theory of the internal structure of functional relationships. *Econometrica 15,* 361–373, 1947.
Meese, R.: Dynamic factor demand schedules for labour and capital under rational expectations. *Journal of Econometrics 14,* 141–148, 1980.
Pindyck, R. & Rotemberg, J.: Dynamic factor demands, energy use, and the effects of energy price shocks. Energy Laboratory Working Paper No. MIT-EL 82-024 WP. MIT, Cambridge, 1982.
Sargent, T.: Estimation of dynamic labour demand schedules under rational expectations. *Journal of Political Economy 86,* 1009–1044, 1978.
Schramm, R.: The influence of relative prices, production conditions and adjustment costs on investment behaviour. *Review of Economic Studies 37,* 361–375, 1970.

Aggregating Heterogeneous Capital Goods in Adjustment-cost Technologies

Charles Blackorby
William Schworm*

University of British Columbia, Vancouver, BC, Canada

Abstract

This paper deals with the existence of an aggregate adjustment-cost technology that character-izes the feasible intertemporal paths of an aggregate capital stock, an aggregate investment rate and aggregate net outputs. The results indicate that only very restrictive adjustment-cost technologies can be aggregated consistently. Therefore the use of aggregative models cannot be justified by functional structure assumptions except in relatively uninteresting circum-stances, so that alternative justifications and interpretations should be investigated.

I. Introduction

Aggregate measures of an economy's capital stock, rate of investment, or technology are intended to usefully summarize aggregate technological relations in the economy. These aggregate relations, however, are conse-quences of the optimizing decisions about many heterogeneous fixed and variable factors of production by many independent producers. In general, there are no measures of aggregate capital, aggregate investment, and an aggregate technology that can consistently reflect the relations among the heterogeneous inputs of a set of firms.

This paper is concerned with the existence of an aggregate adjustment-cost technology that characterizes the feasible intertemporal paths of an aggregate capital stock, an aggregate investment rate, and aggregate net outputs. The firms in the economy are assumed to have adjustment-cost technologies that determine feasible intertemporal paths for a vector of heterogeneous capital stocks, a vector of investment rates, and a vector of net outputs. In the aggregate model, there is a scalar capital stock that aggregates the heterogeneous capital owned by all the firms and there is a scalar aggregate investment rate that determines the rate of change of the aggregate capital stock. The aggregate technology describes the feasible

---

* The research on this paper began while the second author was visiting the Research Department of the Bank of Canada. We thank Larry Epstein and a referee of this journal for comments.

values of the aggregate capital stock, the aggregate investment rate and the aggregate net outputs at each instant. We define consistent aggregation to mean that the wealth achievable in the aggregate model by choice of the scalar investment rate is equal to the wealth achievable in the disaggregate model by choice of the vector of investment rates by each firm. In this paper, we find necessary and sufficient conditions for consistent aggregation in adjustment-cost models.

The adjustment-cost model of investment introduced by Eisner & Strotz (1963) has been extensively utilized in both theoretical and empirical analyses. Frequently, the model is interpreted as describing the dynamic behavior of an industry or economy. Also, in empirical research the model has been applied to data that has been aggregated over types of capital and over firms. Our results provide the conditions under which these applications of the adjustment-cost model can be rationalized.

Fisher (1965, 1968a, 1968b), Gorman (1968, 1981), Stigum (1967), and Whitaker (1968), have investigated the analogous aggregation issues in a static framework. Although the static aggregation conditions are quite restrictive, there are a large class of interesting technologies that satisfy these conditions. Unfortunately, this class of technologies does not satisfy the aggregation requirements in our dynamic context.

Our results indicate that only very restrictive adjustment-cost technologies can be aggregated consistently. The most stringent requirement is imposed by aggregating heterogeneous types of capital. Heterogeneous types of capital can be aggregated into a single capital aggregate in an adjustment-cost technology only if the capital aggregate is a weighted sum of the different types of capital. This implies that the different types of capital are perfect substitutes in production.[1]

The results of this paper suggest that the use of aggregative models cannot be justified by functional structure assumptions except in relatively uninteresting circumstances. This suggests that alternative justifications for the use of aggregate models and alternative interpretations of the results of empirical research with aggregate data should be investigated.

In Section II, the adjustment-cost model is specified and our maintained regularity conditions are described. We present our results in three sections. In Section III, we represent the conditions for consistent aggregation across types of capital. In Section IV, we present the conditions for aggregation across firms. In Section V, the conditions for simultaneous aggregation over firms and different types of capital are described. Proofs of the theorems are in the Appendix.

---

[1] Epstein (1982) has posed a different aggregation problem in an adjustment cost context and found that no technologies are consistent with his aggregation requirements.

II. A Description of the Economy

The economy consists of F firms with technology sets S^f, $f=1,\ldots,F$ containing elements $(X^f, K^{f\cdot}, I^{f\cdot})$ where X^f is a vector of variable outputs and inputs, $K^{f\cdot}=(K^{f1},\ldots,K^{fM})$ is a vector of M different types of capital stocks, and $I^{f\cdot}=(I^{f1},\ldots,I^{fM})$ is a vector of investment rates. We represent these sets by net-revenue functions

$$A^f(P, K^{f\cdot}, I^{f\cdot}):=\max_{X^f}\{P\cdot X^f\mid(X^f, K^{f\cdot}, I^{f\cdot})\in S^f\} \tag{1}$$

where P is a vector of present-value prices. Under suitable regularity conditions A^f is an equivalent representation of S^f; see Gorman (1968) and Diewert (1974). We assume that each A^f satisfies conditions:
(a) twice continuously differentiable, (b) nondecreasing, convex, and linearly homogeneous in P, (c) increasing in $K^{f\cdot}$, (d) concave in $(K^{f\cdot}, I^{f\cdot})$ (e) strictly concave in I^{fm} for $m=1,\ldots,M$, and (f) achieves a maximum in $I^{f\cdot}$ for all $P\geq0, K^{f\cdot}\geq0$, and $-\infty<I^{f\cdot}<+\infty$. $\tag{2}$

Each firm chooses a vector of investment paths so as to maximize the present value of net receipts subject to the equations of motion. These wealth functions are defined by

$$V^f(\{P\},\{Q\},K^{f\cdot}):=\max_{\{I^{f\cdot}\}}\int_0^\infty[A^f(P, K^{f\cdot}, I^{f\cdot})-QI^{f\cdot}]\,dt, \tag{3a}$$

subject to

$$\dot{K}^{fm}=I^{fm}\quad\text{and}\quad K^{fm}\geq0, K^{fm}(0)\text{ given},\quad m=1,\ldots,M, \tag{3b}$$

where Q is the vector of present-value prices of investment goods. The notation, $\{P\}$ and $\{Q\}$, denotes the time path of P and Q, respectively, on the interval $[0,+\infty)$. We restrict our analysis to a set of admissible price paths **P** defined by

$(\{P\},\{Q\})\in\mathbf{P}$ implies, (a) P and Q are continuous functions of time, (b) each wealth function is finite, and

(c) $\lim_{t\to\infty}\dfrac{\partial}{\partial K^{fm}}V^f(\{P\},\{Q\},K^{f\cdot})=0, m=1,\ldots,M.$ $\left.\begin{array}{c}\\\\\\\end{array}\right\}\tag{4}$

Conditions (2) and (4) can be relaxed substantially without altering our main results but the proofs would become more complicated. The strict concavity of the profit function in $I^{f\cdot}$ captures the notion of adjustment costs and insures that investment functions are single-valued. The existence of a maximum in $I^{f\cdot}$ insures that there is some vector of investment rates that eliminates the marginal adjustment costs. The restrictions on the admissible price paths enables us to ignore issues about existence and tranversality. Our assumptions (2) about the profit functions insure that the admissible set of prices **P** is sufficiently large and connected to justify the procedures in the proof.

III. Aggregation of Types of Capital in Adjustment-Cost Models

In this section, we investigate the conditions under which a capital aggregate and an investment aggregate of heterogeneous machines exist in an adjustment-cost technology.

The aggregate model has an adjustment-cost technology characterized by the aggregate profit function, B^f, with image $B^f(P, k^{f\sigma}, i^{f\sigma})$, where $k^{f\sigma}$ and $i^{f\sigma}$ are scalars representing firm f's capital aggregate and investment aggregate. The rate of change of the aggregate capital stock is equal to the aggregate rate of investment. There is a price of aggregate investment denoted by q^f. This aggregate price is firm-specific since it is a price index that depends, in general, on the technology of the firm. The wealth in the aggregate model is defined as follows:

$$W^f(\{P\}, \{q^f\}, k^{f\sigma}) = \max_{\{i^{f\sigma}\}} \int_0^\infty \{B^f(P, k^{f\sigma}, i^{f\sigma}) - q^f i^{f\sigma}\}\, dt \tag{5a}$$

subject to $\dot{k}^{f\sigma} = i^{f\sigma} \geqslant 0, k^{f\sigma}(0)$ given. $\tag{5b}$

The technology of the firm f is said to be consistent with aggregation over types of capital if the following condition is satisfied for all admissible $(\{P\}, \{Q\}, K^{f\cdot})$:

$$W^f(\{P\}, \{q^f\}, k^{f\sigma}) = V^f(\{P\}, \{Q\}, K^{f\cdot}) \tag{6a}$$

where

$$k^{f\sigma} = \mathcal{H}^{f\sigma}(K^{f\cdot}), \tag{6b}$$

and

$$q^b = \mathcal{Q}^f(Q), \tag{6c}$$

where $\mathcal{H}^{f\sigma}$ and $\mathcal{Q}^f$ are continuous and nondecreasing, and $\mathcal{H}^{f\sigma}$ is differentiable. The consistency requirement is that the wealth achievable in the aggregate problem by control of the scalar aggregate investment rate is equal to the wealth achievable in the disaggregate problem by control of the vector of investment rates for each type of capital for all admissible price paths and initial capital stock vectors. The aggregate capital stock can only depend on the vector of capital stocks, $K^{f\cdot}$, and the aggregate investment goods price can only depend on the vector of investment goods prices, Q.

The following theorem states the restrictions on a firm's profit function that are necessary and sufficient for consistent aggregation.

Theorem 1. *There exist functions* W^f, $\mathcal{H}^{f\sigma}$, *and* $\mathcal{Q}^f$ *such that* (6) *is satisfied if and only if there exists a function* B^f *such that*

$$A^f(P, K^{f\cdot}, I^{f\cdot}) = B^f(P, k^{f\sigma}, i^{f\sigma}) \tag{7a}$$

where

$$k^{f\sigma} = \sum_{m=1}^{M} \alpha^{fm} K^{fm} \tag{7b}$$

and

$$i^{f\sigma} = \sum_{m=1}^{M} \alpha^{fm} I^{fm} \tag{7b}$$

for all admissible $(P, K^{f\cdot}, I^{f\cdot})$. *If* (7) *holds, then*

$$q^f = \mathcal{Q}^f(Q) = \min\left\{\frac{Q^1}{\alpha^{f1}}, \ldots, \frac{Q^M}{\alpha^{fM}}\right\}, \tag{8a}$$

and

$$\lambda^{*f} = \lambda^{*fm}/\alpha^{fm}. \tag{8b}$$

For consistent aggregation, the aggregate profit, $B^f(P, k^{f\sigma}, i^{f\sigma})$, must be equal to the disaggregate profit, $A^f(P, K^{f\cdot}, I^{f\cdot})$ for all admissible values for $(P, K^{f\cdot}, I^{f\cdot})$. Therefore, requiring that the aggregate model be consistent with the disaggregate model given that optimal investment paths are chosen is equivalent to requiring consistency for arbitrary vectors of investment paths. This is a consequence of the duality between price paths, $\{Q\}$, and investment paths, $\{I^{f\cdot}\}$, which enables us to induce any investment path consistent with an adjustment cost technology by an appropriate choice of the price paths.

In addition, consistent aggregation requires that the capital aggregate be a weighted sum of the different types of capital and that the investment aggregate be a weighted sum of the different types of investment. The weight used in computing aggregate investment and aggregate capital must be the same. Therefore, all types of machines must be perfect substitutes in production if there exists a capital aggregate in an adjustment cost technology.

The aggregate price index for investment goods, q^f, is the unit cost of obtaining aggregate investment. That is, the investment price index function, $\mathcal{Q}^f$, is defined by

$$\mathscr{D}^f(Q)\, i^{f\sigma} = \min_{I^{f\cdot}} \{ Q \cdot I^{f\cdot} \,|\, \mathscr{I}^{f\sigma}(I^{f\cdot}) \geqslant i^{f\sigma} \}, \tag{9}$$

where $\mathscr{D}^f$ has as its image (7 b).

The l.h.s. of (9) has the specified structure if and only if $\mathscr{I}^{f\sigma}$ is homothetic. Since aggregate investment is a linear function of $I^{f\cdot}$, the unit cost function, $\mathscr{I}^f$, is a minimum function with q^f equal to the minimum value of Q^m/α^{fm} for $m = 1, \ldots, M$.

The shadow value of each type of capital, denoted λ^{*fm}, is equal to the shadow value of the aggregate capital stock, λ^{*f}, multiplied by the weight of this type of capital used in calculating the aggregate capital stock. This structure of the multipliers given in (8 b) is a consequence of the additivity of the aggregate capital stock as expressed in (7 b).

The technologies that are consistent with aggregation imply quite restrictive investment behavior. The firm's disaggregated investment decisions are the solutions to the following problem:

$$\max_{I^{f\cdot}} \left\{ B^f\!\left(P, \sum_{m=1}^{M} \alpha^{fm} K^{fm}, \sum_{m=1}^{M} \alpha^{fm} I^{fm} \right) - \sum_{m=1}^{M} (Q^m - \lambda^{fm})\, I^{fm} \right\}. \tag{10}$$

Necessary conditions for an optimal investment vector are that

$$B_i^f(P, k^{f\sigma}, i^{f\sigma})\, \alpha^{fm} - Q^m + \lambda^{fm} \leqslant 0, \tag{11}$$

with equality if $I^{fm} > 0$ for all $m = 1, \ldots, M$.

Substituting the relationship (8 b) and rearranging yields

$$B_i^f(P, k^{f\sigma}, i^{f\sigma}) + \lambda \leqslant Q^m/\alpha^{fm}, \tag{12}$$

with equality if $I^{fm} > 0$ for all $m = 1, \ldots, M$.

The l.h.s. of (12) is the same for all m. Therefore, the condition (12) can hold with equality for more than one m if and only if the set $\{Q^1/\alpha^f, \ldots, Q^m/\alpha^{fM}\}$ has more than one minimal element. As a consequence of the linearity of $I^{f\sigma}$, investment is positive at any time t only for those types of machines that have the minimal price per efficiency unit, Q^m/α^{fm}.

If a firm's technology is consistent with aggregation, then the optimal investment paths can be found by a two-stage decision process. First, compute the investment price index at each time point by solving (9) for arbitrary aggregate investment, $i^{f\sigma}$. Then, solve (5) to obtain the optimal time path for aggregate investment. Finally, use (9) again to determine the optimal investment path for each type of machine given the optimal aggregate investment rate. Notice that only the choice of the aggregate investment rate is a dynamic problem. The investment price and the optimal disaggregate investment paths given the optimal aggregate investment paths are determined by the solution to the static optimization problem in (9).

IV. Aggregation over Firms

In this section, we ask for the existence of an aggregate industry technology that is defined in terms of aggregate industry variables. We do not require that there exist aggregates over different types of capital or different types of net outputs. Therefore, the industry technology set, S, has elements $(X, k^{\sigma \cdot}, i^{\sigma \cdot})$, where $k^\sigma = (k^{\sigma 1}, \ldots, k^{\sigma M})$ and $i^{\sigma \cdot} = (i^{\sigma 1}, \ldots, i^{\sigma M})$.

The industry profit function is denoted by $A(P, k^{\sigma \cdot}, i^{\sigma \cdot})$. Industry wealth is defined by

$$V(\{P\}, \{Q\}, k^{\sigma \cdot}) = \max_{\{i^{\sigma \cdot}\}} \int_0^\infty \{A(P, k^{\sigma \cdot}, i^{\sigma \cdot}) - Q \cdot i^{\sigma \cdot}\} \, dt, \tag{13a}$$

subject to $\dot{k}^{\sigma m} = i^{\sigma m}$, $k^{\sigma m} \geqslant 0$, $k^{\sigma m}(0)$ given $m = 1, \ldots, M$. \hfill (13b)

The following theorem is a straightforward generalization of Theorem 1 in Blackorby & Schworm (1982 a).

Theorem 2. *There exist a wealth function V and aggregator functions $\mathcal{K}^{\sigma m}$ for $m = 1, \ldots, M$ such that*

$$V(\{P\}, \{Q\}, k^{\sigma \cdot}) = \sum_{f=1}^F V^f(\{P\}, \{Q\}, K^{f \cdot}) \tag{14a}$$

where $k^{\sigma m} = \mathcal{K}^{\sigma m}(K^{\cdot m})$ for $m = 1, \ldots, M$ \hfill (14b)

for all admissible $(\{P\}, \{Q\}, K)$, where $K = (K^{1 \cdot}, \ldots, K^{f \cdot})$, if and only if there exist functions, V^m and $\mathcal{K}^{fm}$ for $m = 1, \ldots, M$ and V^{fo} such that

$$V^f(\{P\}, \{Q\}, K^{f \cdot}) = \sum_{m=1}^M V^m(\{P\}, \{Q\}) \, \mathcal{K}^{fm}(K^{fm}) + V^{f0}(\{P\}, \{Q\}) \tag{15}$$

for all $(\{P\}, \{Q\}, K^{f \cdot})$ for $f = 1, \ldots, F$.

If (15) is satisfied then the aggregate wealth function is given by

$$V(\{P\}, \{Q\}, k^{\sigma \cdot}) = \sum_{m=1}^M V^m(\{P\}, \{Q\}) \, k^{\sigma m} + V^0(\{P\}, \{Q\}) \tag{16a}$$

where $k^{\sigma m} = \sum_{f=1}^F \mathcal{K}^{fm}(K^{fm})$ \hfill (16b)

and $V^0 = \sum_{f=1}^F V^{f0}$. \hfill (16c)

To be consistent with aggregation across firms, each firm must have a wealth function that is affine in the vector of transformed capital stocks of each type, $\mathcal{K}^{fm}(K^{fm})$. The transformation of each type of capital can be firm-specific. The marginal value of each type of transformed capital, however, must be the same for all firms. The implied aggregate wealth function is affine in the aggregate capital stocks of each type.

The next theorem states the conditions on the profit function that are necessary and sufficient for consistent aggregation. This theorem is a generalization of Theorem 3 in Blackorby & Schworm (1982 *a*).

Theorem 3. *There exist functions V and $\mathcal{K}^{om}$ for m=1,...,M such that* (14) *holds if and only if there exist functions A^m for m=1,...,M with images $A^m(P, \mathcal{K}^{fm}(K^{fm}), Z^m)$ which are linearly homogeneous in $(\mathcal{K}^{fm}(K^{fm}), Z^m)$ where Z^m is a M-dimensional vector and a function A^{f0} with image $A^{f0}(P, Z^0)$ such that*

$$A^f(P, K^{f\cdot}, I^{f\cdot}) = \max_{Z^\cdot} \left\{ \sum_{m=1}^{M} A^m(P, \mathcal{K}^{fm}(K^{fm}), Z^m) + A^{f0}(P, Z^0) \,\middle|\, \sum_{m=0}^{M} Z^m = I^{f\cdot} \right\} (17)$$

for all $(P, K^{f\cdot}, I^{f\cdot})$ for f=1,...,F where $Z^\cdot = (Z^0, Z^1, ..., Z^M)$.

If (17) is satisfied then the aggregate net revenue function is given by

$$A(P, k^{\sigma\cdot}, i^{\sigma\cdot}) = \max_{Z^\cdot} \left\{ \sum_{m=1}^{M} A^m(P, k^{\sigma m}, Z^m) + A^0(P, Z^0) \,\middle|\, \sum_{m=0}^{M} Z^m = i^{\sigma\cdot} \right\} \quad (18\,a)$$

where

$$A^0 = \sum_{f=1}^{F} A^{f0}. \tag{18 b}$$

To be consistent with aggregation, the profit function for each firm must be the optimal value function for a certain investment allocation problem. To interpret the allocation problem, suppose that a firm has $M+1$ plants with each plant using a single type of capital except one plant which uses no capital at all. Each capital-using plant has a profit function denoted by A^m for $m=1,...,M$ and the plant without capital has a profit function denoted by A^{f0}. There is a given amount of investment I^{fm} for $m=1,...,M$ to be allocated among the $M+1$ plants. Equation (17) states that $A^f = \sum_{m=1}^{M} A^m + A^{f0}$ when investment for each type of capital is allocated optimally among the $M+1$ plants. The profit function for each of the capital-using plants is linearly homogenous in the capital-investment vector and is the same for all firms. The interpretation of (18) is analogous.

For a more detailed discussion of the results of this section, see Blackorby & Schworm (1982 *a*, 1982 *b*).

V. Aggregating over Firms and Types of Capital

In this section, we investigate conditions under which there exists an aggregate capital stock and an associated aggregate investment rate that represents the capital stocks and investment rates of all firms for all types of capital. In addition, we ask that there be an aggregate technology set described in terms of these aggregate variables that consistently represents the technological possibilities of the industry.

The aggregate technology is characterized by the profit function, B, with image, $B\,(p, k, i)$. The capital aggregator function, $\mathcal{K}$, with image, $k = \mathcal{K}(K)$, and the investment goods price index function, $\mathcal{Q}$, with image, $q = \mathcal{Q}(Q)$. Define aggregate wealth as

$$W(\{P\}, \{q\}, k) = \max_{\{i\}} \int_0^\infty \{B(P, k, i) - qi\}\, dt \tag{19a}$$

subject to $k = i$, $k \geq 0$, $k(0)$ given. $\tag{19b}$

A set of firm technologies represented by A^f, $f = 1, \ldots, F$, are said to be consistent with aggregation if the following conditions are satisfied for all admissible $(\{P\}, \{Q\}, K)$:

$$W(\{P\}, \{q\}, k) = \sum_{f=1}^{F} V^f(\{P\}, \{Q\}, K^{f \cdot}) \tag{20a}$$

where $k = \mathcal{K}(K)$ $\tag{20b}$

and $q = \mathcal{Q}(Q)$ $\tag{20c}$

where $\mathcal{K}$ and $\mathcal{Q}$ are continuous and nondecreasing, and $\mathcal{K}$ is differentiable. We require that the wealth obtained in the disaggregated economy by control of the FxM investment rates is also obtained in the aggregate model by control of the scalar i. In addition the aggregate capital stock is a function of the vector of capital stocks of each type owned by each firm and the aggregate investment price index is a function of the prices of the different types of capital. The wealth functions that are consistent with aggregation are described in the following theorem.

Theorem 4. *There exist functions W, $\mathcal{K}$ and $\mathcal{Q}$ such that* (20) *holds if and only if there exist functions V^k and $\mathcal{K}^{f\sigma}$ and $V^{f\sigma}$ for $f = 1, \ldots, F$ such that*

$$V^f(\{P\}, \{Q\}, K^{f\cdot}) = V^k(\{P\}, \{q\})\, k^{f\sigma} + V^{f0}(\{P\}, \{q\}) + \bar{V}^f(\{P\}, \{Q\}) \tag{21a}$$

where

$$k^{f\sigma} = \mathcal{K}^{f\sigma}\{K^{f\cdot}\} = \sum_{m=1}^{M} \alpha^m K^{fm} \tag{21b}$$

and

$$q = \mathcal{Q}(Q) = \left\{ \frac{Q^1}{\alpha^1}, \ldots, \frac{Q^M}{\alpha^M} \right\} \tag{21 c}$$

and

$$\sum_{f=1}^{F} \bar{V}^f(\{P\}, \{Q\}) = 0 \tag{21 d}$$

for all $(\{P\}, \{Q\}, K^{f\cdot})$ *and for all* $f=1, \ldots, F$.

If (21) is satisfied, then the aggregate value function is given by

$$W(\{P\}, \{q\}, k) = V^k(\{P\}, \{q\}) k + V^0(\{P\}, \{q\}) \tag{22 a}$$

where

$$k = \mathcal{K}(K) = \sum_{f=1}^{F} k^{f\sigma} = \sum_{m=1}^{M} \alpha^m \sum_{f=1}^{F} K^{fm}, \tag{22 b}$$

$$q = \mathcal{Q}(Q) = min \left\{ \frac{Q^1}{\alpha^1}, \ldots, \frac{Q^M}{\alpha^M} \right\}, \tag{22 c}$$

and

$$V^0 = \sum_{f=1}^{F} V^{f0}. \tag{22 d}$$

If wealth functions V^f, $f=1, \ldots, F$ are consistent with aggregation, then each firm has a capital stock aggregate over different types of capital. This capital stock aggregate is a weighted sum of the firm's capital of each type where the weights are the same for every firm. Therefore, the capital aggregator function, $\mathcal{K}^{f\sigma}$, is the same for every firm. The wealth function of each firm is affine in the capital stock aggregate and the shadow value of the aggregate capital stock, $V^k(\{P\}, \{q\})$, is the same for every firm. Therefore, consistency in aggregation implies that each type of capital has the same value in every firm.

Also, it is necessary that each firm have an investment goods price index which is the minimum of the price per efficiency unit, Q^m/α^m, over types of machines. Since the efficiency weights α^m, $m=1, \ldots, M$ are the same for all firms, the investment goods price index is the same for all firms.

The value function of each firm must be expressible as the sum of three terms. The first term is linear in the capital aggregate $k^{f\sigma}$ with a coefficient, $V^k(\{P\}, \{q\})$, which depends on the price index and is the same for all firms. The second term, $V^{f0}(\{P\}, \{q\})$, is firm specific independent of capital stocks, and depends on the investment goods prices, Q, only through the investment goods price index. The third term, $\tilde{V}^f(\{P\}, \{Q\})$ is firm-specific, independent of capital stocks, and can depend on the vector of investment goods prices, Q. However, the terms, $\tilde{V}^f$ for $f=1,\ldots,F$ must sum to zero so that they have no effect on the aggregate technology.

If the technologies of the firms are consistent with aggregation, then the aggregate model is described by (22). The industry aggregate capital stock is an unweighted sum of each firm's aggregate capital stock. The industry price index for investment goods is the price index for each of the firms. The aggregate wealth function is affine in the aggregate capital stock, k, and depends on investment goods prices only through the price index, q.

One surprising fact is that the existence of a capital aggregate at the industry level does not imply the existence of a firm aggregate over types of capital. Although each firm has a component of its technology, represented by $V^k(\{P\}, \{q\})\,k^{f\sigma} + V^{f\sigma}(\{P\}, \{q\})$, in which there is an investment and capital stock aggregate, each firm also can have a component of its technology represented by $\tilde{V}^f(\{P\}, \{Q\})$ in which there is no investment or capital stock aggregate. Since $\Sigma_{f=1}^F \tilde{V}^f = 0$, the component of the technology in which disaggregated investments cannot be aggregated must cancel out when summed over firms so that they do not affect the aggregate technology.

In order to compare the effects of aggregating over firms and aggregating over goods, we assume that each firm has an aggregate capital stock and associated aggregate investment rate. In this case, $\tilde{V}^f = 0$ for $f=1,\ldots,F$ in (21 a). The next theorem states the conditions on the profit functions that are necessary and sufficient for aggregation across types of capital within each firm's technology and for aggregation across firms.

Theorem 5. *The wealth function of each firm $f=1,\ldots,F$ satisfies (21) with $\tilde{V}^f = 0$ if and only if there exist functions, B^f, B^k, and B^{f0} such that*

$$B^f(P, k^{f\sigma}, i^{f\sigma}) = A^f(P, K^{f\cdot}, I^{f\cdot}) \tag{23 a}$$

$$k^{f\sigma} = \sum_{m=1}^M \alpha^m K^{fm}, \tag{23 b}$$

$$i^{f\sigma} = \sum_{m=1}^M \alpha^m I^{fm}, \tag{23 c}$$

and

$$B^f(P, k^{f\sigma}, i^{f\sigma}) = \max_{(i^k, i^0)} \{B^k(P, k^{f\sigma}, i^k) + B^{f0}(P, i^0) \mid i^k + i^0 = i^{f\sigma}\} \tag{24}$$

where B^k is linearly homogeneous in its last two arguments.

The aggregate wealth function satisfies (22) *if and only if there exist functions B^k and B^0 such that the aggregate profit function can be written as*

$$B(P, k, i) = \max_{(i^k, i^0)} \{ B^k(P, k, i^k) + B^0(P, i^0) \,|\, i^k + i^0 = i \} \tag{25}$$

where B^k is linearly homogeneous in its last two arguments.

Since we are requiring a capital aggregate over types of capital for each firm, Theorem 1 implies that for each $f = 1, \ldots, F$ there exists a profit function B^f such that $B^f(P, \Sigma_{m=1}^{M} \alpha^{fm} K^{fm}, \Sigma_{m=1}^{M} \alpha^{fm} I^{fm}) = A^f(p, k^{f\cdot}, I^{f\cdot})$. Aggregation across firms requires, in addition, that the investment goods price index is the same for all firms. As a consequence of the form of the investment goods price index as stated in (21c), the weights used to aggregate capital and investment are the same for every firm: $\alpha^{fm} = \alpha^m$ for $f = 1, \ldots, F$ and $m = 1, \ldots, M$. This describes the required structure of the firm's profit function in the capital stock vector, $K^{f\cdot}$, and the investment vector, $I^{f\cdot}$.

Aggregation over firms, however, implies that each function, B^f, has additional structure in the aggregate variables described by (24). There must exist a function B^k which is independent of f and, linearly homogeneous in $(k^{f\sigma}, i^k)$ and a function B^{f0} which is independent of $k^{f\sigma}$ which sum to B^f when $i^{f\sigma}$ is allocated optimally to B^k and B^{f0}. This implies that the technology set of the firm is the sum of a capital dependent technology set which is a cone and a technology set which is independent of capital.

If the aggregate wealth function satisfies the conditions (22) for consistent aggregation, then the aggregate profit function has the structure given in (25). This is analogous to the structure (24) imposed on the firm's profit functions.

VI. Conclusion

The results of this paper indicate that only in extremely restrictive cases can aggregate data be treated as if it were generated by a single adjustment cost technology with an aggregate capital stock and investment rate. Heterogeneous types of capital can be aggregated only if the types are perfect substitutes in production. In addition, if there is to be an economy-wide capital aggregate, the rates of substitution in production between different types of capital must be the same for every firm. Although these conditions are restrictive, they are implicitly maintained in all research that interprets regression coefficients computed from aggregate data as estimates of parameters of an adjustment cost technology.

It is interesting to observe that the conditions for aggregating heterogeneous capital derived in this paper are the conditions frequently assumed in models of vintage capital. In these models, a standard assumption is that aggregate capital is a weighted sum of capital of each vintage; see Nickell (1978) for examples and further references. Our results, however, show that if these capital aggregates are consistently aggregated over firms, then additional restrictions are imposed on the technologies.

We believe that the conclusion to be drawn from our results is that parameter estimates obtained from aggregate data should not be treated as a characteristic of an aggregate adjustment cost technology. Rather, alternative interpretations should be developed which take explicit account of the heterogeneity of capital and firms.

Appendix

Proof of Theorem 1

Bellman's equation and (6) imply that

$$H^f(P, k^{f\sigma}, q^f - \lambda^{*f}) = G^f(P, K^{f\cdot}, Q - \Lambda^{*f\cdot}) \tag{A.1}$$

where

$$H^f(P, k^{f\sigma}, q^f - \lambda^f) = \max_{i^{f\sigma}} \{B^f(P, k^{f\sigma}, i^{f\sigma}) - (q^f - \lambda^f) i^{f\sigma}\} \tag{A.2}$$

and

$$G^f(P, K^{f\cdot}, Q - \Lambda^{f\cdot}) = \max_{I^{f\cdot}} \{A^f(P, K^{f\cdot}, I^{f\cdot}) - (Q - \Lambda^{f\cdot}) I^{f\cdot}\} \tag{A.3}$$

and

$$\lambda^{*f} = \frac{\partial}{\partial k^{f\sigma}} W^f(\{P\}, \{q^f\}, k^{f\sigma}) \tag{A.4}$$

and

$$\Lambda^{*f\cdot} = (\lambda^{*f1}, \dots, \lambda^{*fM}) \text{ where } \lambda^{*fm} = \frac{\partial}{\partial K^{fm}} V^f(\{P\}, \{Q\}, K^{f\cdot}). \tag{A.5}$$

Differentiation of (6a) with respect to K^{fm} implies

$$\lambda^{*f} \frac{\partial}{\partial K^{fm}} \mathcal{H}^{f\sigma}(K^{f\cdot}) = \lambda^{*fm} \tag{A.6}$$

for $f = 1, \dots, F$ and $m = 1, \dots, M$. Substituting (A.6) into (A.1) yields

$$H^f(P, k^{f\sigma}, \gamma^{*f}) = G^f(P, K^{f\cdot}, \Gamma^{*f\cdot}) \tag{A.7a}$$

where

$$\gamma^{*f} = q^f - \lambda^{*f} \tag{A.7b}$$

and

$$\Gamma^{*f\cdot} = (\Gamma^{*f1}, \ldots, \Gamma^{*fM}) \tag{A.7c}$$

where

$$\Gamma^{*fm} = Q^m - \lambda^{*f} \frac{\partial}{\partial K^{fm}} \mathcal{H}^{f\sigma}\{K^{f\cdot}\} \tag{A.7d}$$

Next, notice that the vector $\Gamma^{*f\cdot}$ can be made to take on any value in $\mathbf{R}_+^M$ by appropriate choice of Q and future price paths. To see this, suppose that Q^1 is varied to vary Γ^{*f1}. Since the change in Q^1 affects λ^{*f}, change future prices so that λ^{*f} remains constant. Then, Γ^{*fm} for $m=2,\ldots,M$ remains constant while Γ^{*f1} is changed. As a consequence, (A.7a) is satisfied for all values of the multipliers, λ^{*f} and λ^{*fm}, $m=1,\ldots,M$ and, hence

$$H^f(P, k^{f\sigma}, \gamma^f) = G^f(P, K^{f\cdot}, \Gamma^{f\cdot}) \tag{A.8a}$$

for all $\Gamma^{f\cdot}$ in $\mathbf{R}_+^M$ where

$$k^{f\sigma} = \mathcal{H}^{f\sigma}(K^{f\cdot}) \tag{A.8b}$$

and

$$\gamma^f = \Gamma^{f\sigma}(\Gamma^{f\cdot}) \tag{A.8c}$$

where $\Gamma^{f\sigma}$ is linearly homogeneous. By Theorem 3.8 in Blackorby, Primont & Russell (1978), (A.8) and (A.3) imply that $I^{f\cdot}$ is homothetically separable from its complement in A^f. Also, (A.8) and (A.3) imply $K^{f\cdot}$ is separable from its complement in A^f. Hence, there exist functions $\bar{A}^f$, $\mathcal{H}^{f\sigma}$, and $\mathcal{I}^{f\sigma}$ such that

$$A^f(P, K^{f\cdot}, I^{f\cdot}) = \bar{A}^f(P, \mathcal{H}^{f\sigma}(K^{f\cdot}), \mathcal{I}^{f\sigma}(I^{f\cdot})). \tag{A.9}$$

Next, note that (A.8), (A.2), and (A.3) imply that A^f and B^f have the same concave conjugate and, hence,

$$B^f(P, k^{f\sigma}, i^{f\sigma}) = \bar{A}^f(P, \mathcal{H}^{f\sigma}(K^{f\cdot}), \mathcal{I}^{f\sigma}(I^{f\cdot})). \tag{A.10}$$

for all $(P, K^{f\cdot}, I^{f\cdot})$. This proves the necessity of (7a).

Since $k^{f\sigma} = i^{f\sigma}$ and $k^{f\sigma} = \mathcal{H}^{f\sigma}(K^{f\cdot})$ and $i^{f\sigma} = \mathcal{I}^{f\sigma}(I^{f\cdot})$, we have that

$$\sum_{m=1}^{M} \left\{ \frac{\partial}{\partial K^{fm}} \mathcal{H}^{f\sigma}(K^{f\cdot}) \right\} I^{fm} = \mathcal{I}^{f\sigma}(I^{f\cdot}) \tag{A.11}$$

for all $I^{f\cdot}$. Since the r.h.s. of (A.11) depends only on $I^{f\cdot}$, the LHS cannot depend on $K^{f\cdot}$, hence $\frac{\partial}{\partial K^{fm}}\mathcal{H}^{f\sigma}(K^{f\cdot})=\alpha^{fm}$. Equations (7b) and (7c) follow immediately. Then, (A.6) implies (8b) and (8a) follows from (7c) by duality. This proves necessity and sufficiency is obvious.

Proof of Theorem 4

Condition (20) implies that $K^{f\cdot}$ is separable from its complement and $\{Q\}$ is separable from its complement in V^f for $f=1,\ldots,F$. Hence, there exist functions W^f, $\mathcal{H}^{f\sigma}$, and $\mathcal{Q}^f$ such that

$$W^f(\{P\},\{\mathcal{Q}^f(Q)\},\mathcal{H}^{f\sigma}(K^{f\cdot}))=V^f(\{P\},\{Q\},K^{f\cdot}) \tag{A.12}$$

for $f=1,\ldots,F$. The application of Theorem 1 implies that there exists a function B^f such that

$$A^f(P,K^{f\cdot},I^{\cdot})=B^f(P,k^{f\sigma},i^{f\sigma}) \tag{A.13a}$$

where

$$k^{f\sigma}=\sum_{m=1}^{M}\alpha^{fm}K^{fm}, \tag{A.13b}$$

$$i^{f\sigma}=\sum_{m=1}^{M}\alpha^{fm}I^{fm}, \tag{A.13c}$$

and

$$q^f=\mathcal{Q}^f(Q)=\min\left\{\frac{Q^1}{\alpha^{f1}},\ldots,\frac{Q^M}{\alpha^{fM}}\right\} \tag{A.13d}$$

for $f=1,\ldots,F$. But condition (20) can be satisfied only if $\mathcal{Q}^f=\mathcal{Q}$ for all $f=1,\ldots,F$. Hence $\alpha^{fm}=\alpha^m$ for $f=1,\ldots,F$ and $m=1,\ldots,M$. This proves (21b) and (21c) are necessary and reduces the aggregation requirements (20) to the following:

$$W(\{P\},\{q\},\mathcal{H}(K))=\sum_{f=1}^{F}W^f(\{P\},\{q\},\mathcal{H}^{f\sigma}(K^{f\cdot})). \tag{A.14}$$

The application of Theorem 2 implies that (21) is necessary. The proof of sufficiency and (22) is immediate.

Proof of Theorem 5

That (23) is necessary has been proved in (A.13). The necessity of (24) is implied by Theorem 3. Sufficiency of (23) and (24) follows from Theorem 1 and Theorem 3 and direct calculations. That (25) is necessary and sufficient is proved by an analogous argument.

References

Blackorby, C. & Schworm, W.: Aggregate investment and consistent intertemporal technologies. *Review of Economic Studies 49*, 595–614, 1982 a.

Blackorby, C. & Schworm, W.: Rationalizing the use of aggregates in natural resource economics. In *Economic Theory of Natural Resources* (ed. W. Eichhorn et al.), Physica-Verlag, Würzburg, Wien, 1982 b.

Bliss, C.: *Capital theory and the distribution of income*. North Holland-Elsevier, Amsterdam, New York, 1975.

Diewert, W.: Applications of duality theory. In *Frontiers of quantitative economics*, 11 (ed. M. Intriligator and D. Kendrick). North Holland, Amsterdam, 1974.

Eisner, R. & Strotz, R.: Determinants of business investment. In *Commission on money and credit: Impacts of monetary policy*, pp. 60–183. Prentice-Hall, Englewood Cliffs, 1963.

Epstein, L.: Aggregating quasi-fixed factors. *The Scandinavian Journal of Economics 85* (2), 191–205, 1983.

Fisher, F.: Embodied technical change and the existence of aggregate capital stock. *Review of Economic Studies 35*, 417–428, 1968 a.

Fisher, F.: Embodied technology and the existence of labour and output aggregates. *Review of Economic Studies 35*, 391–412, 1968 b.

Gorman, W. Measuring the quantities of fixed factors. In *Value, capital and growth* (ed. J. Wolfe). Edinburgh, 1968.

Gorman, W.: Aggregates, activities, and overheads. Technical Report No. 390, IMSSS, Stanford, 1982.

May, K. O.: The aggregation problem for a one-industry model. *Econometrica 14*, 232–244, 1946.

Nickell, S.: *The investment decisions of firms*. Nisbet/Cambridge, Cambridge, 1978.

Stigum, D.: On certain problems of aggregation. *International Economic Review 8*, 1967.

Whitaker, J.: Captial aggregation and optimality conditions. *Review of Economic Studies 35*, 429–442, 1968.

Dynamic Factor Demands under Rational Expectations*

Robert S. Pindyck and Julio J. Rotemberg

Massachusetts Institute of Technology, Cambridge, MA, USA

Abstract

We model the industrial demands for structures, equipment, and blue- and white-collar labor in a manner consistent with rational expectations and stochastic dynamic optimization in the presence of adjustment costs, but allowing generality of functional form. We represent the technology by a translog input requirement function that specifies the amount of blue-collar labor needed to produce an output level given quantities of three quasi-fixed factors: non-production workers, equipment, and structures. A complete description of the production structure is obtained by simultaneously estimating the input requirement function and three stochastic Euler equations. We find adjustment costs are small in total but large on the margin, and differ considerably across factors.

I. Introduction

Understanding the way in which tax changes, changes in relative factor prices, and changes in aggregate output affect investment and employment over time requires a model of the production structure that incorporates dynamic adjustment of "quasi-fixed" factors, i.e. a dynamic model of factor demands. Such a model is developed in this paper in a way that is consistent with rational expectations and dynamic optimization in the presence of adjustment costs, while allowing for generality of functional form.

Dynamic factor demand models are certainly not new to the literature. The "flexible accelerator" and related models of investment demand have been widely used in empirical applications, although they are generally based on *ad hoc* descriptions of the dynamic adjustment process.[1] Berndt, Fuss & Waverman (1980) and Morrison & Berndt (1981) developed dynam-

---

* Research leading to this paper was supported by the National Science Foundation under Grant No. SES-8012667 to R. S. Pindyck and Grant No. SES-8209266 to J. J. Rotemberg. This financial support is greatly appreciated. We also want to thank Ernst Berndt and Dale Jorgenson for providing us their data, George Pennacchi for his superb research assistance, Lawrence Summers for helpful conversations, and two anonymous referees for their comments and suggestions.

[1] As Lucas (1967) and Treadway (1971) have shown, under certain conditions the flexible accelerator is consistent with dynamic optimization in the presence of adjustment costs. For a survey of this and related models, together with an assessment of their empirical performance, see Clark (1979).

ic models in which capital is quasi-fixed and subject to quadratic adjustment costs, but their approach utilizes an explicit solution to the optimal investment problem. In so doing it imposes the assumption that producers have static expectations regarding the evolution of factor and output prices, and requires that the underlying cost function be quadratic. Kennan (1979) and Meese (1980) estimated dynamic factor demand models in which producers have rational expectations, but Kennan imposed the restriction of a linear production structure, and Meese imposed a quadratic production structure. Epstein & Denny (1983) estimate the factor demands implied by a fairly general prespecified value function. However, in their approach, firms act as though they knew their future environment (prices, output, and interest rates) with certainty.[2]

In an earlier paper (1983) concerned primarily with energy demand, we demonstrated an alternative approach that allows for a general production structure and dynamic optimization under uncertainty. It works as follows. In a stochastic environment, firms that have rational expectations and maximize the expected sum of discounted profits also minimize the expected sum of discounted costs. Given any restricted cost function, one can derive the stochastic Euler equations (one for each quasi-fixed factor) that hold for this latter dynamic optimization problem. These Euler equations are just first-order conditions, and although they do not provide a complete solution to the optimization problem, they can be estimated directly for any parametric specification of the technology.

Our approach is to represent the technology by a translog restricted cost function, and then estimate the Euler equations, together with the cost function itself and the static demand equations for any flexible factors, using three-stage least squares. This permits us to test structural restrictions such as constant returns, and to test the over-identifying restrictions implied by rational expectations. The estimated equations then provide a complete empirical description of the production technology, including both short-run (only flexible factors adjust) and long-run (all factors fully adjust) elasticities of demand. The parameter estimates are fully consistent with rational expectations, and in particular with firm behavior that utilizes the solution to the underlying stochastic control problem.[3]

In our earlier paper we used US manufacturing data for the period

---

[2] For a survey of some of the recent work in dynamic factor demand modelling, see Berndt, Morrison & Watkins (1981).

[3] Since we do not actually solve the stochastic control problem (beyond writing the first-order conditions), we cannot calculate optimal factor demand trajectories corresponding to particular stochastic processes for prices. Stochastic control problems of this sort are generally difficult, if not impossible, to solve, and this raises the question of whether rational expectations provides a realistic behavioral foundation for studying investment behavior and factor demands in general.

1948–1971 to estimate a model in which capital and labor were treated as quasi-fixed factors, and energy and materials as flexible factors. We found adjustment costs on capital to be very important, but adjustment costs on labor appeared negligible. One might think that this latter result was due to our aggregation of white-collar (skilled) and blue-collar (unskilled) labor, and we explore this question here.

In this paper we utilize the same methodological approach described above, but both the model and data are different, and we focus on a number of different issues. Here we ignore the role of energy and materials, but we disaggregate labor (into white-collar and blue-collar) and capital (into equipment and structures). This disaggregation turns out to be quite revealing. We find that adjustment costs for white-collar labor are statistically significant, but quite small in magnitude. We also find that adjustment costs on structures and equipment are quite different, and that structures and equipment enter the production structure differently. In addition, this paper studies the role of financing in more detail, and deals explicitly with the effects of both corporate and personal taxes on factor demands. We allow for both debt and equity financing, and *estimate* the extent to which firms borrow to finance the marginal dollar of investment. Finally, we estimate the model with data for the period 1949–1976, thereby including those more recent years during which factor prices and rates of return fluctuated widely.

Our basic methodological approach is summarized in the next section. There we specify the translog restricted cost function (since blue-collar labor is the only flexible factor this boils down to an input requirement function, and there are no static demand equations), and derive the stochastic Euler equations for the quasi-fixed factors. Section III briefly summarized the estimation method, and discusses the treatment of various taxes and other issues related to the data. Estimation results are presented and discussed in Section IV.

II. The Models

Before presenting the details of our particular model specifications, it is useful to briefly review our general approach to estimating the production structure of a firm facing adjustment costs and making input choices in an uncertain environment. Let us assume that at time τ the firm chooses levels of n variable inputs whose quantities and nominal prices are given by the vectors $\mathbf{V}_\tau = (V_{i\tau})$ and $\mathbf{v}_\tau = (v_{i\tau})$ respectively, and m quasi-fixed inputs whose quantities are given by the vector $\mathbf{X}_\tau = (X_{i\tau})$. These inputs yield the single output Q_τ. The technology can therefore be represented by a restricted cost function C_τ which specifies the minimum expenditure on variable factors needed to produce Q_τ, given the amounts of quasi-fixed factors $\mathbf{X}_\tau$:

$$C_\tau = C(\mathbf{v}_\tau, \mathbf{X}_\tau, Q_\tau, \tau),\tag{1}$$

with C increasing and concave in $\mathbf{v}$ but decreasing and convex in $\mathbf{X}$, and the dependence on τ capturing technical progress.

By definition, the firm incurs costs of adjusting the quasi-fixed factors. We assume these adjustment costs are convex and external to the firm,[4] and we represent them in nominal terms by $P_\tau h(\Delta \mathbf{X}_\tau)$, where P_τ is the price of output and $\Delta \mathbf{X}_\tau = X_\tau - X_{\tau-1}$. The firm also makes direct outlays for its use of quasi-fixed factors, and because of tax and financing considerations these expenditures may be spread through time. We therefore assume that outlays (net of adjustment costs) for quasi-fixed factors at τ, H_τ, are a function of the current and past quantities of those factors:

$$H_\tau = H(\mathbf{X}_\tau, \dots, \mathbf{X}_{\tau-T}).\tag{2}$$

We assume the firm maximizes its expected present discounted value of profits. As shown in our earlier paper (1983), this implies that the firm minimizes the expected present discounted value of costs. Thus at time t the firm chooses a contingency plan for the vector of quasi-fixed factors to minimize:

$$\min_{\{\mathbf{X}\}} \mathcal{E}_t \sum_{\tau=t}^\infty R_{t,\tau}[C_\tau + P_\tau h(\Delta \mathbf{X}_\tau) + H_\tau]\tag{3}$$

where $\mathcal{E}_t$ denotes the expectation conditional on information available at t, and $R_{t,\tau}$ is the discount factor applied at t for costs incurred at τ.[5]

By taking the derivative of (3) with respect to X_{it} and setting it equal to zero, it is easily seen that the minimization yields the following Euler equations, or first-order conditions, for $i = 1, \dots, m$:

$$\mathcal{E}_t\left[\frac{\partial C_t}{\partial X_{it}} + P_t \frac{\partial h(\Delta \mathbf{X}_t)}{\partial X_{it}} - R_{t,t+1} P_{t+1} \frac{\partial h(\Delta \mathbf{X}_{t+1})}{\partial X_{it}} + \sum_{j=0}^T R_{t,t+j} \frac{\partial H_{t+j}}{\partial X_{it}}\right] = 0\tag{4}$$

These Euler equations just state that the net change in expected discounted costs from hiring one more unit of X_i at t is zero. That change is the sum of

---

[4] As in Gould (1968). For a survey of the treatment of adjustment costs, see Söderström (1976). We implicitly assume that costs of adjustment are incurred only when the *net* quantity of X_{it} changes. This assumption was relaxed in our earlier paper (1983), where our point estimates suggest that, indeed, only net changes in X_{it} lead to adjustment costs. We also estimated the current models relaxing this requirement, without affecting our results significantly.

[5] Note that while the expectation in (3) treats not just future input prices but also future output as random variables, output is not predetermined. The random variable Q_τ is given by the contingency plan that maximizes expected profits. For a more detailed discussion of this point, see Pindyck & Rotemberg (1983).

the increase in variable costs (which is negative), the extra costs of adjustment at t, the expected discounted value of the extra expenditures which the firm must incur by holding (at t only) one extra unit of X_i, minus the expected discounted value of the savings in future costs of adjustment. Note that the last term in eqn. (4) is a general expression for what is usually referred to as the rental rate on capital.

By Shepherd's Lemma we have the following additional first-order conditions, which take the form of static demand equations for the flexible factors:

$$V_{it} = \partial C_t / \partial v_{it}, \quad i = 1, \ldots, n. \tag{5}$$

As we discuss in more detail later, our approach is to estimate equations (1), (4), and (5) simultaneously using an instrumental variables procedure.

In this paper we focus on four production inputs: equipment, structures, and white-collar and blue-collar labor. Our model pertains to the US manufacturing sector, which we treat as a single firm[6] that takes input prices as given. Data for other inputs (e.g. energy and raw materials) were not available for the time period we consider, and we assume that such inputs are not substitutable for labor and capital. In particular, we assume that expenditures on blue-collar workers (the only variable input) depend only on the wage of those workers, the levels of the other three inputs, and output.[7]

Since there is only one variable input, the restricted cost function (1) takes the form of an input requirement function, which we specify in translog form:

$$\begin{aligned}
\ln B_t = {} & \alpha_0 + \alpha_1 \ln L_t + \alpha_2 \ln E_t + \alpha_3 \ln S_t + \alpha_4 \ln Q_t + \tfrac{1}{2}\gamma_{11}(\ln L_t)^2 \\
& + \gamma_{12} \ln L_t \ln E_t + \gamma_{13} \ln L_t \ln S_t + \gamma_{14} \ln L_t \ln Q_t + \tfrac{1}{2}\gamma_{22}(\ln E_t)^2 \\
& + \gamma_{23} \ln E_t \ln S_t + \gamma_{24} \ln E_t \ln Q_t + \tfrac{1}{2}\gamma_{33}(\ln S_t)^2 + \gamma_{34} \ln S_t \ln Q_t \\
& + \tfrac{1}{2}\gamma_{44}(\ln Q_t)^2 + \lambda t
\end{aligned} \tag{6}$$

where B_t, L_t, E_t, S_t, and Q_t are the levels of blue-collar labor, white-collar labor, equipment, structures and output at t. The term λt allows for neutral technical progress. (The restrictions of the α's and γ's required for this translog function to be decreasing and convex in L_t, E_t and S_t are not imposed in the estimation.)

---

[6] Or, equivalently, as consisting of many competitive firms whose aggregate technology is given by our model.
[7] This assumption is justified if the production function is of the Leontief form in two composite inputs, the first of which is a function of the levels of labor and capital while the second is a function of the other inputs.

Costs of adjustment are assumed to be quadratic in ΔL_t, ΔE_t, and ΔS_t.[8] In particular,

$$h = h_L(\Delta L_t) + h_E(\Delta E_t) + h_S(\Delta S_t) = \tfrac{1}{2}\beta_L(\Delta L_t)^2 + \tfrac{1}{2}\beta_E(\Delta E_t)^2 + \tfrac{1}{2}\beta_S(\Delta S_t)^2.$$

Note that cross effects—i.e. changes in one factor affecting costs of adjusting other factors—are neglected. Letting w_t and b_t be the hourly wage to white-collar and blue-collar workers respectively, the Euler equation for white-collar labor is then given by:

$$[b_t(1-\theta_t)B_t/L_t](\alpha_1+\gamma_{11}\ln L_t+\gamma_{12}\ln E_t+\gamma_{13}\ln S_t+\gamma_{14}\ln Q_t)$$
$$+w_t(1-\theta_t)+P_t\beta_L(L_t-L_{t-1})-\beta_L\,\mathcal{E}_t[R_{t,t+1}P_{t+1}(L_{t+1}-L_t)] = 0 \tag{7}$$

where θ_t is the corporate income tax rate (wages are tax deductible in the US).

The importance of tax and financing considerations becomes clear when we consider equipment. Let e_t be the purchase price of a unit of equipment. Suppose the firm buys a unit of equipment at t with the intention of keeping it until it is fully depreciated. If the firm borrows the present discounted value of the depreciation allowances its after-tax payment would be $e_t \times (1-c_{Et}-z_{Et})$, where c_{Et} is the investment tax credit on equipment and z_{Et} is the present discounted value of the depreciation allowance. If the firm wants an extra unit of equipment at t without affecting the level of capital in subsequent periods, it will purchase $(1-\delta_E)$ fewer units of equipment at $t+1$, where δ_E is the physical depreciation rate for equipment, thereby saving $(1-\delta_E)e_{t+1}(1-c_{E,t+1}-z_{E,t+1})$.[9] So far the only debt the firm incurs is offset by the depreciation allowances. However, we would like to allow for the possibility that a fraction d of $e_t(1-c_{Et}-z_{Et})$ is borrowed for the purchase of the marginal dollar's worth of equipment, and for simplicity we assume (perhaps unrealistically) that this *marginal* debt is repaid after one year. (However, the firm is also allowed to borrow unspecified amounts on *inframarginal* units of equipment.) Given this treatment of taxes and financing, and assuming that factors are productive in the period in which they are purchased, the Euler equation for equipment is:

$$[b_t(1-\theta_t)B_t/E_t](\alpha_2+\gamma_{12}\ln L_t+\gamma_{22}\ln E_t+\gamma_{23}\ln S_t+\gamma_{24}\ln Q_t)$$
$$+(1-d)e_t(1-c_{Et}-z_{Et})+P_t\beta_E(E_t-E_{t-1})$$

---

[8] We also estimated versions of the model assuming adjustment costs are quadratic in $\Delta L/L_{t-1}$, $\Delta E/E_{t-1}$, and $\Delta S/S_{t-1}$, without significantly affecting the results.

[9] This assumes the firm purchases some equipment at $t+1$. If the firm bought an extra unit of equipment at t with the intention of *selling* $(1-\delta_E)$ units at $t+1$, it would be unlikely to borrow the expected present value of the depreciation allowances. Instead it would pay $e_t(1-c_{Et}-\bar{z}_{Et})$ at t, where $\bar{z}_{Et}$ is the depreciation allowances in the first period, and it would receive $(1-\delta_E)e_{t+1}(1-c_{E,t+1})$ at $t+1$.

$$+\mathscr{E}_t R_{t,t+1}\{d[1+i_t(1-\theta_{t+1})]e_t(1-c_{Et}-z_{Et})-(1-\delta_E)\,e_{t+1}(1-c_{E,t+1}-z_{E,t+1})$$

$$-P_{t+1}\beta_E(E_{t+1}-E_t)\}=0 \tag{8}$$

where i_t is the pre-tax rate of interest paid at $t+1$ on marginal borrowing at t.[10]

A similar analysis for structures yields the following Euler equation for that factor:

$$[b_t(1-\theta_t)\,B_t/S_t](\alpha_3+\gamma_{13}\ln L_t+\gamma_{23}\ln E_t+\gamma_{33}\ln S_t+\gamma_{34}\ln Q_t)$$

$$+(1-d)\,s_t(1-c_{St}-z_{St})+P_t\beta_S(S_t-S_{t-1})+\mathscr{E}_t R_{t,t+1}$$

$$\times\{d[1+i_t(1-\theta_{t+1})]s_t(1-c_{St}-z_{St})-(1-\delta_S)\,s_{t+1}(1-c_{S,t+1}-z_{S,t+1})$$

$$-P_{t+1}\beta_S(S_{t+1}-S_t)\}=0 \tag{9}$$

where δ_S, s_t, c_{St}, and z_{St} are, respectively, the physical depreciation rate, the purchase price, the investment tax credit, and the present value of depreciation allowances for structures.

The model given by equations (6)—(9) is our "preferred" specification. One might argue, however, that the distinction between equipment and structures is somewhat artificial, since any capital that cannot be easily removed is classified as a structure. We therefore estimate an alternative model for which equipment and structures are aggregated into a single measure of capital. The blue-collar labor input requirement function is again specified to be translog:

$$\ln B_t = \phi_0+\phi_1\ln L_t+\phi_2\ln K_t+\phi_3\ln Q_t+\tfrac{1}{2}\psi_{11}(\ln L_t)^2+\psi_{12}\ln L_t\ln K_t$$

$$+\psi_{13}\ln L_t\ln Q_t+\tfrac{1}{2}\psi_{22}(\ln K_t)^2+\psi_{23}\ln K_t\ln Q_t+\tfrac{1}{2}\psi_{33}(\ln Q_t)^2+\lambda t \tag{10}$$

where K_t is the quantity of aggregate capital.

Letting δ_K, k_t, c_{Kt}, and z_{Kt} denote, respectively, the physical depreciation rate, purchase price, investment tax credit, and present discounted value of depreciation allowances for this capital, the Euler equations are now given by:

$$[b_t(1-\theta_t)\,B_t/L_t](\phi_1+\psi_{11}\ln L_t+\psi_{12}\ln K_t+\psi_{13}\ln Q_t)+w_t(1-\theta_t)$$

$$+P_t\beta_L(L_t-L_{t-1})-\beta_L\,\mathscr{E}_t[R_{t,t+1}P_{t+1}(L_{t+1}-L_t)]=0 \tag{11}$$

---

[10] If revenues at $t+1$ get discounted at t at the rate $i_t(1-\theta_{t+1})$, then $R_{t,t+1}=1/(1+i_t(1-\theta_{t+1}))$, and the fraction d that is debt financed is irrelevant to the firm. However, it is more reasonable to assume that future costs incurred by firms get discounted at the rate of return on equity. This is the rate at which share-holders, whose objectives the firm represents, discount future revenues and costs.

$$[b_t(1-\theta_t)B_t/K_t](\phi_2+\psi_{12}\ln L_t+\psi_{22}\ln K_t+\psi_{23}\ln Q_t)+(1-d)k_t(1-c_{Kt}-z_{Kt})$$
$$+P_t\beta_K(K_t-K_{t-1})+\mathscr{E}_tR_{t,t+1}\{d[1+i_t(1-\theta_{t+1})]k_t(1-c_{Kt}-z_{Kt})$$
$$-(1-\delta_K)k_{t+1}(1-c_{K,t+1}-z_{K,t+1})-P_{t+1}\beta_K(K_{t+1}-K_t)\}=0 \qquad (12)$$

III. Estimation Method and Data

We obtain parameter values for "Model 1" by simultaneously estimating the input requirement function (6) and the Euler equations (7), (8), and (9), and for "Model 2" by simultaneously estimating the input requirement function (10) and the Euler equations (11) and (12). Note that because there is only one variable factor in each model, no static demand equations are estimated.

The estimation is done using three-stage least squares, which, if the error terms are conditionally homoscedastic, is equivalent to the generalized instrumental variables procedure of Hansen (1982) and Hansen & Singleton (1982). That procedure minimizes the correlation between variables known at t (the instruments) and the residuals of the estimating equations. These residuals result from using the actual values of the prices and quantities at time $t+1$ in the Euler equations (7), (8), (9), (11) and (12). The minimized value of the objective function of this procedure provides a statistic J, which is distributed as chi-squared, and which can be used to test the over-identifying restrictions of the model, as well as structural restrictions such as constant returns.

This instrumental variables procedure is a natural one to apply to the Euler equations. This is because the residuals of those equations can be viewed as expectational errors which, if agents have rational expectations, have mean zero conditional on information available at t. The residuals of the input requirement function, however, cannot be interpreted in the same way, since in theory that function should provide an exact description of the technology. In practice that function will not fit the data exactly, and the errors are likely to be correlated with variables known at t. We will assume that this function holds in expectation with respect to some smaller conditioning set (i.e. set of instruments). We take that set to exclude current variables appearing in the input requirement function or Euler equations.

We estimate the models using annual data for the US manufacturing sector for the years 1949–1976. Quantities and wage rates for blue- and white-collar labor are those compiled in Berndt and Morrison (1979).[11] The purchase prices and quantities of equipment and structures were construct-

---

[11] These data incorporate some embodied technical progress since employment levels are corrected for the educational achievement of the work force.

ed by Ernst Berndt using a perpetual inventory method, and assuming a physical depreciation rate for equipment of 0.135 and for structures of 0.071. (In "Model 2" equipment and structures are aggregated using a Divisia Index). Since no data for gross output in manufacturing is available for the period of our study, we used the level of the gross domestic product of manufacturing from the National Income and Product Accounts. The price index P_t came from the same source.

We assume that the 1-period discount rate $R_{t,\,t+1}$ is equal to $1/(1+r_e)$, where r_e is the after-tax return on equity.[12] This return is constructed from the identity:

$$r_e = r_d(1-\theta_p)+r_c(1-\theta_c),\tag{13}$$

where r_d and r_c are respectively the dividend yield and capital gains rate (we use data on the Standard and Poor's 500 Index for both), θ_p is the marginal personal tax rate (we use data reported by Seater (1980), and θ_c is the *effective* tax rate on capital gains (based on the estimates of Feldstein & Summers (1979), we set $\theta_c=0.047$). As for the interest rate i_t, we use the rate on commercial paper. The investment tax credit and present discounted value of depreciation allowances are computed by Jorgenson & Sullivan (1981), who use data on the term structure of interest rates to obtain z.

The following instruments are used in the estimation of both models: a constant, and the lagged detrended values of the following variables: rate of return on equity, the hourly compensation of both types of workers, the purchase prices of equipment and structures, the present discounted value of their depreciation allowances, as well as the logarithms of the quantities of blue-collar labor, white-collar labor, structures, equipment, and output.

IV. Estimation Results

For our "prefered" specification, both capital and labor are disaggregated, so that there are three quasi-fixed factors. Recall that the model for this specification ("Model 1") is given by the input requirement function (6) and the three Euler equations (7), (8), and (9). We also estimate the alternative specification in which equipment and structures are aggregated; this model ("Model 2") is given by the input requirement function (10) and the Euler equations (11) and (12). Each of these models was estimated first in its unrestricted form, then with the restrictions of homotheticity imposed, and finally with the restrictions of constant returns (CRTS).[13]

---

[12] We also estimated the models using $R_{t,\,t+1}=1/(1+r_{cp})$, where r_{cp} is the after-tax return on commercial paper, but we obtained significantly poorer results.

[13] Note that the homothetic and constant returns versions are estimated *using the covariance matrix obtained from the estimation of the unrestricted model,* thereby permitting us to test these restrictions.

Table 1. *Parameter estimates for Model 1 (B; L, S, E)*
Asymptotic standard errors in parentheses

	Unrestricted	Homothetic	CRTS
α_0	−12.1166	−3.7658	7.8492
	(2.6060)	(1.1064)	(1.2135)
α_1	4.4941	3.9380	−0.7089
	(0.3352)	(0.3413)	(0.6326)
α_2	0.00075	−0.003389	0.001997
	(0.00090)	(0.00132)	(0.000541)
α_3	−0.000677	0.000141	0.001844
	(0.00082)	(0.00106)	(0.000652)
α_4	0.5907		
	(0.9379)		
γ_{11}	−0.7502	−0.6492	0.03281
	(0.0614)	(0.0608)	(0.1642)
γ_{12}	3.010×10^{-5}	0.000486	0.000513
	(0.00016)	(0.000213)	(0.000123)
γ_{13}	−0.000103	0.000175	0.000352
	(0.000138)	(0.000159)	(0.000142)
γ_{14}	0.3416		
	(0.04815)		
γ_{22}	0.000191	−0.000050	0.000289
	(0.000129)	(0.00013)	(0.000113)
γ_{23}	−0.000253	−0.000007	−0.000164
	(9.624×10^{-5})	(0.000071)	(7.878×10^{-5})
γ_{24}	−0.000167		
	(0.000194)		
γ_{33}	0.000563	−0.000718	−0.000261
	(0.000277)	(0.000374)	(0.000104)
γ_{34}	6.181×10^{-5}		
	(0.000173)		
γ_{44}	−0.5045		
	(0.1782)		
λ	−0.01295	−0.000059	−0.02890
	(0.00302)	(0.0023)	(0.001186)
d	1.2733	1.2430	1.1938
	(0.09859)	(0.1012)	(0.09526)
β_L	0.000318	0.000318	0.000191
	(5.243×10^{-5})	(0.00005)	(0.000189)
β_E	0.00476	0.00538	0.003159
	(0.00238)	(0.00384)	(0.002264)
β_S	0.009238	0.02547	0.2021
	(0.009418)	(0.01264)	(0.00868)
θ		0.42446	
		(0.03682)	
J	54.45	141.45	418.22
EQ 6 SSR	0.02186	0.05364	0.06721
D.W.	1.181	0.773	0.737
EQ 7 SSR	0.17229	0.19518	3.2188
D.W.	1.727	1.769	0.218
EQ 8 SSR	0.01858	0.0530	0.03566
D.W.	1.766	0.685	0.912
EQ 9 SSR	0.01272	0.02103	0.02079
D.W.	2.771	1.797	1.715

Table 2. *Parameter estimates for Model 2 (B; L, K)*
Asymptotic standard errors in parentheses

	Unrestricted	Homothetic	CRTS
ϕ_0	−10.9216	−4.782	7.7565
	(2.3371)	(1.021)	(1.3809)
ϕ_1	4.5063	4.362	−0.7034
	(0.3342)	(0.331)	(0.7172)
ϕ_2	−0.003493	−0.00134	−0.01004
	(0.003411)	(0.00303)	(0.001362)
ϕ_3	0.1395		
	(0.8566)		
ψ_{11}	−0.7527	−0.7611	0.03160
	(0.06122)	(0.0595)	(0.1863)
ψ_{12}	0.000709	0.00063	0.002714
	(0.000611)	(0.00049)	(0.000347)
ψ_{13}	0.3473		
	(0.04810)		
ψ_{22}	0.000885	−0.00124	0.001593
	(0.000656)	(0.00044)	(0.00046)
ψ_{23}	−0.001416		
	(0.000659)		
ψ_{33}	−0.4247		
	(0.1620)		
λ	−0.01213	−0.00200	−0.02427
	(0.002614)	(0.00165)	(0.000721)
d	1.5977	1.5655	1.4381
	(0.1752)	(0.1610)	(0.1635)
β_L	0.000315	0.000309	0.000185
	(0.000052)	(0.000053)	(0.000223)
β_K	0.01768	0.02301	0.01047
	(0.003304)	(0.00370)	(0.002753)
θ		0.51087	
		(0.02569)	
J	34.81	61.39	447.83
EQ 10 SSR	0.02154	0.0353	0.09893
D.W.	1.160	0.901	0.506
EQ 11 SSR	0.1717	0.1834	3.2225
D.W.	1.708	1.487	0.217
EQ 12 SSR	0.08443	0.1059	0.2643
D.W.	1.647	1.842	0.568

For Model 1, the parameter restrictions implied by homotheticity are: $\alpha_4 = \theta(1 - \alpha_1 - \alpha_2 - \alpha_3)$, $\gamma_{14} = -\theta(\gamma_{11} + \gamma_{12} + \gamma_{13})$, $\gamma_{24} = -\theta(\gamma_{12} + \gamma_{22} + \gamma_{23})$, $\gamma_{34} = -\theta(\gamma_{13} + \gamma_{23} + \gamma_{33})$, and $\gamma_{44} = -\theta(\gamma_{14} + \gamma_{24} + \gamma_{34})$. These restrictions imply that when output increases by 1 percent all factor inputs will increase by θ

percent in long-run equilibrium. For Model 2, the parameter restrictions implied by homotheticity are: $\phi_3=\theta(1-\phi_1-\phi_2)$, $\psi_{13}=-\theta(\psi_{11}+\psi_{12})$, $\psi_{23}=-\theta(\psi_{12}+\psi_{22})$, and $\psi_{33}=\theta(\psi_{13}+\psi_{23})$. Finally, for both models constant returns to scale requires that in addition $\theta=1$.

Parameter estimates are shown in Table 1 for Model 1, and in Table 2 for Model 2. Both models satisfy the condition of monotonicity and convexity for all but the first four years of data. Observe that for the unrestricted version of Model 1 the value of J is 54.45. Under the null hypothesis that the model is valid, J is distributed as chi-square with number of degrees of freedom equal to the number of instruments (13) times the number of equations (4) minus the number of parameters (20). The critical 5% level of the chi-square distribution with 32 degrees of freedom is 46.2, so that the over-identifying restrictions are rejected, throwing some doubt on the validity of the estimated standard errors.[14] For Model 2 the value of J is 34.81. For this model there are 39–14=25 degrees of freedom, the critical 5% level of the chi-square distribution is 37.7, and the over-identifying restrictions can be accepted.

To test for homotheticity, we use the difference in the values of J with and without the parameter restrictions imposed. That difference is 87.0 for Model 1, and 26.3 for Model 2. These numbers are well above the critical 5 percent values of the chi-square distribution with four and three degrees of freedom respectively, so that homotheticity is overwhelmingly rejected. The estimates for θ are near 0.5 for both models, suggesting important economies of scale.

The fact that θ is significantly different from 1 constitutes a rejection of CRTS under the maintained hypothesis of homotheticity. We also test CRTS directly by comparing the J statistics for CRTS imposed with those of the unrestricted models. The differences in the values of J are 363.8 for Model 1, and 413.0 for Model 2, which are much larger than the critical 5 percent chi-square values with five and four degrees of freedom, again rejecting CRTS.[15]

Our unrestricted estimates allow us to compute how much output would increase if all inputs were increased by 1%. For the 1976 data point, Model 1 shows a 1.66% increase in output, and Model 2 shows a 1.64% increase. We thus find increasing returns to scale that are large but not unreasonable.

The parameter estimates have interesting implications for the role of

---

[14] Failure of the over-identifying restrictions in this model is inconsistent with the hypothesis that firms are optimizing with rational expectations. It could imply the existence of systematic optimizing or forecasting errors on the part of firms, or a mis-specification of our input requirement function.

[15] Note that this puts into question empirical q-theory models of investment that equate marginal and average q.

Table 3. *Adjustment costs*

	Percentage marginal adjustment cost (avg.)[a]	Percentage total adjustment cost (avg.)[a]
Model 1		
L	0.03	0.001
E	0.23	0.007
S	0.34	0.005
Model 2		
L	0.03	0.001
K	2.14	0.056

[a] Computations are explained in the text.

adjustment costs. Observe that all of the adjustment cost parameters have the correct sign, and all are statistically significant except the one for structures in Model 1 (although this parameter is numerically large). The importance of adjustment costs is best understood by comparing their value as a total fraction of expenditures on a particular quasi-fixed factor with their value on the margin. This is done in Table 3. In the first column we take the average annual change in the stock of each quasi-fixed factor over the sample period, compute the marginal adjustment cost for that average

Table 4. *Elasticities*

Model 1 (B; L, S, E)					
Long-run elasticity of demand for	With respect to				
	P_B	P_L	P_E	P_S	Q
B	-1.4505	1.4505	-1.493×10^{-5}	1.734×10^{-5}	0.3575
L	2.3105	-2.3106	0.000126	1.0007×10^{-5}	0.9938
E	-0.1554	0.8166	-0.5221	-0.1390	1.0582
S	0.2708	0.09809	-0.2107	-0.1582	0.5282
Short-run elasticity of demand for	With respect to				
	L	E	S	Q	
B	-0.6278	-9.7065×10^{-5}	-6.4045×10^{-5}	0.98158	
Model 2 (B; L, K)					
Long-run elasticity of demand for	With respect to				
	P_B	P_L	P_K	Q	
B	-1.4674	1.4676	-0.000229	0.3513	
L	2.3381	-2.3385	0.000394	1.0187	
K	-1.6851	1.8186	-0.1335	0.7275	
Short-run elasticity of demand for	With respect to				
	L	K	Q		
B	-0.62769	-0.000136	0.99086		

annual change using the parameter estimates of Tables 1 and 2, and then divide by the average rental rate for the factor. This provides a measure of percentage marginal adjustment costs. In the second column we compute total adjustment costs for each factor in each year as a fraction of the total expenditure on that factor, and then average these figures over the sample period. This provides a measure of percentage total adjustment costs. Observe that while adjustment costs are small as a total percentage of expenditures, they are quite large on the margin for capital. This means that the firm's cost minimization problem is very much a dynamic one. However, adjustment costs for white-collar labor, both on the margin and as a percentage of total cost, are small. We also found very small adjustment costs for labor in our earlier paper (1983), in which labor is aggregated.

Our estimates also have implications for the role of financing. In particular the parameter d specifies the fraction of the after-tax cost of a dollar of capital that is debt financed at the margin. However, our estimates of d are implausibly high since they are significantly greater than one for both models. While the parameter d applies only at the margin and thus the inframarginal investments may well lead to lower borrowing, these values seem high nonetheless.

Further insight into the production structure can be obtained by examining the elasticities of factor demands.[16] These elasticities were calculated for the 1976 sample point, and are presented in Table 4.[17]

A number of things should be mentioned about these elasticities. First, note that there is consistency across the two models. Elasticities of blue- and white-collar labor demand with respect to the two wage rates and output are almost identical across the two models, and in Model 2, the elasticities of demand for capital with respect to its own price and output are about midway between the corresponding elasticities for equipment and structures in Model 1.

Second, note that the elasticities are generally reasonable, both in magnitude and in sign. The short-run elasticities with respect to other factor inputs are negative in both models, as required by monotonicity. In Model 1, blue-collar labor and equipment are complementary inputs in the long run, as are structures and equipment, and in Model 2 blue-collar labor and

---

[16] Intermediate- and long-run elasticities, i.e. those that apply when quasi-fixed factors have partially or fully adjusted, must be interpreted with caution. The reason is that if prices evolve stochastically, the adjustment path for any particular discrete change in a price, as well as the long-run expected equilibrium, are solutions to a stochastic control problem (and in some cases a long-run expected equilibrium may not exist). Since it is typically infeasible to obtain such solutions, we must compute elasticities by implicitly assuming that firms ignore the variance of future prices in responding to price changes. These elasticities can therefore be best viewed as a description of the technology.

[17] The formulas used to calculate these elasticities are available from the authors on request.

the capital aggregate are complements in the long run. As one would expect, structures is relatively price inelastic, and in particular less elastic than equipment. The small own-price elasticity for the capital aggregate in Model 2 is disturbing by itself, and also when contrasted with the much larger values found in our earlier study (1983). The elasticities of demand for white-collar labor are large, but still reasonable.[18]

Although we do not do so here, one could use the models presented in this paper to simulate the effects of changes in factor prices or output—but only in a deterministic context. As explained in Pindyck and Rotemberg (1983), such simulations are carried out by numerically solving the deterministic control problem that corresponds to the minimization in eqn. (3). A solution to the control problem can be obtained by finding initial conditions for the quasi-fixed factors which yield steady-state values for those factors (i.e. values which satisfy the associated transversality conditions) when the Euler equations and input requirement function are together solved recursively through time. Note that for Model 1, in which there are three quasi-fixed factors, this involves searching over a three-dimensional grid of initial conditions.

V. Conclusions

The model of factor demands presented in this paper is consistent with rational expectations and dynamic optimization in the presence of adjustment costs. With the possible exception of the parameter which describes the manufacturing sector's financing decisions, our estimates are quite plausible. We obtain reasonable elasticity estimates, and find that equipment is a complementary factor to both blue-collar labor and structures, while other factor pairs are substitutes. As in our previous paper, we strongly reject constant returns to scale. Finally, we find that adjustment costs are important at the margin, especially for equipment and structures.

It is important to keep in mind that our model has a number of limitations, some of which are suggestive of further work. First, we aggregate across goods, factors, and time. The numerous outputs produced under the heading of manufacturing are treated as a single good. Factor diversity is in fact richer than the two types of labor and capital we consider. Also, our use of annual data requires the implicit assumption that seasonal fluctuations are such that average output is only a function of average factor use over the year.

---

[18] A surprising result in both models is that the elasticity of each type of labor with respect to its own price is nearly the negative of the elasticity with respect to the price of the other type. This is a result of the coincidental fact that for the later data points, the labor price ratios are nearly equal to the ratios of the slopes of the demands.

Second, our model imposes constraints on firms' financial policies. Although we allow for the different tax consequences of debt and equity financing, we ignore the term structures of the debt that firms incur when they purchase new capital. Finally, we only allow for limited forms of technical progress. Expanding the model to include other forms of technical progress might significantly affect the parameter estimates.

References

Berndt, Ernst R., Fuss, Melvyn A. & Waverman, Leonard: Dynamic adjustment models of industrial energy demand: Empirical analysis for US manufacturing, 1947–74. Research Project No. 683–1, Final Report, Electric Power Research Institute, Palo Alto, California, November 1980.

Berndt, Ernst R. & Morrison, Catherine J.: Income redistribution and employment effects of rising energy prices. *Resources and Energy 2*, 131–150, 1979.

Berndt, Ernst, Morrison, Catherine & Campbell Watkins, G.: Dynamic models of energy demand: An assessment and comparison. In *Measuring and modelling natural resource substitution* (ed. E. Berndt and B. Field). MIT Press, Cambridge Massachusetts, 1981.

Clark, Peter K.: Investment in the 1970's: Theory, performance, and prediction. *Brookings Papers on Economic Activity 1*, 74–113, 1979.

Epstein, Larry G. & Denny, Michael G. S.: The multivariate flexible accelerator model: Its empirical restrictions and an application to US manufacturing. *Econometrica 51*, March 1983.

Feldstein, Martin & Summers, Lawrence: Inflation and the taxation of capital income in the corporate sector. *National Tax Journal 32*, 445–470, December 1979.

Hansen, Lars Peter: Large-sample properties of method of moments estimators. *Econometrica 50*, 1029–1054, July 1982.

Hansen, Lars Peter & Singleton, Kenneth: Generalized instrumental variables estimation of nonlinear rational expectations models. *Econometrica 50*, 1269–1286, September 1982.

Jorgenson, Dale W. & Sullivan, Martin A.: Inflation and corporate capital recovery. In *Depreciation, inflation, and the taxation of income from capital* (ed. C. R. Hulten), pp. 171–233. The Urban Institute Press, Washington, 1981.

Kennan, John: The estimation of partial adjustment models with rational expectations. *Econometrica 47*, 1441–1456, November 1979.

Lucas, Robert E.: Optimal investment policy and the flexible accelerator. *International Economic Review 8*, 78–85, February 1967.

Meese, Richard: Dynamic factor demand schedules for labor and capital under rational expectations. *Journal of Econometrics 14*, 141–158, 1980.

Morrison, Catherine J. & Berndt, Ernst R.: Short-run labor productivity in a dynamic model. *Journal of Econometrics 16*, 339–365, 1981.

Pindyck, Robert S. & Rotemberg, Julio J.: Dynamic factor demands and the effects of energy price shocks. *American Economic Review*, to appear, 1983.

Seater, John: Marginal federal personal and corporate income tax rates in the US. 1909–1975. Research Papers of the Philadelphia Federal Reserve Bank, Number 57, November 1980.

Söderström, Hans T.: Production and investment under costs of adjustment: A survey. *Zeitschrift für Nationalökonomie 76*, 369–388, 1976.

Treadway, Arthur B.: On the multivariate flexible accelerator. *Econometrica 39*, 845–855, September 1971.

The Divisia Index of Technological Change, Path Independence and Endogenous Prices

Murray Brown and Richard Greenberg*

State University of New York, Buffalo, NY, USA

Abstract

A general equilibrium model is presented which contains the same assumption base as that for the Divisia index of total factor productivity (DITFP). The conditions under which the DITFP is independent of path are derived. The unique feature of this paper is that a condition is added to those already in the literature for the DITFP to be path independent.

I. Introduction

The Divisia Index of total factor productivity (DITFP) is known to possess many desirable properties; see Richter (1966) and Usher (1974). Yet, it suffers from an extremely serious defect: since it is a line integral, it depends in general on the path over which the integral is taken. That is, suppose there are two paths connecting a point with itself. Since the integral is not path independent, a Divisia index calculated for one of the paths does not return to its initial point. This implies that if technology were unchanged, the DITFP would register a nonzero residual. This bias can become arbitrarily large or small if the economy executes cycles from the initial point.

Hulten (1973) has given necessary and sufficient conditions for the absence of path dependence in the DITFP for a single sector production unit that takes prices as given. These are: the relevant functions satisfy the Leontief conditions on consistent aggregation (weak separability), the aggregate is linear homogeneous and the first order equilibrium conditions must hold. However, Hulten did not consider the implications for the DITFP entailed by a general equilibrium framework.

In the present paper we embed the production unit into a simple general equilibrium model and enquire into the conditions under which the DITFP for all production units is path independent. The condition for path independence is that the differential form underlying the DITFP be exact (its curl

---

* The authors wish to thank Edwin Burmeister, Winston Chang, Dale Jorgenson and an anonymous referee for their comments.

must vanish), a condition that is tested by examining the coefficients of the changes in inputs and outputs. In Hulten's model, the coefficients are allowed to change from one equilibrium to another but they cannot be explicitly expressed in terms of outputs and inputs. However, in a general equilibrium model, these coefficients can be found explicitly and hence the conditions under which the curl of DITFP vanishes can be readily calculated.

The unique feature of our paper is that this procedure allows us to add a condition to those already in the literature for the DITFP to be path independent. We can summarize our results by noting that the following conditions yielding an unbiased DITFP are sufficient: (*a*) the rate of interest (profit) be zero; or (*b*) both intersectoral and intrasectoral aggregation conditions are satisfied (which is implied by (*a*)); or (*c*) prices are constant on the path between the initial and comparison points. Condition (*a*) is new in the present context though it has appeared in related problems before (see below).

We proceed as follows. A general equilibrium model that contains the same assumption base in the large as that for the DITFP is presented in Section II. It permits us to do comparative steady-state analysis quite simply. Though no apologies are required for the simplicity of the model since it is easily generalizable, the analysis is unrealistic in assuming that the observed data are generated by steady-state equilibria. Of course that is the assumption underlying the Norsworthy et al. paper (1979, pp. 395–6), so that the present work preserves continuity in that respect. In any event, the model in Section II is a standard one, it introduces some simple general equilibrium considerations and it also discusses the curl condition.

The conditions under which the DITFP is independent of path are derived. Here, a very simple two-sector general equilibrium version of the model is used with and without the consumption sector suppressed. The principal result is obtained by calculating the curl of the differential form underlying the DITFP. Section III contains some remarks linking the new result obtained here to the literature.

II. The DITFP with Endogenous Prices

Aside from the criticisms of the Divisia index that are data related (namely, the index tends to accumulate errors of measurement), its principal shortcoming is asserted to be that it is not path independent. Hulten (1973) develops conditions for the DITFP to be path independent but he does not avail himself of relations that emerge from a general equilibrium model. Our results do precisely that and though they are derived by means of a simple general equilibrium model, they can easily be generalized.

Consider the zero profit condition (price equals cost) at the sectoral level with no depreciation:

$$p_j y_j = \varrho_j + r \sum_i^n p_i \varkappa_{ij} \quad (j = 1, 2, ..., n) \tag{1}$$

where y_j and p_j are per capita output and price relative to the wage rate of the jth sector, L_j is the jth sector's labor input, $\varrho_j = L_j/L$, $\Sigma_j \varrho_j = 1$, and the $\varkappa_{ij}$ represents the use of the ith capital good in the jth sector in per capita terms. We can immediately add the expressions in (1) to obtain an aggregate zero profit condition:

$$\sum_j p_j y_j - 1 - r \sum_j \sum_i p_i \varkappa_{ij} = 0. \tag{2}$$

Consumption has been suppressed here but its presence or lack of presence in what follows is not material (see below).[1] Write out the total differential of (2), placing the changes in quantities on the l.h.s.:

$$\sum_j p_j \, dy_j - r \sum_j \sum_i p_i \, d\varkappa_{ij} = - \sum_j y_j \, dp_j + r \sum_j \sum_i \varkappa_{ij} \, dp_i + \sum_j \sum_i p_i \varkappa_{ij} \, dr, \tag{3}$$

where d indicates the total change in each variable.

Examination of the l.h.s. of (3) indicates that it is in fact the differential form from which the DITFP is derived (see below). In the absence of technical advances, it should vanish. That is, with no technical advances the l.h.s. of (3) vanishes by virtue of the satisfaction of the sectoral first order conditions where each sector takes prices as given but obviously that in itself does not assure path independence since the equilibrium prices may differ between the initial and terminal points over which the DITFP is calculated.

In order to make this more evident, rewrite the l.h.s. of (3) for a two-sector economy as

$$p_1(dy_1 - r \, d\varkappa_{11} - r \, d\varkappa_{12}) + p_2(dy_2 - r \, d\varkappa_{21} - r \, d\varkappa_{22}). \tag{4}$$

---

[1] Evidently, (2) is not an identity. It is an expression for zero profits that results from assuming that factors of production are paid the value of their marginal products in competitive equilibrium where all outputs are produced by a constant returns to scale technology and where all net own rates of return equal r. It is only a national income identity when r is defined by (2). Since r is taken to be given exogenously in the heterogeneous capital model used here, (2) does not hold identically.

This does not mean that r need be the only exogenous variable. In fact, rather than r, we could have specified the real wage rate exogenous but since the factor price frontier allows us to take $dw/dr < 0$ for $w > 0$, $r > 0$, it is immaterial which variable is chosen to be exogenous; see Morishima (1964, p. 61). Moreover, in the theory of noninduced technical change, advances in technology are also taken as exogenous a procedure which is consistent with the measurement of technological change by the chain index method.

Formally, the integral of the expression in (4) is called a line integral which is zero along any closed curve if and only if (4) is an exact derivative; the line integral is then independent of path. The necessary and sufficient conditions that (4) be exact are that its curl vanishes; see Lass (1957, pp. 178–9).[2]

In order to understand the meaning of the curl it is perhaps instructive to view a physical analog. We can define work as the integral of a force field over a particular path. So, too, we can describe the DITFP as the integral of the vector of outputs less the vector of inputs over a time path. In the physical analog, if we begin at a particular point and traverse a closed path until we return to the starting point, there will be no work performed if the force field is conservative by virtue of Stokes theorem. So, too, the DITFP should be conservative in that if we begin at a particular state of technology and return to it at some future time the measure of the net technological change should be zero. For a force field to be conservative it must have a curl of zero. Therefore, a conservative measure of technological change, and thus an unbiased one, must also have a curl identically equal to zero.

Suppose that all prices are constant between the initial and terminal points for which the DITFP is to be calculated. Then clearly the curl vanishes and the DITFP is path independent. In a simple general equilibrium model with heterogeneous capital goods, as in Brown & Chang (1976), constant (relative) prices obtain if the labor shares (of income) are equal for all sectors. This provides a Hicksian aggregation condition which permits the model to be collapsed into a single sector with a single aggregate capital input. But that is precisely the general equilibrium counterpart of Hulten's partial equilibrium result (1973, pp. 1018 and 1020) which requires the existence of an aggregate in order for the DITFP to be path independent.

Formally, we have

Theorem 1. *The DITFP (4) is path independent if inter- and intra-sectoral aggregation conditions hold.*

---

[2] The vanishing of the curl is equivalent to having the partial derivative of the coefficient of each variable with respect to all other variables equal the partial derivative of the coefficients of the other variables with respect to the first variable. For example:

$$\frac{\partial p_i}{\partial x_{ij}} = -r \frac{\partial p_i}{\partial y_i}$$

Obviously the l.h.s. and r.h.s. of (3) together constitute an exact differential equation since we know that there exists a function, say $\varphi(y, x, p, r)$, such that $d\phi$ is given by (3), that function being (2) from which (3) is derived. A curl of zero (actually the null vector) implies not only path independence of the DITFP (a value of zero around any closed path) but also that the DITFP is both the gradient of some value function (in this case the difference in value between output and payments to inputs) and its exact differential; see Wylie (1966).

Proof. It is sufficient to refer to Brown & Chang (1976), where it is shown that consistent aggregation permits (4) to be written as

$$P\,dY - rP\,dK,$$

where $Y = f(y_1, y_2)$ and $K = g(x_{11}, x_{12}, x_{21}, x_{22})$ are quantity indexes for which f and g are independent of prices, while $P = h(p_1, p_2)$ is a price index for which h does not vary with quantities. Clearly,

$$\frac{\partial P}{\partial K} = 0 = -r\frac{\partial P}{\partial Y} = 0,$$

and the aggregate differential form is exact and hence the curl vanishes.

These conditions are extremely restrictive and in addition they do not lend themselves to empirical verification. Our next theorem, though a special case of Theorem 1, is more useful.

In the general equilibrium context, we can directly calculate the curl and inquire into the conditions under which it vanishes. First, we obtain solutions for equilibrium prices from (1); see Brown & Chang (1976). These are

$$p_j^* = \frac{\varrho_j(y_i - rx_{ii}) + \varrho_i\,rx_{ij}}{\Delta}, \quad j \neq i;\ i, j = 1, 2 \tag{5}$$

where

$$\Delta = \prod_{j=1}^{2}(y_j - rx_{jj}) - r^2 x_{12}\,x_{21}.$$

At the economy-wide level, the expressions in parentheses in (4) are related to the prices by means of (5). This operation combines the equilibrium prices (5) with the differential form (4) and hence we have accounted for the interactions between prices and quantity changes in a general equilibrium representation of the DITFP.[3]

We now state:

Theorem 2. *The DITFP* (4) *is path independent if the interest rate is zero.*

Proof. The price solutions given by (5) represent the equilibrium prices which must hold at every point where net own rates of return on the heterogeneous capital items are equated. Since both (4) and (5) hold at

---

[3] It is assumed that labor is required directly or indirectly to produce every good and that each sector's output is produced by a constant return to scale production function in perfectly competitive markets. For additional restrictions, see Brown & Chang (1976, p. 1186).

Table 1. *Conditions for path independence of DITFP (4)*

Variables	Coefficient	Cross partials of coefficients	Conditions for equality
1. y_j, x_{ij}	$p_j, -rp_j$	$rp_j(y_i-rx_{ii})/\Delta, \ rp_j(y_i-rx_{ii})/\Delta$ $(i\neq j)$	Generally holds
2. y_j, x_{ji}	$p_j, -rp_j$	$rp_j(y_i-rx_{ii})/\Delta, \ p_j(r^2x_{ij})/\Delta$	$r=0$ or $rx_{ij}=(y_i-rx_{ii})$
3. y_j, x_{ij}	$p_j, -rp_i$	$\varrho_j+rp_ix_{ij}, \ -\varrho_j+p_j(y_j-rx_{ij})$	$r=0$ or $\varrho_i=\varrho_j=0$
4. y_j, x_{ii}	$p_j, -rp_i$	$rp_jx_{ji}, \ rp_ix_{ij}$	$r=0$ or $p_jx_{ji}=p_ix_{ij}$
5. y_j, y_i	p_j, p_i	$\dfrac{\varrho_i}{\Delta}-p_i\dfrac{(y_i-rx_{ii})}{\Delta}, \ \dfrac{\varrho_j}{\Delta}-p_j\dfrac{(y_j-rx_{ij})}{\Delta}$	$r=0$ or $rp_ix_{ij}=rp_jx_{ji}$
6. x_{ij}, x_{ji}	$-rp_j, -rp_j$	$\dfrac{-r^2}{\Delta}p_j(y_i-rx_{ii}), \ \dfrac{rp_j}{\Delta}(-r^2x_{ij})$	$r=0$ or $rx_{ij}=y_i-rx_{ii}$
7. x_{ij}, x_{ij}	$-rp_j, -rp_i$	$\dfrac{r}{\Delta}p_i(y_i-rx_{ii}), \ \dfrac{r}{\Delta}(\varrho_i+rp_jx_{ji})$	$r=0$ or $p_i(y_i-rx_{ii})$ $=\varrho_j+rp_jx_{ji}$
8. x_{ij}, x_{ii}	$-rp_j, -rp_i$	$\dfrac{r}{\Delta}[\varrho_i-p_i(y_i-rx_{ii})],$ $=\dfrac{r}{\Delta}[\varrho_j-p_j(y_j-rx_{ij})]$	$r=0$ or $rp_ix_{ij}=rp_jx_{ji}$
9. x_{ji}, x_{ij}	$-rp_j, -rp_i$	$\dfrac{r}{\Delta}(\varrho_j+p_irx_{ij}), \ \dfrac{r}{\Delta}(\varrho_i+p_jrx_{ji})$	$r=0$ or $p_j(y_j-rx_{jj})$ $=p_i(y_i-rx_{ii})$

every equilibrium point, substitute (5) into (4) in order to examine the question of path independence of the DITFP by applying the necessary and sufficient curl condition.

Consider Table 1 which lists the conditions for (4), and thus the DITFP, to be exact. The first column gives the pairs of variables to which the curl operation is to be applied. The second gives the pairs of coefficients; the third gives the results of applying the curl operation; and the fourth column gives conditions for equality required for the curl to vanish. Line (3) indicates that either $r=0$ or $\varrho_i=\varrho_j=0$. But this violates the assumption that labor is required, either directly or indirectly, to produce every good which implies that the activity vectors are not uniquely determined, *inter alia* in the steady, state; see Burmeister & Dobell (1970, pp. 275 ff.). That means that if the assumptions of the model which are required to obtain positive prices are accepted, the condition, $r=0$, is the only alternative if i does not hold. This completes the proof.

Remark 1. The above results neglect the consumption good sector. If we specify such a sector as using both of the capital goods and add it to our little model, and if the steady-state conditions are invoked, as in Burmeister & Dobell (1970), the aggregate zero profit condition becomes

$$p_0 c + (g-r)[p_1 \varkappa_{10} + p_2 \varkappa_{20} + p_1 \varkappa_1 + p_2 \varkappa_2] - 1 = 0,$$

where the zero subscript refers to the consumption sector, $\varkappa_1 = \Sigma_{j=1}^2 \varkappa_{1j}$, and $\varkappa_2 = \Sigma_{j=1}^2 \varkappa_{2j}$. Performing the differentiation operation with reference to the quantities will yield the DITFP which, again, is an exact differential form if its curl vanishes. One condition for that to occur is

$$(g-r)\frac{\partial p_i}{\partial c} = \frac{\partial p_0}{\partial \varkappa_{10}}.$$

But $\partial p_1 / \partial c = 0$, as is easily shown, while

$$\frac{\partial p_0}{\partial \varkappa_{10}} = \frac{r}{c\Delta} \{ r\varkappa_{21} \varrho_2 + \varrho_1(y_2 - r\varkappa_{22}) \}. \tag{6}$$

Since $\Delta > 0$ and all quantities are taken as positive while positive prices require $y_2 - r\varkappa_{22} > 0$, this expression is zero if $r=0$. In other words, even if $r=g$, one still needs $r=0$ for the curl of the DITFP with consumption to vanish. (One also may want to show that if the capital matrix is a diagonal matrix and if the consumption good is only produced by labor, the condition is satisfied but that of course violates the assumption required for positive prices.)

III. Some Remarks on the Literature

Our result intersects with the aggregation literature on capital, labor and output. Burmeister (1976, pp. 500–01) shows that the elasticity of the factor price frontier is equal to relative factor income shares at $r=0$, which in turn is the condition for the DITFP to be an exact differential.

It is known that statisticians tend to eschew the use of the Divisia index; see Usher (1973) and Keynes (1953). Theorists tend to commend it; see Richter (1966) and Hulten (1973). However, Bliss (1975) sides with the statisticians. He argues that the Divisia index of heterogeneous capital within a sector is not path independent unless the Leontief–Solow conditions are satisfied, in agreement with Hulten. In effect, a well-behaved intrasectoral capital index must exist in order not to mismeasure the sectoral production function if one specifies a Divisia capital index in it. As Bliss clearly shows, for discrete changes, that is an implication of the Champernowne result which requires no reswitching in order to employ a Divisia index of heterogeneous capital see also Brown (1980). We are concerned here with intersectoral as well as intrasectoral aggregation by means of chain indexes. That requires something stronger than the satisfaction of the Leontief–Solow condition, for intersectoral aggregation must also be achieved even when changes in prices and quantities are discrete.[4]

IV. Some Open Questions

It has been repeatedly stressed that the aggregation conditions such as those derived by Fisher, Leontief–Solow, Brown & Chang, etc., are stringent and are not likely to be satisfied empirically. Whether the new condition derived here, the interest rate is zero, that underlies the unbiasedness of the DITFP is less stringent than the received conditions for the well-behaved aggregates is an open question. Be that as it may, none of these conditions, to our knowledge, has been tested econometrically. Until that is done, whether the DITFP is substantially free of bias is another open question.

In the meantime, subjective expressions of confidence in alternative measures of technological change are not without value and it is our belief that direct estimates of frontier production functions are more credible than those based on the DITFP; see Forsund & Hjalmarsson (1979). Also, Vogt (1978) has developed a "natural" Divisia index corresponding to a linear path of integration between two points. This confronts the path-independence problem head on and hence provides some encouragement for the

---

[4] The discrete counterpart of (4) employs the Kloek (1976) and Theil (1976) quadratic approximation theorem. As generally applied, the DITFP uses weights which are in fact averages of the beginning and end of period. This incorporates certain second order effects which, it is asserted, improve the index. However, the aforementioned problems of path dependence and bias, to our knowledge, are not shown to be eliminated.

The effect of averaging can be seen by defining s as the ratio of the value of outputs to the payments to inputs ($s = p^T y / (q^T k + 1)$, p is the vector of output prices relative to the wage rate, y is the vector of corresponding per capita output quantities, q is the vector of capital costs relative to the wage rate, k is the vector of per capita capital inputs, and T represents the transpose. The exact differential of the log of s including all second-order terms is:

$$d \log s = w^T(\hat{p}+\hat{y}) - v^T(\hat{q}+\hat{k})$$

$$+ \frac{1}{2} \sum_{i=0}^{n} w_i(\hat{p}_i'+\hat{y}_i)^2 - \frac{1}{2} \sum_{i=1}^{n} v_i(\hat{q}_i+\hat{k}_i)^2$$

$$+ \tfrac{1}{2}[(\hat{p}+\hat{y})^T(ww^T)(\hat{p}+\hat{y}) - (\hat{q}+\hat{k})^T(vv^T)(\hat{q}+\hat{k})].$$

The hatted variables represent rates of change, and w and v represent the vectors of output value weights and input weights of capital, respectively. The weighted average DITFP, say, $\overline{\text{DITFP}}$, would be $\bar{w}^T\hat{y} - \bar{y}^T\hat{k}$ in the above terminology where the bars represent the beginning and end of period average; see Jorgenson & Griliches (1969, p. 33).

The $\overline{\text{DITFP}}$ obviously contains prices at the beginning and the end of the comparison periods. But these prices are equilibrium prices as in (5), so that the derivation of the conditions for path independence are more complicated than above; they will involve their partial differentiation at two points rather than one.

retention of the Divisia index, albeit in a form that only remotely resembles the traditional Divisia index. But Vogt's version, too, must evetually be embedded in a general equilibrium model and the conditions under which it is satisfied in that context is still another open question.

References

Bliss, C. J.: *Capital theory and the distribution of income*. Amsterdam, North-Holland, 1975.

Brown, Murray: The measurement of capital aggregates: A post reswitching problem. In *The measurement of capital* (ed. Dan Usher). National Bureau of Economic Research, The University of Chicago Press, 1980.

Brown, M. & Chang, W.: Capital aggregation in a general equilibrium model of production. *Econometrica 44*, November 1976.

Burmeister, E.: The factor-price frontier and duality with many primary factors. *Journal of Economic Theory, 12* June 1976.

Burmeister, E. & Dobell, A. R.: *Mathematical theories of economic growth*. New York, 1970.

Førsund, F. R. & L. Hjalmarsson: Frontier production functions and technical progress: A study of general milk processing in Swedish dairy plants. *Econometrica 47*, July 1979.

Hulten, C. H.: Divisia Index Numbers. *Econometrica 41*, November 1973.

Jorgenson, D. W. & Griliches, Z.: The explanation of productivity changes. *Rev. Econ. Stud.*, May 1969.

Keynes, J. M.: *A treatise on money*, vol. 1. Macmillan, London, 1953.

Kloek, T.: On quadratic approximations of cost of living and real income index numbers. Report 6710, Econometric Institute, Netherlands School of Economics, 1967.

Lass, H.: *Elements of pure and applied mathematics*. McGraw-Hill, New York, 1957.

Morishima, M.: *Equilibrium, stability and growth*. Clarenden, Oxford, 1964.

Norsworthy, J. R., Harper M. & Kunze, K.: The slowdown in productivity growth: Analyses of some contributing factors. *Brookings Papers on Economic Activity*, 2, 1979.

Richter, M. K.: Invariance axioms and economic indexes. *Econometrica, 34*, October 1966.

Theil, H.: *Theory and measurement of consumer demand*, vol. 1. North-Holland, Amsterdam, 1976.

Usher, D.: The suitability of the divisia index for the measurement of economic aggregates. *Review of income and wealth 20*, 273–88, 1973.

Vogt, A.: Divisia indexes on different paths. In *Applications of economic indexes* (ed. W. Eichhorn et al.). Würzburg, Vienna, 1978.

Wylie, C. R.: *Advanced engineering mathematics*. 3rd ed. McGraw-Hill, New York, 1966.

PART IV OTHER ASPECTS

On the Dynamics of Production under Cost Uncertainty

Jon Vislie*

University of Oslo, Norway

Abstract

In planning the production of many large projects which usually take a long time to complete, entrepreneurs are often faced with several aspects of uncertainty. We derive the *ex ante* optimal plan for production of a large capital unit with production factors whose prices might change at some unknown future date. Two different plans are derived. The first, the noncommitment plan, is the best *ex ante* policy or strategy which specifies one path conditional on the nonoccurrence of the date when the unit cost changes, and another path given that the date of change has occurred. It is shown, given the assumptions in the paper, that the optimal input path when the date of change is known will start at a lower level than the conditional optimal input path when the date of change is unknown *ex ante*. The second plan is a so-called commitment plan. It is determined in such a way that the entrepreneur, for various reasons, has to pursue the policy which is announced initially. This plan is suboptimal if no commitments are to be made.

I. Introduction

In considering the production process for construction of a large capital unit, say a tanker, a plant or a complex machine, we cannot avoid observing that the completion of such a large capital object takes time. Since this applies to a large number of productive activities in real life, these observations should be taken into account in working out a theory of production.

The issue of the production of large capital units was first raised in an analytically convenient way by Haavelmo in his book on investment theory; see Haavelmo (1960, Chapter 12). Some of Haavelmo's ideas were elaborated in more detail by Vislie (1982 a), where attention was focused on determination of the length of the production period and the associated optimal input path, for a given payment schedule (revenue function) and fixed and known factor prices throughout the production period.

Some other aspects of the entrepreneur's production planning problem are considered in this paper. We focus on the input structure of the problem, when there is uncertainty in future factor prices which enters the

---

* I am grateful to Michael Hoel and Aanund Hylland for stimulating discussions and two anonymous referees for useful comments on an earlier version of this paper.

problem in two ways.[1] First, *the points in time* when some factor prices change are stochastic *ex ante*. Second, the *new* factor prices which the entrepreneur faces at these dates are also stochastic as viewed from the date of planning.

Throughout the paper we are concerned with the cost structure of the problem and the associated optimal input path when the entrepreneur faces the two types of uncertainty mentioned above. The relationship between the length of the production period and some payment schedule is not explicitly taken into account. Since a production program of the type we have in mind (say the construction of a specific tanker) will usually be implemented when the entrepreneur's bid or offer has been accepted by the buyer (or the principal), the cost structure itself is crucial to whether the entrepreneur's bid will be accepted or not. Assume, for ease of exposition, that the principal has asked for a cost estimate, given a certain date of delivery and a revenue function. The entrepreneur's problem is then to work out a cost estimate, given the end-point of the production period (equal to the date of delivery) and some revenue function or payment schedule.

In Section II, the model is presented for the case where the date of change is known *ex ante*, while the factor prices or unit costs prevailing after this date are not (for reasons to be explained later). Uncertainty is introduced in Section III. At the planning point in time the entrepreneur is uncertain about the exact date of change and the corresponding factor prices prevailing after this date. We then derive the optimal *ex ante* plan when the entrepreneur is able to pursue this policy (the noncommitment case). This optimal plan or strategy now consists of two input paths; one conditional on that the change has not yet occurred and one conditional on that the date of change has occurred. Throughout the paper the entrepreneur is assumed to be risk neutral.[2] We also compare how this plan will differ from the optimal plan when no uncertainty exists. We then turn to a situation where the entrepreneur has to make commitments such that the plan announced initially has to be followed. Some conclusions and generalizations are presented in Section IV.

---

[1] Other kinds of uncertainty are ignored. However, with proper modifications, our model has other applications as well. One time-consuming activity, familiar to many readers, is research activity, where other kinds of uncertainty than the two mentioned in the text are involved. In planning a research project, we know that both the rate of progress and the result itself are stochastic *ex ante*. These aspects of uncertainty are ignored in the production planning problem analyzed in this paper. For an extensive presentation of various aspects of R & D, see Kamien & Schwartz (1982).

[2] Similar questions have been analyzed by Dasgupta & Heal (1974) and Dasgupta & Stiglitz (1981) in the context of resource depletion under technological uncertainty about the date of introduction of a back-stop technology.

II. The Model When the Date of Change is Known *Ex Ante*

At each point in time t during the period of construction, energy, raw materials and equipment are used in fixed proportions to labor, denoted $N(t)$, to produce a product or value added per unit of time $X(t)$. The technology which relates the labor input to the product or value added per unit of time at t, is given by the function F, which is twice differentiable, strictly increasing and strictly concave for all $N \geqslant 0$:

$$X(t) = F(N(t)), \tag{1}$$

where $F(0)=0$, $F'>0$ and $F''<0$ for all finite values of $N \geqslant 0$. Furthermore, we assume $F'(0)=\infty$ and $F'(\infty)=0$. The F-function can be interpreted as a production function, although the product at t is not the final output, but value added in the capital object under construction.

The production process starts at $t=0$ and ends at $t=T$, where T is now fixed by assumption.[3] At the end-point of the production period T, the final output or the capital object is completed; i.e.

$$\int_0^T F(N(t)) \, dt = 1, \tag{2}$$

where the Figure 1 on the r.h.s. of (2) indicates one unit of the object in question.

At the planning point in time, the cost per unit of labor is w_0, which is known to the entrepreneur. At $t=T_0'<T$, the unit cost will change, where T_0' is now known, while the unit cost prevailing after T_0' is not known *ex ante*. One reason for such an assumption could be that through contractual agreements, the entrepreneur has been promised delivery of necessary inputs at given prices until $t=T_0'$, which is the expiration date of these contracts, while the input prices prevailing after T_0', are uncertain. Assume that the entrepreneur has some well-defined subjective probability distribution for w, the random unit cost after the date of change, with an expected value equal to $\bar{w}$. If now $\bar{w}>w_0$, the labor input path which minimizes the total discounted cost of completing the capital object during $[0, T]$, will be given by

$$QF'(\tilde{N}(t)) = w_i e^{-rt} \quad \text{for every } t \in [0, T] \tag{3}$$

where r is a constant rate of interest, $w_i=w_0$ for all $t \in [0, T_0')$ and $w_i=\bar{w}$ for all $t \in (T_0', T]$ and Q is a positive, constant shadow price associated with the integral constraint (2). Due to our assumptions, it is easily seen that the

---

[3] In Vislie (1982 *a*), T itself is a control variable, determined in such a way that total discounted profit is maximized.

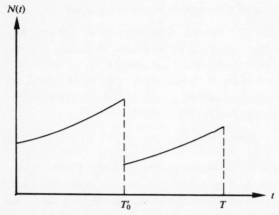

Fig. 1. The optimal input path $\tilde{N}(t)$ when T_0' is known *ex ante*, $T_0'<T$ and $\bar{w}>w_0$.

optimal input path $\tilde{N}(t)$ will be increasing with t, but will jump downwards at $t=T_0'$, as illustrated in Figure 1.

It can now be shown that as $\bar{w}/w_0$ increases when T_0' is known *ex ante*, the left part of the path $\tilde{N}(t)$ is shifted upwards, while the right or lower part is shifted downwards. This should be rather obvious. Furthermore, if T_0' were reduced, then both parts of $\tilde{N}(t)$ would be shifted upwards. As $T_0' \rightarrow 0$, the left part will ultimately disappear and the lower part will approach the limit path. This is the optimal path when $\bar{w}$ prevails during the entire production period, and it will be independent of the value of the unit cost.

We now turn to our main topic, namely, the optimal input profile when the date of change T_0 is not known *ex ante*.

III. The Date of Change T_0 is Unknown

In contrast to the preceding section, we now assume that the entrepreneur has imperfect knowledge about the exact date of change. As before, we assume that at the planning point in time the cost per unit of labor w_0 is known. However, the entrepreneur believes that this unit cost will change at some time and with some probability during $[0, T]$. For ease of exposition assume that, with probability one, there will be at most one change in the unit cost during the fixed production period. The point in time when such a change occurs is denoted T_0, and the entrepreneur regards T_0 as a random variable, as viewed from the date of planning. The entrepreneur has a well-defined subjective probability density function $s(\tau)$, defined for all nonnegative values of τ, and $s(\tau)$ is continuous everywhere. The distribution function is given by

$$Pr(T_0 \leq \tau) = \int_0^\tau s(v)\, dv = S(\tau), \tag{4}$$

where $S'(\tau) \equiv s(\tau) \geq 0$ for all $\tau \in [0, \infty)$, and

$$\int_0^\infty s(v)\, dv = 1. \tag{5}$$

The cost per unit of N at t, where $t \in [0, T]$, will therefore be a random variable. With some probability it will be equal to w_0 at t, as viewed from the planning point in time. More precisely, the probability for $w=w_0$ at t is equal to the probability for $T_0 > t$, that is, with probability $1-S(t)$, the unit cost at t will be qual to w_0. Hence, with probability $S(t)$ the unit cost will have changed before t. At the planning point in time, the entrepreneur is uncertain about the new value of the unit cost at t, given that the change has occurred. Assume that the entrepreneur has some well-defined subjective probability distribution for the unit cost at t, given that the change occurs at $T_0 = \tau \leq t$. This is defined as

$$G(a|\tau \leq t) = Pr(w_t \leq a|T_0 = \tau \leq t) = \int_0^a g(w|\tau)\, dw,$$

where $g(w|\tau)$ is the subjective conditional probability density function for w, conditional on that the date of change occurs at τ. The conditional expected value of w, conditional on that the change occurs at τ, defined as $\bar{w}(\tau)$, will in general be some function of τ.[4] However, for ease of exposition, we assume that the probability distribution for the new value of the unit cost at t, given that the change occurs at $T_0 = \tau \leq t$, is stationary or independent of when the change takes place. This means that the entrepreneur *ex ante* has some firm opinion about the future expected unit cost, given that a change has occurred, and this expected unit cost, $\bar{w}$, is independent of the date of change itself.

The Optimal Behavior in the Absence of Commitment

We now turn to the following question: What is the entrepreneur's best *ex ante* strategy when taking into account that the unit cost might change at an unknown future point in time? Assume that the entrepreneur is free to act according to the strategy derived, i.e. he is not forced to make any commit-

---

[4] The subjective probability distribution $G(w|\tau)$ depends explicitly on τ. The reason for such dependence is that the entrepreneur assigns different probability distributions for w for different values of τ. For instance, he could believe that the conditional probability density function $g(w|\tau)$ moves to the right for increasing values of τ, implying that the conditional expected unit cost $\bar{w}(\tau)$ increases with τ.

ments to the effect that a plan must be announced initially and that this plan cannot be deviated from. Furthermore, what will he do at the point in time when uncertainty is resolved, i.e. when the date of change actually occurs? After having stated some of the properties of this plan, it will be compared to the one derived when the date of change is known *ex ante*. The problem is to find a time path for N with properties such that, as long as the date of change has not occurred, it will be optimal to follow exactly this path. In other words, if the date of change did not take place during the period $[0, T]$, the entrepreneur will be able to complete the project by pursuing the plan and will not regret his choice, given the information he had initially and the information he acquired during the production period. Whenever the date of change occurs during the period $[0, T]$, he will pursue that policy which minimizes the expected discounted cost from that date to the end-point T, given that the project should be completed at T and given the degree of fulfillment at the date of change.

The optimal policy, as viewed from the planning point in time, from τ to T where τ is an arbitrary date of change, is therefore given by

$$V(Z(\tau)) = \frac{\min}{N} \int_{\tau}^{T} e^{-r(t-\tau)} \bar{w} N(t) \, dt, \tag{6}$$

subject to

$$\int_{\tau}^{T} F(N(t)) \, dt = 1 - Z(\tau), \text{ where } Z(\tau) = \int_{0}^{\tau} F(N(t)) \, dt, \tag{7}$$

where $\bar{w}$ is the expected unit cost after the change, viewed from the planning point in time. As shown in Appendix 2, the optimal path—given that the change has occurred—will be strictly increasing with time, and $V(Z(\tau))$ is strictly decreasing and strictly convex in $Z(\tau)$, and $V(1)=0$.

The optimal policy is now determined by solving the following problem at the planning point in time.

$$\frac{\min}{N} \int_{0}^{T} e^{-rt} [w_0 (1 - S(t)) N(t) + S'(t) V(Z(t))] \, dt, \tag{8}$$

subject to

$$\int_{0}^{T} F(N(t)) \, dt = 1. \tag{9}$$

Suppose that a solution to this problem exists. Then, as demonstrated in Appendix 1, the optimal input use as long as the date of change has not occurred must satisfy

$$\Lambda F'(N^*(t)) = e^{-rt}w_0(1-S(t)) \tag{10}$$

$$\dot{\Lambda} = -e^{-rt}S'(t)\lambda(Z(t)) \leqslant 0. \tag{11}$$

We are now interested in how $N^*(t)$ behaves over time as long as the date of change has not taken place. Differentiating (10) w.r.t. t and using (11) yields, after some manipulation where $\alpha(\tau)$ is defined in Appendix 3:

$$\dot{N}^*(t) = -\frac{F'(N^*(t))}{F''(N^*(t))}\left[r+\alpha(t)+\frac{\dot{\Lambda}(t)}{\Lambda(t)}\right]. \tag{12}$$

By using (10) we can now define

$$P(t) = \frac{\Lambda(t)\,e^{rt}}{1-S(t)} = \frac{w_0}{F'(N^*(t))} \tag{13}$$

as the undiscounted marginal cost of increasing Z at t, conditional on that the date of change has not occurred by then. From (10) and (13) it follows that

$$\frac{\dot{\Lambda}(t)}{\Lambda(t)} = -\alpha(t)\frac{\lambda(Z(t))}{P(t)}, \tag{14}$$

which inserted into (12) yields:

$$\dot{N}^*(t) = -\frac{F'(N^*(t))}{F''(N^*(t))}\left[r+\alpha(t)\left(1-\frac{\lambda(Z(t))}{P(t)}\right)\right]. \tag{15}$$

In a dynamic or along an intertemporal equilibrium, the following arbitrage condition must be satisfied for the production of a large capital object by a risk-neutral entrepreneur.[5] During the period $(t,t+\Delta)$, it should not be possible to transfer labor input from one date to the other in such a way that costs are reduced. In other words

$$P_t(1+r\Delta) = \alpha_t\Delta\lambda+(1-\alpha_t\Delta)P_{t+\Delta}. \tag{16}$$

The l.h.s. is the marginal undiscounted cost of increasing Z at t, evaluated at $t+\Delta$, given that the date of change has not occurred by t, while the r.h.s. of (16) is the conditional expected marginal cost of increasing Z at $t+\Delta$, conditional on the nonoccurrence of the event by t. In a dynamic equilibrium, (16) must hold for all t, as long as the event has not taken place by t. Now, taking limits as $\Delta\to 0$, we get

$$\frac{\dot{P}(t)}{P(t)} = r+\alpha(t)\left(1-\frac{\lambda(Z(t))}{P(t)}\right), \tag{17}$$

which is exactly the expression within brackets in (15).

---

[5] The same basic principle is also discussed by Dasgupta & Stiglitz (op. cit.) in the case of resource depletion under uncertainty.

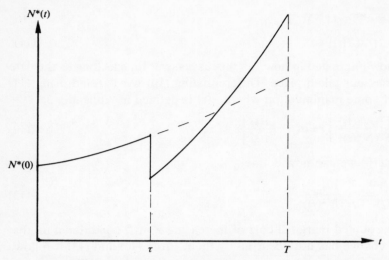

Fig. 2. One possible trajectory for optimal input use when the date of change occurs at τ.

Suppose now that the entrepreneur expects the unit cost after the change to be higher than the current one, $\bar{w}>w_0$, and let τ be some date of change when a higher unit cost is realized. Assume furthermore that the input path $N^*(t)$ is strictly increasing as long as the change has not occurred.[6] This possibility is illustrated in Figure 2, where $N^*(0)$ is determined in such a way that if the date of change does not occur during $[0, T]$, then by pursuing the policy given by this path starting from $N^*(0)$, the project will be completed at T. Due to a higher expected cost after the change than the current cost, we must have $\lambda(\tau^+)>P(\tau^-)$, $\dot{P}/P<r$ and the optimal path conditional on that no change takes place during $[0, T]$ increasing at a lower rate than the path after the change; see (15) and (ix) in Appendix 2. Hence, when the date of change takes place, optimal input use must jump downwards at τ, and during the rest of the production period $N^*(t)$ will increase at a higher rate after τ than before τ.

Thus far, we have demonstrated how, in the production of a large capital object, an entrepreneur should specify his production plan *ex ante* in the presence of future uncertainty as to the date when the unit cost might change and in the absence of any commitments. In what way does the conditional plan differ from the optimal plan in the case where T_0 is known *ex ante*?

Let us first compare the case where $T_0>T$ with certainty; i.e. when the unit cost is w_0 throughout the production period, with the case where the

---

[6] It should be noted that $N^*(t)$ could be strictly decreasing over time. Its behavior over time depends on r, the probability distribution for T_0 and the ratio $\bar{w}/w_0$.

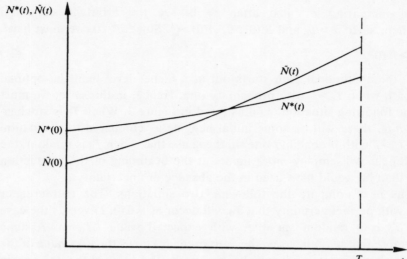

$N^*(t), \tilde{N}(t)$

$\tilde{N}(t)$

$N^*(t)$

$N^*(0)$

$\tilde{N}(0)$

T

t

Fig. 3

entrepreneur believes there is a positive probability for the event $T_0 < T$ and the expected unit cost prevailing after T_0 has occurred is $\bar{w} > w_0$.

From Section II we know that when $w = w_0$ for all $t \in [0, T]$, the optimal input use at every t must satisfy

$$QF'(\tilde{N}(t)) = w_0 e^{-rt}. \tag{18}$$

The value of the shadow price Q, which is positive and constant, is determined in such a way that the project is completed at T by following the path determined in (18). When T_0 is random, (10) and (11) give the necessary conditions for optimal input use, as long as T_0 has not occurred. As before, we assume $N^*(t)$ to be increasing with time and $\Lambda(0)$ determined in such a way that if T_0 does not occur during $[0, T]$, the project will be completed by pursuing the policy given by $N^*(t)$. Consider now the initial situation. From (18), (10) and (13) we have

$$\Lambda(0) F'(N^*(0)) = w_0 = QF'(\tilde{N}(0)). \tag{19}$$

Since $\Lambda(0) = P(0)$ and $\bar{w} > w_0$, we must necessarily have

$$\Lambda(0) = P(0) \geqslant Q. \tag{20}$$

(If $S'(0) > 0$, the inequality in (20) will be strict.) From the definition of $P(0)$ as the marginal current cost of increasing Z at $t=0$, which in an intertemporal optimum should be equal to the expected current marginal cost of increasing Z "just after" $t=0$—see the arbitrage condition (16)—then, since $\bar{w}>w_0$ and $S'(0)>0$, $\Lambda(0)>Q$. Since $F''<0$, we must have

$$N^*(0) > \bar{N}(0),\tag{21}$$

that is, the conditional path starts out at a higher level than the optimal input path when $T_0>T$ with probability one. Hence, in this case, we must have the following situation, as illustrated in Figure 3. When T_0 is stochastic *ex ante*, there will be some initial hedging as compared to a situation where $T_0>T$ with probability one, in the sense that when T_0 is random, the entrepreneur will employ *more* inputs at the beginning of the production period than he would have used in the absence of uncertainty.

Let us next compare the following two situations. The entrepreneur knows with perfect certainty that T_0 will occur at $t_0 \in (0, T)$ versus the case where T_0 is a random variable, with expected value $ET_0=t_0$. Assume furthermore that in both cases, the entrepreneur knows the true value of the unit cost after the date of change has occurred. The value of the unit cost in this sub-period is $w_1>w_0$.

Consider now an arbitrary $t \in (t_0, T)$. The current marginal cost of increasing Z at t when T_0 is known with perfect certainty is Qe^{rt}, while the expected current marginal cost of increasing Z at t, conditional on the nonoccurrence of T_0 at t, is $P(t)$. Since $w_1>w_0$, we must have $Qe^{rt}>P(t)$ for a $t \in (t_0, T]$. This is also true in t_0^+, and since both Qe^{rt} and $P(t)$ are continuous functions of t, the inequality must hold in t_0^-, when the unit cost in the certainty case is $w_0<w_1$. Therefore, we have

$$P(t_0^-)\,F'(N^*(t_0^-)) = w_0 = Qe^{rt_0^-}F'(\bar{N}(t_0^-))\tag{22}$$

and since $P(t_0^-)<Qe^{rt_0^-}$, the optimal input use in the certainty case at t_0^-, $\bar{N}(t_0^-)$, must be higher than when T_0 is stochastic, i.e.

$$\bar{N}(t_0^-) > N^*(t_0^-).\tag{23}$$

When $w_1>w_0$, we have that $\lambda(Z(t))>P(t)$, that is, the marginal cost of increasing Z at a point in time t (and the date of change occurs at t) is higher than the expected marginal cost of increasing Z at t, conditional on the nonoccurrence of T_0 at t. From (17), combined with $\alpha(t)>0$, we then have that $P(t)$ increases by a rate smaller than the interest rate r, and since Qe^{rt} increases by a rate equal to r, we must have $Qe^{rt}>P(t)$ during an interval (t^*, t_0), and $Qe^{rt}>P(t)$ for all $t \in (t_0, T]$. Is it possible that $t^*=0$? The answer is no, since as long as $w_1>w_0$ and $S'(0)>0, P(0)>Q$. We therefore have:

$P(t) > Qe^{rt}$ for all $t \in [0, t^*)$
$Q(t)\,e^{rt} > P(t)$ for all $t > t^*$ where
$t^* \in (0, t_0).$ \hfill (24)

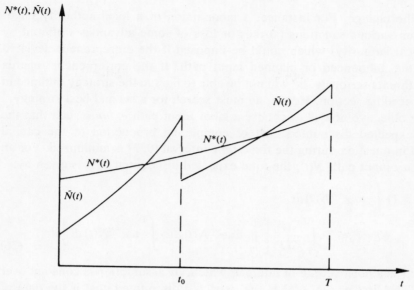

Fig. 4

Hence, it follows that

$$N^*(t) > \tilde{N}(t) \quad \text{for all } t \in [0, t^*)$$
$$\tilde{N}(t) > N^*(t) \quad \text{for all } t \in (t^*, t_0). \tag{25}$$

One possible situation is illustrated in Figure 4. (It should be noted that whether or not $N^*(T)$ is higher than $\tilde{N}(T)$ depends crucially on the parameters involved, especially the interest rate, the ratio w_1/w_0, properties of the probability distribution of T_0 and the production function F. Therefore, the situation in Figure 4 is only one possibility as to the question of how $\tilde{N}(t)$ will move after t_0.)

As in the preceding case, there is some initial hedging in the case of stochastic T_0, since $N^*(t) > \tilde{N}(t)$ at the beginning of the production period. It should be obvious that "the degree of hedging" will depend on the parameters of the model, especially the ratio w_1/w_0, the interest rate and the expected date of change, in addition to the scale properties of the production function. (If the model is specified in more detail, this will become rather evident.)

The Optimal Behavior When an Initial Commitment Has to be Made

Assume that for some reason, the entrepreneur has to make a commitment such that the planned input path derived *ex ante* has to be followed, regardless of when the change occurs and the magnitude of the unit cost after the change. For instance, a labor union or a local authority might threaten various sanctions (strikes or loss of some advantages offered by the local authority) which could be imposed if the entrepreneur deviated from the announced or planned input path. If the entrepreneur regards these threats seriously, he will not be able to pursue the strategy outlined in the preceding section. Hence, he must search for a second-best strategy.

The objective now is to choose a labor input path *ex ante* such that the total expected discounted cost of completing production of the capital object in question during the fixed time interval $[0, T]$ is minimized. For an arbitrary input path $N(t)$, the total expected discounted cost is given by:

$$Pr(T_0 > T) \int_0^T w_0 e^{-rt} N(t) \, dt$$

$$+ Pr(T_0 \leq T) \int_0^T \frac{s(\tau)}{S(T)} \left[\int_0^\tau w_0 e^{-rt} N(t) \, dt + \int_\tau^T \bar{w} e^{-rt} N(t) \, dt \right] d\tau, \tag{26}$$

where r is a positive rate of interest, which, by assumption is constant over time. The first part of (26) is the expected discounted cost if the date of change does not occur within $[0, T]$, while the second part is the expected discounted cost if T_0 occurs before T. $s(\tau)/S(T)$ is the subjective conditional probability for the change to occur at τ, conditional on that the change occurs before T. On integrating (26) by parts, we obtain the following expression for the total expected discounted cost along an arbitrary input path:

$$\int_0^T e^{-rt} N(t) \left[(1 - S(t)) w_0 + S(t) \bar{w} \right] dt, \tag{27}$$

where $(1 - S(t)) w_0 + S(t) \bar{w}$ is the current or undiscounted expected unit cost at t. This is a convex combination of the known unit cost, w_0, and the expected cost after the change, $\bar{w}$, where the weights of the convex combination are the probabilities of the change not having occurred at t and having occurred at t.

The planning problem when commitment is made is therefore:

$$\min_N \int_0^T e^{-rt} N(t) \left[(1 - S(t)) w_0 + S(t) \bar{w} \right] dt$$

s.t.

$$\int_0^T F(N(t)) \, dt = 1, \quad \text{or equivalently} \tag{28}$$

$$\dot{Z}(t) = F(N(t)), \quad Z(0) = 0, \quad Z(T) = 1, \quad \text{where}$$

$$Z(t) = \int_0^t F(N(s)) \, ds, \quad \text{and } F \text{ satisfies the conditions given after (1)}.$$

This problem can be solved by using optimal control theory, with $N(t)$ as the control variable and $Z(t)$ as the state variable.[7]

For every $t \in [0, T]$, the planned or *ex ante* optimal labor input must satisfy the following marginal condition:

$$qF'(\hat{N}(t)) = e^{-rt}[(1-S(t)) w_0 + S(t) \bar{w}], \tag{29}$$

where q is a positive shadow price associated with the differential equation in (28) and constant over time, since the state variable does not enter the Hamiltonian function.[8] The condition in (29) says that at each point in time during the period of construction, the marginal discounted value productivity of labor should equal the discounted expected unit cost.

Using (29) we can state some properties of the planned or committed input path, particularly its dependence on the various parameters involved and its variation over time. The optimal input use at t can be found from (29) as:

$$\hat{N}(t) = (F')^{-1} \left(\frac{e^{-rt}[(1-S(t)) w_0 + S(t) \bar{w}]}{q} \right) = n(\ ), \tag{30}$$

where $n'(\cdot) < 0$ due to strict concavity of F.

The value of the constant shadow price q is now determined in such a way that the terminal constraint is met, that is, such that

$$\hat{Z}(T) = \int_0^T F(n(\cdot)) \, dt = 1. \tag{31}$$

Hence, we can express q as a function of the parameters involved:

$$q = q\left(\underset{-}{T}, \underset{-}{r}, \underset{+}{\frac{w_0}{\bar{w}}}\right), \tag{32}$$

where the signs of the partial derivatives of q w.r.t. the various arguments are indicated and easily verified. For instance, a higher value of the certain unit cost w_0, as compared to the expected cost after the change, will increase the value of q, but $0 < \partial q / \partial w_0 < q/w_0$ must be satisfied in order for the integral constraint in (28) to be met. It is then easily seen from (29) that

---

[7] We will not specify the necessary conditions in detail in this paper. More formal details can be found in Seierstad & Sydsæter (1977) and in Vislie (1982 b).

[8] The Hamiltonian of this problem is $H(Z, N, q, t) = -e^{-rt}[(1-S(t)) w_0 + S(t) \bar{w}] N + qF(N)$. The optimal pair $(\hat{Z}(t), \hat{N}(t))$ satisfies for every $t \in [0, T]$: $H(\hat{Z}(t), \hat{N}(t), q, t) \geqslant H(\hat{Z}(t), N, q, t)$ for all $N \geqslant 0$, $\hat{Z}(0) = 0$, $\hat{Z}(T) = 1$ and $\hat{Z}(t) = F(\hat{N}(t))$. The movement of the shadow price over time is determined by

$$\dot{q}(t) = -H'_Z(\hat{Z}(t), \hat{N}(t), q, t) = 0,$$

as seen from the Hamiltonian above.

as w_0 is higher, *ceteris paribus*, the initial optimal use $\hat{N}(0)$ must go down and, furthermore, the planned path will move downwards for all $t \in [0, t^*)$ and be shifted upwards for all $t \in (t^*, T]$, where t^* is some point in time where $\hat{N}(t)$ is unaffected by the higher value of w_0.

How does $\hat{N}(t)$ behave over time? As shown in Appendix 3, we can now write (29) as:

$$qF'(\hat{N}(t)) = w_0 e^{-\int_0^t \psi(v)\, dv} \left[1 + \frac{S(t)}{1-S(t)} \frac{\bar{w}}{w_0}\right] \tag{29'}$$

where $\psi(v)$ is the risk-adjusted interest rate at v; see Yaari (1965) for a similar formulation. Differentiating (29') w.r.t. time and after some calculations, we get:

$$\dot{\hat{N}}(t) = \frac{F'(\hat{N}(t))}{F''(N(t))}[-r + a(t)(w^*(t) - 1)], \tag{33}$$

where $a(t) \equiv \dfrac{S'(t)}{1-S(t)}$ is the conditional probability for the date of change to occur at t, conditional on that the date of change has not occurred before t, and $w^*(t)$ defined as:

$$w^*(t) \equiv \frac{\bar{w}}{(1-S(t))\, w_0 + S(t)\, \bar{w}}, \tag{34}$$

which is the ratio between the expected unit cost after the change and the expected unit cost at t, as viewed from the planning point in time. (Note that $w^*(0) = \bar{w}/w_0$.)

The behavior of the commitment path $\hat{N}(t)$ throughout the production period depends on the parameters involved (r, w_0 and $\bar{w}$) and the properties of the subjective probability distribution for T_0. Several cases are possible. However, it does not seem worthwhile to explore these possibilities in any detail, except to observe that $\hat{N}(t)$ is continuous.

It should be noted that in this commitment plan, when the entrepreneur makes an optimal decision at t, he is *not* allowed to take the information available at t into consideration. Hence, the dynamic aspects of uncertainty *vanish* in this context. This case could be interpreted as one where the entrepreneur faces a given time function for the unit cost, see (34); hence the aspects of uncertainty do not have any significant impact in the commitment case.

Why, then, is such a case of interest? Since the entrepreneur is not allowed to take the information available at t into account when deciding on input use at t, the commitment plan will clearly result in a suboptimum as compared to the noncommitment case. Why explore such suboptimal plans? The commitment case was justified above with reference to the claims of a labor union that the plan should be announced initially and that this plan should be pursued. If the entrepreneur deviated from this plan at some date, the labor union would strike, whereby the entrepreneur would incur heavy losses. The commitment plan is therefore a second-best solution. In several European countries, especially in Norway, labor unions are trying to resist any changes in production plans, etc. which entrepreneurs find worthwhile due to changes in prices and other parameters. If the entrepreneur in question faces a well-organized labor union and takes threats of sanctions seriously, he will be forced to pursue the second-best solution or the commitment plan.

IV. Conclusion

We have analyzed the optimal planning of production of a large capital object during a given production period, when the entrepreneur is faced with uncertainty about the future unit cost. At the planning point in time, he does not know when the date of change will occur. On the basis of his subjective probability beliefs about future events, an *ex ante* optimal policy was derived, both for the case of commitment (the *ex ante* announced input path had to be followed for some reason) and for the noncommitment case (the entrepreneur could pursue the best *ex ante* policy). While the commitment path was everywhere continuous, we found that in the absence of any commitments, the *ex ante* optimal policy or strategy was discontinuous in any date of change. Furthermore, the optimal input path when the date of change is known was shown to start from a lower level than the conditional optimal input path for the case where the date of change was unknown *ex ante*. In this sense there is *initial hedging* in the uncertainty case as compared to the certainty case (where the unit cost is known *ex ante* for the entire production period); that is, uncertainty induced the entrepreneur to concentrate more input at the beginning of the production period.

We have studied a highly special case where there is at most one price change during $[0, T]$. The problem could have been posed in a more general form, by assuming the unit cost to be given by some stochastic process $w(t)$. The optimization problem would then have been a stochastic dynamic optimization problem with two state variables: the degree of completion, $Z(t)$, and the unit cost $w(t)$. This general problem should deserve some interest. However, the special case analyzed above has the advantage that the impact of future uncertainty on optimal input use can easily be determined.

Appendix 1

Assume that the problem in (8)–(9) has a solution. The Hamiltonian associated with this problem is then

(i) $H = -e^{-rt}[w_0(1-S(t))N + S'(t)V(Z)] + \Lambda F(N)$

where Λ is a shadow price associated with the integral constraint (9). The optimal input use as long as the date of change has not occurred is then given by: for every t until the date of change takes place, the following conditions must be satisfied:

(ii) $\Lambda F'(N^*(t)) = e^{-rt}w_0(1-S(t))$

(iii) $\dot{\Lambda} = -H_Z = e^{-rt}S'(t)V'(Z(t))$
$= -H_Z = -e^{-rt}S'(t)\lambda(Z(t))$

since $V'(Z_t) = -\lambda(Z_t)$; see Appendix 2.

Appendix 2

For any date of change $\tau \in [0, T]$, the optimal policy from τ to T is given by $V(Z(\tau))$ in (6) if such a solution exists, which is assumed. Let τ be the date of change. The optimal policy $N^*(t)$ after the change is given by: for any $t \in [\tau, T]$, the following must be satisfied:

(i) $\lambda F'(N^*(t)) = \bar{w}e^{-r(t-\tau)}$

(ii) $\dot{\lambda} = -H_Z = 0 \Rightarrow \lambda(t) = \lambda > 0$ after the date of change, where the Hamiltonian associated with (6)–(7) is given by

(iii) $H = -e^{-r(t-\tau)}\bar{w}N + \lambda F(N)$

(iv) $\displaystyle\int_\tau^T F(N^*(t))\, dt = 1 - Z(\tau).$

From i) we have

(v) $N^*(t) = (F')^{-1}\left(\dfrac{\bar{w}e^{-r(t-\tau)}}{\lambda}\right) \equiv n\left(\dfrac{\bar{w}e^{-r(t-\tau)}}{\lambda}\right)$

where $n'(\cdot) < 0$ due to $F'' < 0$.

Inserting $N^*(t) = n(\cdot)$ into (iv), we can express λ as a function of the various parameters

(vi) $\lambda = \lambda(T, \tau, \bar{w}, r, Z(\tau))$
        $ - \; + + \; - \; -$

where we have indicated the signs of its partial derivatives.

From (6) we now easily find

(vii) $\dfrac{\partial V(Z_\tau)}{\partial Z_\tau} = -\lambda < 0$,

and from vi) it follows that

(viii) $\dfrac{\partial^2 V(Z_\tau)}{\partial Z_\tau^2} = -\dfrac{\partial \lambda}{\partial Z_\tau} > 0$.

Since $\lambda(Z_\tau)$ is the shadow price or marginal cost of increasing Z_τ, given that the date of change has occurred at τ, we observe that the minimal expected cost of completing a fraction $1 - Z(\tau)$ from τ to T is strictly decreasing and strictly convex in Z_τ.

From i) on differentiating w.r.t. t, we find:

(ix) $\dot{N}^*(t) = -r\dfrac{F'(N^*(t))}{F''(N^*(t))}$,

and due to strict concavity of F, $N^*(t)$ must obviously be strictly increasing with time, after the change has occurred.

Appendix 3

From (29) we have

$$qF'(\hat{N}(t)) = w_0(1 - S(t))\, e^{-rt}\left[1 + \frac{S(t)}{1 - S(t)}\frac{\bar{w}}{w_0}\right]$$

$$= w_0 e^{-rt + \ln(1 - S(t))}\left[1 + \frac{S(t)}{1 - S(t)}\frac{\bar{w}}{w_0}\right]$$

$$= w_0 e^{-\int_0^t (r(v) + a(v))\, dv}\left[1 + \frac{S(t)}{1 - S(t)}\frac{\bar{w}}{w_0}\right]$$

where

$$a(v) = -\frac{d}{dv}\ln(1 - S(v)) = \frac{S'(v)}{1 - S(v)}$$

is the conditional probability for the change to occur at v, conditional on that the change has not occurred before v. Denoting $\psi(v) = r(v) + a(v) = r + a(v)$ as the risk-adjusted interest rate, we get (29').

References

Dasgupta, P. & Heal, G.: The optimal depletion of exhaustible resources. *Review of Economic Studies*, Symposium on the Economics of Exhaustible Resources, pp. 3–28, 1974.

Dasgupta, P. & Stiglitz, J.: Resource depletion under technological uncertainty. *Econometrica* 49 (1), 85–104, 1981.

Haavelmo, T.: *A study in the theory of investment*. University of Chicago Press, Chicago, 1960.

Kamien, M. I. & Schwartz, N. L.: *Market structure and innovation*. Cambridge University Press, Cambridge, 1982.

Seierstad, A. & Sydsæter, K.: Sufficient conditions in optimal control theory. *International Economic Review 18* (2), 367–391, 1977.

Vislie, J.: A production model for a large project. *Scandinavian Journal of Economics 84* (1), 13–25, 1982 *a*.

Vislie, J.: A note on an intertemporal cost function for a class of dynamic problems. *Economics Letters 9* (3), 215–219, 1982 *b*.

Yaari, M. E.: Uncertain lifetime, life insurance, and the theory of the consumer. *Review of Economic Studies 32* (2), 137–150, 1965.

Production and Maintenance: Joint Activities of the Firm*

Derek Bosworth and Clive Pugh

Loughborough University, Leicestershire, England

Abstract

The degree of capital utilisation and the implications of variations in utilisation for the costs of the firm are dealt with in this paper. In particular, increased utilisation will generally result in a more rapid depreciation of the capital stock, other things being equal, and depreciation is a component of the user cost of capital. It is argued that observed rates of depreciation based on capital consumption published in official sources and used in constructing measures of the user cost of capital significantly understate the true rate of depreciation because firms undertake maintenance activities. Thus, the reduction in depreciation caused by maintenance activities is viewed in this analysis as a joint production activity of the firm.

I. Introduction

The initial work on employment functions, based heavily on an inverted production function, tended to play down the role of capital services in the production process,[1] if anything, capital utilisation was treated as synonymous with hours per employee.[2] The separation of the labour services input into its two constituent parts, employment and hours, led to the unanticipated (but, unfortunately, all too consistent) finding of increasing returns to hours in the production process.[3] The search for a means of obviating this largely unacceptable result has been one of the reasons for a more detailed examination of the role played by capital utilisation.[4] These new lines of research, in conjunction with the movement toward more generalised factor demand models, resulted in the interrelated[5] and simultaneous[6] factor demand systems.

---

* The research reported in this paper is, in part, the result of work carried out on a project, "Optimal Capital Utilisation in British Manufacturing Industry", funded by the Leverhulme Trust. The authors wish to thank an anonymous referee for useful comments provided on an earlier draft of this paper.
[1] Particularly in empirical work, see e.g. the work of Brechling (1965) and Ball & St. Cyr (1966).
[2] See e.g. Hazledine (1976), p. 5.
[3] Feldstein (1967) and Craine (1972).
[4] Ireland & Smyth (1969) and Nadiri & Rosen (1969).
[5] Nadiri & Rosen (1969).
[6] See eg. Briscoe & Peel (1975), Hazledine (1974) and Morgan (1979).

To some degree, these early, largely static[7] factor demand models are now beginning to be superseded by dynamic factor demand systems.[8] Nevertheless, the static models still form the backbone of the literature in this area and, indeed, are still to be fully explored. These models have a great deal left to offer in understanding the relationship between production and employment and continue to be a useful 'test-bed' for further developments in the theory. The work to extend the theory to look at the contributions of particular education levels, ages, skills or occupations,[9] has been paralleled by an increasing emphasis on fuel and raw material inputs following the fuel crisis of the 1970s.[10] More recently, the theoretical framework has been extended to incorporate shiftworking.[11] Some of these developments, particularly those associated with the disaggregation of fuels and raw materials (where the ease of substitution between inputs is central), have been associated with increasingly general underlying technologies, culminating in the translog functions. In other instances, such as the models incorporating shiftworking (where the role of substitution is not so central), the authors have been able to use much simpler functional forms.

This paper is concerned with the degree of capital utilisation and the implications of variations in utilisation for the costs of the firm. In particular, increased utilisation will generally result in a more rapid depreciation of the capital stock, other things being equal, and depreciation is a component of the user cost of capital. It is argued below that observed rates of depreciation based on capital consumption, published in official sources[12] and used in constructing measures of the user cost of capital[13] significantly understate the true rate of depreciation because firms undertake maintenance activities. Thus, the reduction in depreciation caused by maintenance activities is viewed in this paper as a joint product of the firm,[14] and

---

[7] A "dynamic element" is generally introduced in an *ad hoc* manner by the adoption of a lagged adjustment mechanism, in order to reflect the partial adjustment of inputs to their desired levels because of the costs of adjustment.

[8] See e.g. Berndt, Fuss & Waverman (1979) and McIntosh (1981).

[9] See e.g. Layard, et al. (1971), Dougherty (1972), Skolnick (1975) and Freeman & Medoff (1977).

[10] See e.g. Binswanger (1974), Humphrey & Moroney (1975), Halvorsen (1976; 1977), Duncan & Binswanger (1976) and Fuss (1977).

[11] Bosworth & Dawkins (1981) and Bosworth (1981).

[12] Central Statistical Office, *National Income and Expenditure* (annually).

[13] Briscoe & Peel (1975), Cable (1971) and Wilson (1980).

[14] The treatment of maintenance as a joint production activity gives rise to the expectation that there are other activities of the firm that should be treated in an analogous manner. Most "support" activities of the firm might be treated in a broadly similar way. See, for example, the first steps towards this, taken by Leicester (1971) and Crum (1976) in their *ad hoc* models of the "non-production" activities of the firm. See also the work of Schott (1978) in the analysis of R & D activities.

it is particularly important in the light of the magnitude of capital costs and the number of maintenance employees in more capital intensive firms.[15]

Section II outlines a general framework that can be used to investigate the role of capital utilisation and explores the links between depreciation and maintenance. Section III develops these principles in an explicit mathematical form, where maintenance is treated as a joint activity of the firm. Finally, Section IV outlines the main conclusions and discusses further avenues of research.

II. A Factor Demand Model: Shiftwork and Maintenance

(i) *An Interrelated Factor Demand Model Framework*

An interrelated factor demand model of the Nadiri & Rosen (1969) type provides a framework for examining the role played by maintenance activities. The production function can be written as the general function,

$$Y = f(K, U, L, H),\tag{1}$$

where Y denotes output of the firm's product per period; K is the stock of capital used in production; U is the degree to which the capital stock is utilised; L denotes the total number of production workers; and H is the average hours worked per production employee.

It has been argued by certain authors that, in such a model, H and U both indicate the degree to which the capital stock is utilised.[16] In this case, the production function has only three input variables. This argument has been dealt with elsewhere,[17] however, as U and H are linked through shiftworking, S, where S denotes the number of shifts. The relationship linking U, H and S is the wage-utilisation envelope, formed from the shiftwork-overtime combinations that produce the lowest wage cost associated with ensuring a constant level of manning over a period of U hours (where U is assumed to be the operating hours of the capital stock).[18] Thus, whilst it cannot be assumed that $U=H$, both S and H are determined by the wage-utilisation envelope once U is given (i.e. $U=H \cdot S$). Thus, equation (1) can be rewritten,

$$Y = f(K, E, U),\tag{2}$$

---

[15] For a more complete discussion of the importance and trends in maintenance work, see Bosworth & Dawkins (1982).
[16] Hazledine (1976).
[17] Bosworth (1981).
[18] Clearly, as the model incorporates the concept of shiftworking, these may not be the same workers at every point during the operating day: one worker can replace another as the shift-crews change over.

where, in this instance, E denotes the number of employees on the main-shift; $E \cdot S$ is the total number of workers employed; and U is the number of hours the plant is operated.

This model retains the basic characteristics of the Nadiri and Rosen (1969) system. In particular, higher levels of utilisation result in reduced amounts of capital for a given output level. Thus, the capital bill, pK, is reduced as K falls, *other things being equal,* where p denotes the user cost of capital. A natural consequence would be that, if other things were equal, U would be expanded to a level consistent with continuous working of capital, U^X. In the Nadiri & Rosen model, utilisation is terminated at some level $U \leqslant U^X$ by offsetting increases in the user cost of capital, p, arising from the more rapid depreciation of capital at higher levels of utilisation, $\partial p / \partial U \geqslant 0$. In the modified form of the model, increased labour costs (arising from the need to pay shift and overtime premia) augment the higher depreciation costs to terminate U, at less than its physical maximum.[19]

The central theme of this paper is concerned with the role of maintenance in production and its impact on the resulting model of factor demands. Maintenance enters the model in two ways. First, it affects the rate of depreciation and, therefore the life expectancy of capital; we return to this in Section II (iii) below. Second, it may influence the current level of output by ensuring the continuity of factor services. For any given level of other inputs, higher levels of maintenance will reduce breakdowns and lost production. Hence equation (2) can be rewritten,

$$Y = f(K, E, U, M), \tag{3}$$

where M denotes the amount of maintenance activity. Two special cases may be worthy of further consideration: first, where maintenance lengthens the life of capital, but does not contribute to current output; second, where maintenance does not influence the life expectancy of capital, but makes a positive contribution to current output.[20] In the former case, maintenance may be considered more as a joint production activity of the firm, where its output is future capital services.

(ii) *The Wage-Utilisation Frontier*

Once the optimal level of utilisation is isolated, the optimal number of shifts and level of overtime hours per shift can be determined from the wage-utilisation envelope,

$$w = \omega(U) = \omega(H, S), \tag{4}$$

---

[19] Bosworth (1981, pp. 260–4).

[20] These ideas appear to be more consistent with the generalised theory of costs proposed by Alchian (1959), but which have, as yet, found limited following in the literature.

where w, the wage rate is influenced by the size of shift and overtime premia. It has been shown that the wage-hours submodel of the Ball and St. Cyr (1966) system is a special case of the wage-utilisation function, where the number of shift crews is constrained to unity (i.e. there is only a single, day "shift").

The shape of the envelope itself, however, is the subject of investigation at the present time.[21] In the context of the majority of industrial firms, the positively sloped part of the relationship in the interval between normal hours, U^N, worked by a single shift, and maximum operating hours, U^X, is of particular interest (i.e. between approximately 40 and 168 hours per week). This part of the relationship might be approximated by one of the three functional forms, a–c, shown in Figure 1. Increased attention has focused on the curve below U^N, because of growing interest in short-time working. This part of the relationship may be represented in two principal ways, as shown in Figure 1. The first is a backward continuation of the wage-utilisation function prevailing to the right of U^N (e.g. a, b or c). The function in this region may represent the case of full time workers on short-time, but not covered by guaranteed payment provisions, or part-time workers. The second, is a new, negatively sloped curve such as d, which applies where $U < U^N$ and guaranteed payments become operative.

(iii) *User Cost of Capital, Depreciation and Maintenance*

The discussion of Section II (i) highlights the simplicity of the assumption about the relationship between the rate of depreciation and the degree of utilisation in the literature. Investigation of the available UK statistics on capital consumption and depreciation only serves to reinforce this point.[22] Depreciation statistics appear to be calculated on the assumption that the capital stock is consumed at a *linear rate* over its expected lifetime.[23] In addition, the estimated lifetime is based on inadequate information and cannot be assumed to reflect variations over time in either the degree of utilisation or maintenance activity.[24]

If maintenance is treated as a separate element of cost, then the user cost of capital should account for real rates of depreciation, reflecting both the degree of utilisation and the extent of maintenance activities. Thus,

$$p = \mathfrak{p}(i, \delta) = \mathfrak{p}(i, U, M), \tag{5}$$

where i is the rate of interest; δ denotes the rate of depreciation, which is a function of the level of utilisation, U, and maintenance, M. Thus, in

[21] Bosworth (1982).
[22] See e.g. the discussion in Griffin (1979) and Wilson (1980).
[23] Griffin (1979, p. 102).
[24] Ibid. pp. 117–123.

general, it is anticipated that $\partial p/\partial U \geq 0$ and $\partial p/\partial M \leq 0$. In this paper, therefore, attention focuses on a firm that undertakes its own maintenance and the capital services saved in this way can be considered as a joint product of the firm.

It is clear from UK data that maintenance is an important activity within the firm,[25] it is worth pointing out that by the second half of the 1970s, maintenance workers formed nearly 10 per cent of all manual workers.[26] More detailed case-study work has revealed a much higher incidence of maintenance workers for certain plants.[27] In addition, maintenance workers tend to be relatively well paid, reflecting in part overtime, shift and unsocial hours payments. Thus, it may be assumed that,

$$m = m(U), \tag{6}$$

where m is the per unit cost of maintenance activity and U is the degree to which capital is utilised on the main production process.

III. Production and Maintenance

This section reports on the development of a model of maintenance, incorporating the main features outlined in Section II. Following Nadiri & Rosen (1969), the goal of the firm is assumed to be one of cost minimisation subject to an output constraint. As the elasticity of substitution is not a central feature, the underlying technology is assumed to be Cobb-Douglas.[28] Thus, the problem is expressed as the unconstrained minimisation of the Lagrangian expression,

$$LG \stackrel{\Delta}{=} \omega(U)EU + p(i, U, M)K + m(U)M +$$

$$\lambda\{\ln Y - \ln A - \alpha \ln K - \beta \ln E - \gamma \ln U - \eta \ln M\}, \tag{7}$$

where A is the technical efficiency parameter and α, β, γ and η are the constant exponents on K, E, U and M in the Cobb-Douglas (α, β, γ, $\eta \geq 0$). The cost element of the expression now has three components: labour, capital and maintenance costs. Total labour costs, $\omega(U)EU$, is comprised of the average wage per hour associated with a work pattern covering U operating hours, $\omega(U)$, multiplied by the total number of man-hours (i.e. the number of men in the plant at any given time, E, multiplied by the length of operating day, U). Total capital costs, $p(i, U, M)K$, are self explanatory,

[25] Bosworth & Dawkins (1982).
[26] Department of Employment, *New Earnings Survey* (annually).
[27] A recent case study of a plant in the chemicals industry, for example, revealed that over half the workforce were maintenance workers, Bosworth & Dawkins (1982).
[28] Cobb & Douglas (1928).

although, it should be added, that, for simplicity, the function $p(\ )$ adopted is of a multiplicative rather than additive form. Total maintenance costs, $m(U)M$, allow the user cost of maintenance to vary with the degree of utilisation.

The first-order conditions for a minimum are shown in equations (8) to (12):

$$\frac{\partial LG}{\partial U} = \frac{dw}{dU} \cdot EU + wE + \frac{\partial p}{\partial U} \cdot K + \frac{\partial m}{\partial U} \cdot M - \frac{\lambda\gamma}{U} = 0 \tag{8}$$

$$\frac{\partial LG}{\partial E} = wU - \frac{\lambda\beta}{E} = 0 \tag{9}$$

$$\frac{\partial LG}{\partial K} = p - \frac{\lambda\alpha}{K} = 0 \tag{10}$$

$$\frac{\partial LG}{\partial M} = \frac{\partial p}{\partial M} \cdot K + m - \frac{\lambda\eta}{M} = 0 \tag{11}$$

and

$$\frac{\partial LG}{\partial \lambda} = \ln A + \alpha \ln K + \beta \ln E + \gamma \ln U + \eta \ln M - \ln Y = 0 \tag{12}$$

This yields a system of five equations in five unkowns: U, E, K, M and λ.

In order to derive solutions for U, K, E and M, it is necessary to specify the user cost variables. It is therefore assumed that,

$$w = w_0 + w_1 U^\theta \tag{13}$$

$$p = bU^\varphi M^\psi \tag{14}$$

and

$$m = cU^\varrho, \tag{15}$$

where w_0, w_1, b, c, θ, φ, ψ and ϱ are given constants. The wage function may be dichotomous at U^N, see Figure 1; either wage regimes a–c prevail for all U, $0 \leqslant U \leqslant U^X$, or they prevail for $U^N \leqslant U \leqslant U^X$ and regime d operates for $0 \leqslant U \leqslant U^N$. The need to respecify the wage-utilisation relationship around U^N should not be interpreted as a weakness of the model, this is precisely what happens in the real world. In the results which follow, the wage-utilisation relationship has been normalised around $U^N = 1$. While the approach is valid whether or not the relationship is normalised in this way, the parameters of equation (13) can be given a more meaningful economic interpretation. In particular, the gradient of the curve is θw_1 at $U = 1$ and this is the initial overtime (shift) premium which comes into play above

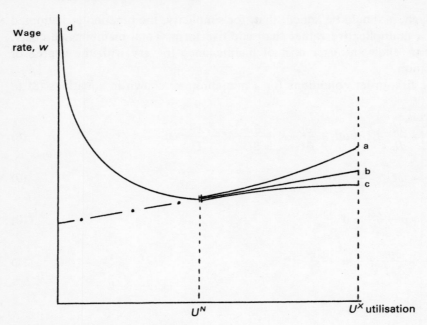

Fig. 1. Wage–utilisation relationship.

normal hours (and analogously the guaranteed wage mark-up for $U<U^N$). In addition, the basic wage can be written $w^N=w_0+w_1$ at $U=1$ independent of the prevailing wage regime. Finally, the mark-up of the basic wage, w^N, over the minimum acceptable wage as $U\to0$, can be written as w_1/w_0 in cases a–c. Hence, in the sequel we will refer to $U=1$ as U^N.

Equation (13) is sufficiently general to incorporate all four cases shown in Figure 1. The parameter signs that appear to be of interest from an economic point of view are as follows:

Case a, $\theta>1$, $w_0>0$ and $w_1>0$;
Case b, $\theta=1$, $w_0>0$ and $w_1>0$;
Case c, $0<\theta<1$, $w_0>0$ and $w_1>0$;
Case d, $\theta<0$, $w_0>0$ and $w_1>0$.

While the signs of θ and w_1 are fairly obvious in each case, the sign of w_0 requires slightly more explanation. In the cases a–c, a negative w_0 will mean that, for a sufficiently small U, the wage rate, w, becomes negative, which is clearly unacceptable from an economic viewpoint and may give rise to special results. These have been investigated, but they are reported on only briefly below. In cases a–c, therefore, the intercept term, w_0, is assumed positive. Turning now to case d, $\theta<0$ implies that $w\to w_0$ as U increases. While $U>U^N$ is not experienced under regime d, it nevertheless seems natural to assume that a negative wage could never be tolerated and, hence, $w_0 > 0$. It should be noted that the interpretation of the parameters differs somewhat between cases a–c and case d.

The user cost of capital term is log-linear in the arguments U and M, where it is assumed higher utilisation increases and higher maintenance reduces the value of the user cost. The rate of interest, i, can be included as a constant (captured within the b term) or as a further multiplicative argument. As this term was not central to the discussion, the former approach was adopted.[29] Finally, $\varrho > 0$ in equation (15), allows the user cost of maintenance to vary with the length of operating day, reflecting the higher overtime, shift or unsocial hours payments made to maintenance workers as utilisation is increased.

Equations (8)–(12) yield an explicit solution for optimal utilisation,

$$U^\theta = \frac{\dfrac{\gamma}{\beta} - 1 - \dfrac{\alpha\varphi}{\beta} - \dfrac{\varrho}{\beta}(\eta - \alpha\psi)}{\theta - \left[\dfrac{\gamma}{\beta} - 1 - \dfrac{\alpha\varphi}{\beta} - \dfrac{\varrho}{\beta}(\eta - \alpha\psi)\right]} \cdot \frac{w_0}{w_1} = \frac{\dfrac{\gamma}{\beta} - \chi}{\theta - \dfrac{\gamma}{\beta} + \chi} \cdot \frac{w_0}{w_1}, \tag{16}$$

where $\chi = 1 + \dfrac{\alpha\varphi}{\beta} + \dfrac{\varrho}{\beta}(\eta - \alpha\psi)$. The production parameters are non-negative,

$$A, \alpha, \beta, \gamma, \eta \geqslant 0. \tag{17}$$

The price parameters associated with capital services and maintenance activities can be written,

$$b, \varphi, c, \varrho > 0; \psi \leqslant 0. \tag{18}$$

Finally, the price parameters associated with labour services vary according to the case adopted,

$$w_0, w_1 > 0 \text{—all cases}$$
$$\theta > 1, \theta = 1, 0 < \theta < 1, \theta < 0 \text{—cases a, b, c, d, respectively.} \tag{19}$$

Using the information from inequalities (17)–(19) in equation (16) indicates two sets of cases where $U > 0$,

$$\chi \geqslant \frac{\gamma}{\beta} \geqslant \chi + \theta \quad (\theta < 0) \tag{20}$$

---

[29] An additive term in i, coupled with multiplicative terms in U and M, causes considerable problems in terms of the intractability of the mathematics.

Table 1. *Direction of the influence of the price parameters*

Derivative	Value of derivative	Sign of derivative	
		Condition 20	Condition 21
$\dfrac{\partial U}{\partial w_0}$	$\left(\dfrac{\left(\dfrac{\gamma}{\beta}-\chi\right)}{\left(\theta-\dfrac{\gamma}{\beta}+\chi\right)}\cdot\dfrac{1}{w_1}\right)\cdot\dfrac{1}{\theta U^{\theta-1}}$	<0	>0
$\dfrac{\partial U}{\partial w_1}$	$-\left(\dfrac{\left(\dfrac{\gamma}{\beta}-\chi\right)}{\left(\theta-\dfrac{\gamma}{\beta}+\chi\right)}\cdot\dfrac{w_0}{w_1^{2}}\right)\cdot\dfrac{1}{\theta U^{\theta-1}}$	>0	<0
$\dfrac{\partial U}{\partial \theta}$	$-\left(\ln U+\dfrac{1}{\left(\theta-\dfrac{\gamma}{\beta}+\chi\right)}\right)\cdot\dfrac{U}{\theta}$	$<0,\ \forall U\leqslant 1$	$<0,\ \forall U\geqslant 1$
$\dfrac{\partial U}{\partial \varphi}$	$-\left(\dfrac{1}{\left(\theta-\dfrac{\gamma}{\beta}+\chi\right)^{2}}\cdot\dfrac{\alpha}{\beta}\cdot\dfrac{w_0}{w_1}\right)\cdot\dfrac{1}{U^{\theta-1}}$	<0	<0
$\dfrac{\partial U}{\partial \psi}$	$\left(\dfrac{1}{\left(\theta-\dfrac{\gamma}{\beta}+\chi\right)^{2}}\cdot\dfrac{\alpha\varrho}{\beta}\cdot\dfrac{w_0}{w_1}\right)\dfrac{1}{U^{\theta-1}}$	>0	>0
$\dfrac{\partial U}{\partial \varrho}$	$-\left(\dfrac{1}{\left(\theta-\dfrac{\gamma}{\beta}+\chi\right)^{2}}\cdot\dfrac{(\eta-\alpha\psi)}{\beta}\cdot\dfrac{w_0}{w_1}\right)\dfrac{1}{U^{\theta-1}}$	<0	<0

and

$$\chi+\theta\geqslant\frac{\gamma}{\beta}\geqslant\chi \quad (\theta>0) \tag{21}$$

where condition (20) holds for case d and condition (21) holds for cases a–c.

Using equation (16) it is possible to isolate the direction of the influence of the various price parameters. Thus, Table (1) explores the signs of the partial derivatives of U with respect to w_0, w_1, θ, ψ and ϱ. The results are presented separately for the cases where guaranteed payments are in operation (condition (20)) and where normal pay, shift and overtime premia are in force (condition (21)). It can be seen that the signs are reversed for the partial derivatives with respect to w_0 and w_1 but are consistent for θ, φ, ψ and ϱ.

The results reported in Table (1) correspond with *a priori* expectations. Increases in w_0, other things being equal, reduce the relative penalty for not being at normal hours, U^N. While w_1 also enters basic pay, it also directly influences the size of overtime and shift premia (e.g. $dw/dU=\theta w_1$ at U^N). Thus, increases in w_1 raise the penalty for not being at U^N. The sign of θ differs between conditions (20) and (21). Thus, the increase in θ

raises the penalty for not being at U^N for $U>U^N$ and lowers it for $U<U^N$. The greater the impact of utilisation on depreciation, via φ, the lower will be optimal utilisation. Increases in ψ reduce the beneficial effects of maintenance on the user cost of capital resulting in higher levels of utilisation. Finally, the higher the cost penalty of maintenance caused by utilisation, via ϱ, the smaller the optimal level of utilisation.

Thus, several important conclusions can be derived from equation (16) and Table 1. In particular the maintenance parameters η and ψ affect optimal utilisation in the same direction. The positive term $\varrho/\beta(\eta-\alpha\psi)$ is subtracted from the numerator and added to the denominator in equation (16). Where maintenance makes a positive contribution to current output, it is a substitute for utilisation. In the case where maintenance reduces depreciation, it appears as a further dimension to the user cost of capital services ignored in traditional factor demand models. Its existence has the effect of reducing the predicted level of optimal utilisation. Thus, traditional models have an omitted variable problem whenever η and/or ψ are non-zero and predict too high a level of utilisation.

A number of other combinations of parameter signs could give rise to a positive value of U in equation (16). For example, on the upward sloping part of the wage-utilisation relationship, it appeared possible that $w_0<0$. This gave rise to two further conditions for $U>0$,

$$\frac{\gamma}{\beta}>\theta+\chi \quad (w_0<0) \tag{22}$$

or

$$\frac{\gamma}{\beta}<\chi \quad (w_0<0) \tag{23}$$

Further examination, however, reveals that condition (23) only produces $U>0$ where $w=w_0+w_1 U^\theta<0$, and can therefore be ignored from an economic viewpoint. While condition (22) appears quite interesting from a mathematical viewpoint (reversing the signs of the majority of the partial derivatives *vis à vis* condition (21). It is of considerably less interst from an economic position: first, it implies that employees would be willing to work some positive number of hours before requiring compensation; second, it is associated with a wage-utilisation function not experienced in UK manufacturing.[30]

It is not necessary, for the purposes of this paper, to obtain explicit values for the remaining variables, M, E and K, since the primary interest is in their variation with respect to certain of the parameters. This behaviour

---

[30] Bosworth (1982).

may be more simply ascertained from the implicit relationships which can be derived from the first order conditions (8)–(12). Specifically, it may be deduced that,

$$\frac{1}{M} \cdot \frac{\partial M}{\partial \xi} = -\varrho \frac{1}{U} \cdot \frac{\partial U}{\partial \xi}, \tag{24}$$

where ξ represents any of the parameters, w_0, w_1, θ, ϱ or φ. In the sequel, ξ will be used in this way without any further reference. The case of ψ is slightly more complicated and the analogous equation to (24) can be written,

$$\frac{1}{M} \cdot \frac{\partial M}{\partial \psi} = -\varrho \cdot \frac{1}{U} \cdot \frac{\partial U}{\partial \psi} - \frac{(\alpha+\beta)}{\left(\dfrac{\eta}{\alpha} - \psi\right)} \cdot \frac{1}{(\alpha+\beta+\eta-\alpha\psi)}, \tag{25}$$

where only ψ is negative. Hence, it is clear from equations (24) and (25) that $\partial M/\partial \xi$ and $\partial U/\partial \xi$ will be of opposite sign. The variation in K can be obtained in a similar manner,

$$\frac{1}{K} \cdot \frac{\partial K}{\partial \xi} = -(\varphi - \varrho\psi) \cdot \frac{1}{U} \cdot \frac{\partial U}{\partial \xi} \tag{26}$$

$$\frac{1}{K} \frac{\partial K}{\partial \psi} = -(\varphi - \varrho\psi) \cdot \frac{1}{U} \cdot \frac{\partial U}{\partial \psi} + \frac{1}{\left(\dfrac{\eta}{\alpha} - \psi\right)} \cdot \frac{\beta\psi+\eta}{\alpha+\beta+\eta-\alpha\psi} \tag{27}$$

Again, it can be seen that, as ψ is negative and all the remaining parameters are positive, $\partial K/\partial \xi$ and $\partial U/\partial \xi$ are also of opposite sign for all ξ. The same is true of $\partial K/\partial \psi$ whenever $\beta\psi+\eta<0$, although it is possible for $\partial K/\partial \psi$ and $\partial K/\partial U$ to have the same sign, for sufficiently large η and small ψ. Interestingly, the sign here turns on the relative contributions of maintenance to current production and to the reduction in the rate of depreciation. Finally,

$$\frac{1}{E} \cdot \frac{\partial E}{\partial \xi} = \left(\frac{\alpha\varphi}{\beta} + \frac{\alpha\varrho}{\beta}\left(\frac{\eta}{\alpha} - \psi\right) - \frac{\gamma}{\beta}\right)\frac{1}{U}\frac{\partial U}{\partial \xi} \tag{28}$$

$$\frac{1}{E} \cdot \frac{\partial E}{\partial \psi} = \left(\frac{\alpha\varphi}{\beta} + \frac{\alpha\varrho}{\beta}\left(\frac{\eta}{\alpha} - \psi\right) - \frac{\gamma}{\beta}\right)\frac{1}{U}\frac{\partial U}{\partial \psi} + \frac{\alpha}{\alpha+\beta+\eta-\alpha\psi} \tag{28}$$

As ψ is negative and the remaining parameters are positive, it is clear from equations (28) and (29) that $\partial E/\partial \psi$ has the same sign as $\partial U/\partial \xi$ and $\partial U/\partial \psi$ whenever $\dfrac{\alpha\varphi}{\beta} + \dfrac{\alpha\varrho}{\beta}\left(\dfrac{\eta}{\alpha} - \psi\right) > \dfrac{\gamma}{\beta}$. This inequality is related to χ, as $\dfrac{\alpha\varphi}{\beta} + \dfrac{\alpha\varrho}{\beta}\left(\dfrac{\eta}{\alpha} - \psi\right) = \chi - 1$, see equation (16), and can be used to provide information about the sign of $\partial E/\partial \xi$ or $\partial E/\partial \psi$. However, from equation (28):

Table 2. *Variations in optimal utilisation and changes in the parameter* ξ

Para-meter	Variable Condition 20					Condition 21			
	U	M	K	E $-1<\theta<0$	$\theta<-1$	U	M	K	E
w_0	−	+	+	+	~	+	−	−	−
w_1	+	−	−	−	~	−	+	+	+
θ	−	+	+	+	~	−	+	+	+
φ	−	+	+	+	~	−	+	+	+
ψ	+	−	~	~	~	+	−	~	~
ϱ	−	+	+	+	~	−	+	+	+

$\partial E/\partial \xi$ and $\partial U/\partial \xi$ are of opposite sign using condition (20) and $-1<\theta<0$; they are of opposite sign using conditions (21) and (22). The sign of $\partial E/\partial \psi$ is more difficult to establish, as there is an additional positive constant, although its value will generally be small $(0 \leqslant \dfrac{\alpha}{\alpha+\beta+\eta-\alpha\psi} \leqslant 1)$.

Table 2 summarises the main results, focusing on conditions (20) and (21), particularly the latter, which are most relevant from an economic viewpoint. It is apparent from the table that, where they can be determined, the signs for U and the other three variables are opposite. Thus, changes in factors prices that have a positive influence on U, have a negative influence on all the remaining variables and vice versa. The indeterminate signs associated with $E(\theta \leqslant -1)$ and ψ require further investigation, in the light of empirical work isolating values for the various parameters.

IV. Conclusions

The concept of joint products tends to be associated with a diversified firm, selling a range of differentiated or quite distinct products. In this paper, it was argued that even single product firms in this traditionally accepted sense are involved in the production of a range of intermediate goods and services that, in certain instances, can be treated as joint production activities. Of these, maintenance is a particularly interesting example, given the importance of maintenance activities in almost every sector of the economy. The output of the maintenance process does not enter the firm's product or product range in the normally accepted sense,[31] and, in this paper, its output has been measured as the ability to maintain output levels

---

[31] Although the resulting improvement in the quality of capital may ensure the continuity of production and availability of the product, and, perhaps to a lesser extent, aid quality control.

with given levels of other inputs and the reduction in the depreciation of the stock of capital used in production.[32]

An interest in capital utilisation grew out of the deficiencies in the early work on production and employment functions. In a similar way the interest in the maintenance process central to this paper arose from a recognition that the existing employment functions took no account of maintenance as a means of reducing the rate of depreciation caused by increased levels of utilisation. While the ensuing discussion has taken the first steps towards rectifying this oversight, a great deal of work remains to be done. The construction of the model quite clearly demonstrates that the average age and life expectancy of capital can be manipulated through utilisation and maintenance. The interrelationships between utilisation, maintenance and depreciation require much closer scrutiny. Such a study would also need to take into account the effects of the ageing of capital, which may also influence both maintenance and the optimal level of utilisation.[33] Further developments along these lines would almost certainly prove more productive using a more dynamic framework, linked to a vintage model of production.

The manner in which maintenance itself enters the model should also be the subject of investigation. The inclusion of a single maintenance variable, M, and its associated price term, $m(U)$, might correspond with a purely labour intensive maintenance process. The next stage of the research is to generalise this term, so that the output of the maintenance process arises out of the use of maintenance capital and labour that may be quite distinct from that used in the main production process. Clearly, other generalisations are also possible, including the adoption of a less restrictive underlying technology of production, in order to examine the role played by such factors as the elasticity of substitution between inputs. In addition, the research might focus specifically on the question of utilisation and maintenance amongst less developed and developing countries. From an empirical point of view, the current research has indicated the need to provide empirical estimates of the parameters that appear in the model, in particular, the contributions of maintenance to production and future supplies of capital services (η and ψ).

Finally, even at this early stage, the work has highlighted severe problems of measurement in official UK data sources. The method of constructing capital consumption series used in calculating depreciation rates appears to preclude the possibility of any meaningful analysis of the relation-

---

[32] The principle outlined in this paper, however, can be applied to other activities and could be used to extend the early work on 'non-production' processes that have begun to appear in the literature. See e.g. Leicester (1971), Crum (1976) and Schott (1978).

[33] Marris (1970).

ships between utilisation, maintenance and depreciation. Disillusionment with the capital consumption series, by implication, also casts grave doubt on the accuracy and validity of the published net capital stock series and other authors' attempts to calculate the user cost of capital. Despite these empirical problems, however, there can be little doubt that the role played by maintenance in the production process deserves considerably more attention than has so far been devoted to it in the economics literature.

References

Alchian, A.: Costs and outputs. In *The Allocation of Economic Resources* (ed. M. Abramovitz et al.). Stanford U.P., Stanford, 1959.

Ball, R. & St. Cyr, E. B. A.: Employment models in UK manufacturing industries. *Review of Economic Studies 33*, 179–207, 1966.

Berndt, E. R., Fuss, M. A. & Waverman, L.: A dynamic model of costs of adjustment and inter-related factor demands, with an empirical application to energy demand in US manufacturing. Paper presented to the European Meeting of the Econometric Society, Athens, Greece, September 1979.

Binswanger, H. P.: The measurement of technical change biases with many factors of production. *American Economic Review 64*, 964–76, 1974.

Bosworth, D. L. & Dawkins, P. J.: *Work patterns: An economic analysis.* Gower Press, Aldershot, 1981.

Bosworth, D. L.: Shiftworking and the specification of factor demand models. *Scottish Journal of Political Economy 28*, 256–65, 1981.

Bosworth, D. L.: The wage utilisation frontier and the structure of labour costs. *Occasional Paper No. 65, Loughborough University of Technology*, 1982.

Bosworth, D. L. & Dawkins, P. J.: *Optimal capital utilisation in British manufacturing industry.* Report to the Leverhulme Trust, 1982.

Brechling, F. P. R.: The relationship between output and employment in British manufacturing industries. *Review of Economic Studies*, 187–216, July 1965.

Briscoe, G. & Peel, D.: The specification of the short-run employment function. *Oxford Bulletin of Economics and Statistics 37*, 115–42, 1975.

Cable, J.: User cost of capital and the effects of investment incentives. *CIEBR Discussion Paper No. 10, University of Warwick*, 1971.

Central Statistical Office: *National Income and Expenditure.* HMSO, London, (annually).

Cobb, C. W. & Douglas, P. H.: A theory of production. *American Economic Review 18*, (supplement), 139–65, 1928.

Craine, R.: On the service flow from labour. *Review of Economic Studies 39–45*, January 1972.

Crum, R. E.: *Non-manufacturing activities in UK manufacturing industry.* Report by the School of Social Studies, University of East Anglia, November 1976.

Department of Employment: *New Earnings Survey.* HMSO, London (annually).

Dougherty, C. R. S.: Estimates of labour aggregation functions. *Journal of Political Economy 80*, 1101–1119, 1972.

Duncan, R. C. & Binswanger, H. P.: Energy sources: Substitutability and biases in Australia. *Australian Economic Papers*, pp. 289–301, December 1976.

Feldstein, M. S.: Specification of the labour input in the aggregate production function. *Review of Economic Studies*, 375–86, October 1967.

Freeman, R. B. & Medoff, J. L.: Substitution between production labour and other inputs in unionised and non-unionised manufacturing. *Discussion Paper No. 581, Harvard Institute of Economic Research, Harvard University*, 1977.

Fuss, M. A.: The demand for energy in Canadian manufacturing: An example of the estimation of production structures with many inputs. *Journal of Econometrics 5*, 89–116, 1977.

Griffin, T.: The stock of fixed assets in the UK: How to make best use of the statistics. In *The measurement of capital* (ed. K. D. Patterson and K. Schott). Macmillan, 1979.

Halvorsen, R.: Demand for electric energy in the U.S. *Southern Economic Journal 42*, 610–625, April 1976.

Halvorsen, R.: Energy substitution in US manufacturing. Vol. LIX, pp. 381–8. November 1977.

Hazledine, T.: Employment and output functions for New Zealand manufacturing industries. *Journal of Industrial Economics 22*, 161–98, 1974.

Hazledine, T.: New specifications for employment and hours functions. Discussion Paper, *Economics Branch, Agriculture Canada*, Ottawa, October 1976.

Humphrey, D. B. & Moroney, J. R.: Substitution among capital, labour and natural resource products in American manufacturing. *Journal of Political Economy 83*, 57–82, 1975.

Ireland, N. J. & Smyth, D. J.: Specification of short-run employment models. *Review of Economic Studies*, 281–5, April 1970.

Layard, P. R. G., Sargan, J. D., Ager, M. E. & Jones, D. J.: *Qualified manpower and economic performance*. Allen Lane, Penguin Press, London, 1971.

Leicester, C. S.: Future manpower requirements of the British economy. In *Models of manpower systems* (ed. A. R. Smith) pp. 13–35. English Universities Press and American Elsevier, 1971.

Marris, R. L.: *Multiple shiftwork*. NEDO, HMSO, London, 1970.

McIntosh, J.: Dynamic inter-related factor demand systems: The United Kingdom 1950–78. *Discussion Paper, Economics Department, University of Essex*, November 1981.

Morgan, P. L.: Employment functions in manufacturing industry. *Discussion Paper, Research and Planning Division, Department of Employment*, May 1979.

Nadiri, M. I. & Rosen, S.: Inter-related factor demand functions. *American Economic Review*, pp. 457–71. September 1969.

Schott, K.: The relations between industrial research and development and factor demands, Vol. 88, pp. 85–106. March 1978.

Skolnik, M. L.: An empirical analysis of substitution between engineers and technicians in Canada. *Industrial Relations 25*, 284–300, 1975.

Wilson, R. A.: The measurement of the user cost of capital. *Research Paper 50, Manpower Research Group, University of Warwick*, July 1980.

Shiftwork and the Choice of Technique under Alternative Maximands*

Alan P. Hamlin and David F. Heathfield

University of Southampton, England

Abstract

Attempts to estimate production functions, measure productivity or analyse investment decisions should explicitly concern themselves with the utilisation rate dimension of the flow of capital services. A number of the results already present in the literature with regard to the traditional profit-maximising firm and the labour-managed firm are presented. It is then argued that the rate of profit, as opposed to its level, is of at least substantial importance to the decision-maker in the context of *ex ante* planning.

I. Introduction

Empirical estimates of the rate of capital utilization in U.K. manufacturing industry suggest that the typical unit of fixed capital is employed at less than 20% of its productive potential.[1] Utilization rates show considerable inter-industry differences with the Engineering and allied industries reaching only 11% whilst the Chemical industry achieves a rate of 45%. Furthermore, utilization rates vary over time, exhibiting an upward trend with moderate cyclical fluctuations.

Under these circumstances it is particularly important that attempts to estimate production functions, to measure productivity or to analyse investment decisions should explicitly concern themselves with the utilization rate dimension of the flow of capital services. Some of the issues raised in respect of production function and productivity studies are discussed in Heathfield (1980); the present paper sets out to examine the simultaneous choice of capital stock and utilization rate in a range of simple models of the *ex ante* planning stage of investment.

There has, of course, been a substantial tradition of work in this area

---

* We gratefully acknowledge the comments of two anonymous referees on an earlier version of this paper.
[1] See Heathfield (1972). The utilization rates quoted are absolute rather than relative; on this distinction see Foss (1963).

which is sometimes couched in terms of the analysis of shiftwork—e.g. Marris (1964) and Alexander & Sproas (1959) and sometimes in terms of the optimal idleness of capital—e.g. Winston & McCoy (1974), Betancourt & Clague (1975, 1977, 1981). Winston & McCoy (1974) present their discussion by reference to the traditional profit-maximising firm faced with the continuous choice of the length of the working day. Betancourt & Clague (1975, 1981) also concentrate attention on the profit-maximising firm whilst in their 1977 paper they analyse the case of a labour-managed firm concerned to maximise the basic (i.e. day shift) income per worker when faced with the choice of single or double shift working. The first objective of the present paper is to bring together a number of the results already present in the literature for these cases of the traditional profit-maximising firm and the labour-managed firm.

The second and more novel objective is to argue that the rate of profit, as opposed to its level, will be of at least substantial importance to the decision-maker in the context of *ex ante* investment planning. Consequently, we explore the impact of specifying the rate of profit as the firm's maximand so as to compare the implications for the choice of technique as between the three classes of firms. The comparative static responses of a profit-rate maximising firm to changes in their environment are, in qualitative terms, symmetric with those found in respect of the labour-managed firm and, therefore, broadly similar to those of the traditional profit level maximising firm. However, our interest lies not only in the routine comparison of qualitative results but also in the comparison of decisions which might be expected to flow from differently motivated enterprises faced with identical decision problems. It is this comparison across maximands which can be seen as the purpose of presenting results for each type of firm within the framework of a single, simple model; and it is in this respect that significant differences between the types of firms studied arise.

The arguments in support of viewing the rate of profit as a potentially plausible maximand are presented in Section II. In Section III the three variants of the basic model and their basic properties are presented and compared. Some concluding comments are offered in Section IV.

II. The Rate of Profit

The hypothesis of maximisation of the rate of profit has a somewhat chequered history in the theory of the firm,[2] and we do not wish to argue that it is an appropriate behavioural assumption in all contexts. Our claim is the much more limited one that, in the particular circumstances of an *ex*

---

[2] See, for example, Lutz & Lutz (1951), Gabor & Pearce (1952), Harcourt (1968) and Amey (1969).

ante choice amongst mutually exclusive alternative production strategies, the rate of profit will be of at least considerable importance to the firm and may form a perfectly plausible maximand in its own right.

If all the alternative production strategies open to the firm involve the same quantity of capital, there can clearly be no distinction between decision criteria based on the level of profits or the rate of profit. However, typically, alternative strategies require different amounts of capital so that both the level and rate of profit will be of interest to the decision-maker. If, for example, there are just two alternative strategies requiring $K_1(K_2)$ units of capital and yielding $r_1(r_2)$ rate of profit, strategy 1 will be selected if:

$$K_1 r_1 > K_2 r_2 + (K_1 - K_2) r_0$$

or

$$K_1(r_1 - r_0) > K_2(r_2 - r_0),$$

where r_0 is the opportunity cost of investment funds. In this case, then, neither the level of profit $(k_i r_i)$ nor the rate of profit (r_i) will be a completely adequate guide to decision-making, both will be important. However, if faced with the choice between $k_i r_i$ and r_i as the single most useful simple maximand, we argue that the rate of profit may be chosen.

In making this argument we may first distinguish between two classes of essentially capitalist firms. Following Meade (1972),[3] a "joint-stock" firm is one in which owners of capital group together to hire other factors and sell output retaining all surplus for themselves; an "entrepreneurial" firm, on the other hand, is one in which a pivotal entrepreneur hires all factors and where the surplus is the reward to that entrepreneur. Clearly the joint-stock firm is directly analogous to the labour-managed firm, and it is therefore clear that the rate of profit on capital invested forms an entirely natural and appealing maximand for this type of firm in precisely the manner of the maximand of earnings per worker in the case of the labour-managed firm.

In the case of the entrepreneurial firm, decision-making authority is vested in the single entrepreneur and is therefore divorced from the owner-ship of capital. Thus, the entrepreneur may be expected to pursue his own interests, giving rise to the various notions of "managerial capitalism" and, in the simplest case, the traditional maximand of the level of profit. Note however, that the entrepreneur is insulated from the interests of the capital owners by an essentially perfect capital market. Our argument concerning the plausibility of the rate of profit maximand in an entrepreneurial firm

---

[3] See also Dubravcic (1970).

thus depends on the existence of what we consider to be a realistic degree of imperfection in the market for investment funds.

We suggest that the entrepreneur's view of the capital market is one of a number of potential lenders each with a fixed maximum sum to invest and a subjective reservation rate of return in mind, confronted by entrepreneurs each armed with a prospectus. A prospectus, in this context, is a financial forecast based on a particular chosen production strategy and includes, *inter alia*, details of the capital requirement, the rate of return offered to investors, and the predicted profitability of the project. The entrepreneur will be uncertain of the numbers of lenders and entrepreneurs in the market, the sums available to lenders, the distribution of reservation rates of return, and the content of other entrepreneurs' prospectives.

Clearly each lender can be expected to seek the best available rate of return on their own funds but, furthermore, a lender may be expected to prefer a prospectus which indicates a high rate of profit over one predicting more limited returns even though such profits over and above the promised rate of return on capital invested become the property of the entrepreneur. Thus, a prospectus offering a 10% return out of a 15% rate of profit may be chosen over a prospectus offering 10% out of 11% even if the absolute level of profit is higher in the second case.

In attempting to attract lender's funds in such an uncertain capital market, an entrepreneur can be expected to design his prospectus so as to offer both a high rate of return on capital invested and a high rate of profit. The major means available to the entrepreneur to influence the content of the prospectus is the *ex ante* choice of production technique. This line of argument therefore suggests that in the *ex ante* choice of production strategy, the rate of profit will be of at least substantial interest to the entrepreneurial capitalist, and may form a plausible maximand in its own right as it does in the case of the "joint-stock" capitalist firm.

III. The Models

In keeping with our emphasis on the *ex ante* choice amongst mutually exclusive production strategies under alternative maximands, we confine ourselves to the study of employment, investment and shiftworking/utilization decisions in a putty clay world in which all relevant prices and total planned output are taken as fixed. Furthermore, we follow Betancourt & Clague (1977) in specifying the shiftwork/utilization decision in terms of a discrete choice amongst alternative shift regimes where each shift within any particular regime is of equal length and productivity. The putty of the models is represented by a constant return to scale instantaneous flow, constant elasticity of substitution function written as:

$$y_n^{-\theta} = \gamma^{-\theta}[\delta k_n^{-\theta} + (1-\delta)\, l_n^{-\theta}], \tag{1}$$

where y_n is output per shift under an n shift regime
k_n is the capital stock under an n shift regime
l_n is employment per shift under an n shift regime.

Total planned "daily" output is fixed by assumption at Y, so that:

$$Y = ny_n. \tag{2}$$

The three models to be viewed differ from each other in respect of the specified maximands. In the cases of the traditional profit-maximising firm and the labour-managed firm the major results are already available in the literature[4] so that coverage here will be restricted to a brief summary of results in the context of our basic model which will allow relevant comparisons to be drawn with the results derived for the profit-rate maximising firm. Initially, however, the three models may be outlined separately.

(a) *The Traditional Profit-level Maximising Firm*
This maximand can be written as:

$$\text{Max } \pi_n = PY - nw_n l_n - rqk_n, \tag{3}$$

where π_n is the level of profit under an n shift regime
P is the fixed price of output
w_n is the average wage per shift under an n shift regime
q is the unit cost of capital
r is the rate of interest.

The maximisation of (3) subject to (1) and (2) allows the maximum level of profit attainable under an n shift regime to be written as

$$\pi_n^* = PY\left\{1 - \frac{1}{P\gamma(1-\delta)}\left[\delta\left(\frac{n\delta}{rq(1-\delta)}\right)^{-\sigma\theta} + w_n^{\sigma\theta}(1-\delta)\right]^{1/\sigma\theta}\right\}, \tag{4}$$

where $\sigma = 1/(1+\theta)$ and is the elasticity of substitution. The following results may then be derived.
(i) Defining $\varrho = w_2/w_1$ as a measure of the wage premium associated with shift working,[5] two shifts will be preferred to one if:

$$\delta\left(\frac{\delta}{rq(1-\delta)}\right)^{-\sigma\theta}(2^{-\sigma\theta}-1) < w_1^{\sigma\theta}(1-\delta)(1-\varrho^{\sigma\theta}) \tag{5}$$

for $\theta > 0$, whilst if $\theta < 0$ the inequality in (5) is reversed.

---

[4] For further references to this literature see Winston (1974), Betancourt & Clague (1981).
[5] Recall that W_2 is the *average* wage per shift with two shifts. The mark-up between the two shifts is therefore $(2\varrho - 1)$.

(ii) For all values of the elasticity of substitution, increasing the shift premium (ϱ) tends to reduce the number of shifts worked.

(iii) The qualitative impact of changes in the basic wage on the number of shifts worked depends crucially on the value of the elasticity of substitution; see Winston and McCoy (1974). Denoting the r.h.s. of (5) A, we have:

$$\frac{\partial A}{\partial w_1} = \sigma\theta w_1^{\sigma\theta-1}(1-\delta)(1-\varrho^{\sigma\theta}) < 0, \tag{6}$$

so that increasing the basic wage with $\theta > 0$ will tend to reduce the number of shifts worked, whilst if $\theta < 0$ the inequality in (5) is reversed so that increasing basic wages tends to increase the number of shifts worked.

(iv) For all nonunitary values of the elasticity of substitution, the optimal level of total employment is a decreasing function of the number of shifts worked.

Defining total employment under an n shift regime as $E_n = nl_n$, we have:

$$\left(\frac{E_1}{E_2}\right)^\theta = \frac{[rq(1-\delta)/w_1\delta]^{\sigma\theta}+(1-\delta)/\delta}{[rq(1-\delta)/2\varrho w_1\delta]^{\sigma\theta}+(1-\delta)/\delta}. \tag{7}$$

(v) Increasing shift premia results in decreasing total employment within any particular shift regime, but increased employment at the frontier between regimes.

(vi) Increasing the basic wage results in decreasing total employment within any particular shift regime.

However, the impact of increased basic wages at the frontier between regimes depends on the elasticity of substitution. If $\theta < 0$, increased basic wages imply more shifts and hence falling total employment; whilst if $\theta > 0$, fewer shifts and hence rising total employment will result.

(b) *The Labour-managed Firm*

Following Betancourt & Clague (1977) we model the labour-managed firm's objective in terms of the maximisation of the basic (i.e. day shift) earnings per worker (V_n). Furthermore, we assume, with Betancourt and Clague, that the shift premia are fixed so as to ensure that the required numbers of shift workers can be found. This maximand can then be written as:

$$\text{Max } V_n = \frac{PY - rqk_n}{l_n n\varrho_n}, \tag{8}$$

where ϱ_n is the natural extension of ϱ to the n shift case. Denoting the optimal value of a variable by means of an asterisk, the maximisation of (8) subject to (1) and (2) provides the following statement of the maximum basic earnings per worker and an n shift regime:

$$v_n^* = \frac{rq(1-\delta)}{n\varrho_n\delta}\left(\frac{K_n^*}{l_n^*}\right)^{1+\theta} \tag{9}$$

where

$$K_n^* = \left(\frac{\delta P}{rq}\right)^\sigma (n\gamma)^{-\sigma\theta} Y \tag{10}$$

$$l_n^* = \frac{Y(1-\delta)^{1/\theta}}{n\gamma}\left[1-\delta\left(\frac{rq}{\delta Pn\gamma}\right)^{\sigma\theta}\right]^{-1/\theta}. \tag{11}$$

The following results may then be derived and compared to those presented in the preceding subsection.

(i) Two shifts will be preferred to one if:

$$\frac{1-\varrho^{\sigma\theta}}{2^{-\sigma\theta}-\varrho^{\sigma\theta}} < \delta\left(\frac{rq}{\sigma P\gamma}\right)^{\sigma\theta} \tag{12}$$

for all nonunitary values of the elasticity of substitution.

(ii) Increasing the shift premium tends to reduce the number of shifts worked.

(iii) The qualitative impact of changes in the cost of capital on the number of shifts worked depends crucially on the value of the elasticity of substitution. Denoting the RHS of (12) B, we have:

$$\frac{\partial B}{\partial(rq)} = \theta\sigma\delta(rq)^{\sigma\theta-1}(\delta P\gamma)^{-\sigma\theta} \gtrless 0 \text{ as } \theta \gtrless 0, \tag{13}$$

so that increasing the costs of capital with $\theta>0$ tends to increase the number of shifts worked whilst, with $\theta<0$ the impact is to reduce the number of shifts.

(iv) For all nonunitary values of the elasticity of substitution the optimal level of total employment is a decreasing function of the number of shifts worked.

$$\left(\frac{E_1}{E_2}\right)^\theta = \frac{1-\delta(rq/\delta P\gamma)^{\sigma\theta} 2^{-\sigma\theta}}{1-\delta(rq/\delta P\gamma)^{\sigma\theta}}. \tag{14}$$

(v) Increasing the shift premia has no effect on total employment within any particular shift regime, equation (11); but at the frontier between shift regimes, increasing premia result in fewer shifts and hence a higher level of total employment.

(vi) Increasing the cost of capital results in increasing total employment within any shift regime. At the frontier between regimes an increase in the cost of capital will result in increased (decreased) total employment if $\theta<0$ (>0).

(c) *The Rate of Profit-Maximising Firm*

We may first offer the basic results derived from this model in a manner similar to that adopted in the previous subsections.

Defining R as the rate of profit, the maximand may be written:

$$\text{Max } R_n = \frac{PY - nw_n l_n}{qk_n} - r. \tag{15}$$

The maximisation of (15) subject to (1) and (2) yields the following statement for the maximum rate of profit attainable under an n shift regime:

$$R_n^* = \frac{n}{q}\left(\frac{1-\delta}{\delta}\right)^{1/\theta}\left[(P\gamma)^{\sigma\theta}(1-\delta)^{-\sigma} - w_n^{\sigma\theta}\right]^{1+(1/\theta)}. \tag{16}$$

(i) If $\theta > 0$, two shifts will be preferred to one if:

$$(1-\delta)^{-\sigma}\left(\frac{P\gamma}{w_1}\right)^{\sigma\theta}(2^{\sigma\theta}-1) > (2\varrho)^{\sigma\theta}-1, \tag{17}$$

whilst if $\theta < 0$, the inequality in (17) is reversed.

(ii) For all values of the elasticity of substitution, increasing the shift premium tends to reduce the number of shifts worked.

(iii) The impact of basic wage variations on shiftworking will again depend upon the value of the elasticity of substitution. Denoting the l.h.s. of (17), C we have.

$$\frac{\partial C}{\partial w_1} = -\sigma\theta(1-\delta)^{-\sigma}(P\gamma)^{\sigma\theta}w_1^{-\sigma\theta-1}(2^{\sigma\theta}-1) < 0, \tag{18}$$

so that increasing the basic wage with $\theta > 0$ tends to reduce the number of shifts worked whilst, if $\theta < 0$ this impact is reversed.

(iv) The optimal level of total employment is a decreasing function of the number of shifts worked. In fact:

$$\frac{E_1}{E_2} = \varrho^\sigma > 1. \tag{19}$$

(v) Increasing the shift premium results in decreasing total employment within any particular shift regime, but increased employment at the frontier between regimes.

(vi) Increasing the basic wage implies decreasing total employment within any particular shift regime. At the frontier between regimes the impact depends upon the elasticity of substitution. For $\theta > 0$ ($\theta < 0$) total employment will be increased (decreased).

(d) *The Models Compared*

The presentation of the preceding subsections bears clear testimony to the similarities between the models studied. In particular, the qualitative comparative static results regarding the profit rate maximising firm's responses to changes in basic wage rates or shift premia, mirror those of the traditional profit-level maximiser and are symmetric with those of the labour-managed firm. However, these similarities should not serve to distract us from the equally real differences which separate the models, and particularly those which distinguish between the two essentially capitalist models.

At the level of qualitative comparative static responses the major distinctions lie in the responses to changes in the user cost of capital (rq) and the price of output (P). From (5) above it is clear that the shiftworking/utilization decision of the profit-level maximiser is unaffected by variations in product price whilst any increase in the user cost of capital will tend to increase the number of shifts worked if $\theta > 0$, and reduce utilization if $\theta < 0$.

$$\frac{\partial n^*}{\partial P} = 0, \frac{\partial n^*}{\partial (rq)} \gtreqless 0 \text{ as } \theta \gtreqless 0, \tag{20}$$

this latter result being the simple analogue of that reported under (a) (iii) above.

In the case of the rate of profit maximister however, we have from (17);

$$\frac{\partial n^*}{\partial P} \gtreqless 0 \quad \text{as} \quad \theta \gtreqless 0, \quad \frac{\partial n^*}{\partial (rq)} = 0, \tag{21}$$

so that the roles of the cost of capital and product price may be seen to be reversed as between the two models. In fact (21) is part of a wider result that, in the context of a profit-rate maximising firm, the cost of capital plays no part in determining factor proportion (capital deepening). Although, of course, the cost of capital does influence capital widening. Again, the obvious comparison is with the role played by product price in the more familiar profit-level maximising model.

However, we suggest that the major differences between the alternative capitalist models—and indeed between either of these models and that of the labour-managed firm—are not to be found in terms of the qualitative, comparative static responses generated. Rather, it is in the comparison of equilibria across alternative models that the true importance of alternative enterprise structures can be assessed. It is clear from the preceding subsections that the decision rules and conditions associated with the alternative models are markedly distinct in terms of functional form so that we would expect firms of each type to come to rather different decisions regarding the choice of production strategy even when they are placed in identical circumstances. The presentation of the three models within a single simple

Table 1. *Numerical example*

	(1) πn Max.	(2) Vn Max.	(3) Rn Max.
E_n^*	95	87	188
qK_n^*	17 100	45 000	5 100
n^*	2	1	2
π	6 865	6 010*	5 233
V	20	89	20
R	40.1 %	13.4 %	102.6 %

* Calculated with wage = 20.

framework allows of some investigation of the potential scale of the differences which result solely from the variations in maximands.

Relative to the profit-level maximising strategy one would expect that the profit-rate maximiser would adopt a more labour-intensive production plan whilst the labour-managed firm would select a more capital-intensive strategy; however, intuition does not provide quite such an obvious guide to the choice of shift regime under the alternative maximands, or to the likely scale of the differences for reasonable parameter values. Table 1 contains a numerical example based on a particular, plausible set of parameters,[6] which sheds some light on these issues. Viewing factor proportions (E_n^*, qK_n^*) first, it is the scale of the variations, rather than the expected qualitative pattern, which we could emphasise. The profit-rate maximiser employs almost twice as many workers as the profit-level maximiser faced with identical technology, prices and output, whilst cutting the fixed capital requirement by 70%. It might be suggested that such large scale shifts in factor employments from their cost-minimising levels reduces the plausibility of the profit rate maximand; but if this is to be argued it seems that the same logic must throw doubt on the labour managed firm where the fixed capital requirement increases relative to the profit level maximiser by some 260% whilst total employment falls by only 8%. The general pattern and scale of these results appear to be fairly robust to plausible variations in parameter values.

The shiftwork/utilization decision, however, is a much more volatile one. For the parameter values incorporated in Table 1, both of the capitalist firms would plan to work two shifts whilst the labour-managed firm would work only a single shift. Inspection of the inequalities (5) (12) and (17) suggests that there is no pattern of results on shiftworking which may be robust across parameter values, and experimentation with alternative para-

---

[6] The parameter values used are $Y=10\,000$, $P=1$, $W_1=20$, $\varrho=1.2$, $r=0.05$, $q=300$, $\delta=0.3$, $\gamma=100$, $\theta=0.7$ (implying an elasticity of substitution of 0.588).

meter values confirms that any pattern of shiftworking across the alternative models is possible within the range of plausible parameters. Thus, it is not possible to assert that one or other of the types of enterprise will utilize capital more fully without specifying with some accuracy the parametric environment in which the enterprises operate.

In order to ensure that the models reported in Table 1 are feasible, we also report the level of profit (π), earnings per worker on the basic shift (v) and the profit rate (R) for each type of firm. Given the parameters utilized, all firms operate satisfactorily on all criteria.

IV. Concluding Comments

We have attempted to argue that rate of profit maximisation is a plausible—though not necessarily compelling—possibility which may be adopted by capitalist enterprises of either the "joint stock" or "entrepreneurial" varieties in the context of *ex ante* investment decision-making involving the choice of technique.

Furthermore, we have attempted to show that the hypothesis of profit-rate maximisation produces significantly different outcomes from those associated with either profit-level maximisation or the maximisation of basic earnings per worker. These differences lie partly in terms of comparative static responses, although here qualitative similarities strongly outnumber the differences; but mostly in terms of the absolute differences between the production plans chosen by each type of firm when placed in a particular environment.

Two final points may help to unite these two themes and place them in context. First, we are not arguing that capitalist firms *should* maximise the rate of profit—clearly such a policy results in production plans which operate at greater than minimum cost. We simply argue that, given the view of the market for investment funds outlined in Section II, it is entirely reasonable to expect at least some capitalist firms to operate their investment planning on the basis of profit-rate maximisation. This point can be reinforced by reference to the numerical example quoted above. Each column of Table 1 can be viewed as an alternative prospectus embodying a particular choice of strategy. Our argument is simply that, in choosing amongst these options with a view to increasing the probability of raising the required investment funds from an uncertain capital market, we would expect at least some entrepreneurs to select column (3) in preference to column (1). Our argument claims no more than this, but it is clear from Table 1 that even if only a relatively small proportion of firms operate strategies of the column (3) type, the consequences for employment, for example, may be substantially different from those expected from the standard cost minimising model.

The second point returns to the volatility of the shiftwork/utilization decision and points out the implication for aggregative empirical investigation of utilisation rates. If an industry which produces an homogeneous product with standard technology is, in fact, made up of a variety of firms pursuing different objectives in the determination of their utilization rate, both static measures of capital utilization and, perhaps more importantly, measure of the impact of parametric changes on utilization will be misleading. This extra dimension of the standard aggregation problem makes it important that empirical studies of utilisation rates be carried out at the individual firm level. A further advantage of such an empirically disaggregated approach is that it would potentially allow of the identification of the empirical significance of profit-rate maximising choices of technique within any industry.

References

Alexander, A. J. W. & Sproas, J.: Shiftworking: An application of the theory of the firm. *Quarterly Journal of Economics*, 1959.

Amey, L. R.: *The efficiency of business enterprises*. Allen and Unwin, 1969.

Betancourt, R. R. & Clague, C. K.: An economic analysis of capital utilization. *Southern Economic Journal*, 1975.

Betancourt, R. R. & Clague, C. K.: The theory of capital utilization in labour-managed enterprises. *Quarterly Journal of Economics*, 1977.

Betancourt, R. R. & Clague, C. K.: *Capital utilization*. Cambridge University Press, 1981.

Dubravcic, D.: Labour as entrepreneurial input: An essay in the theory of the producer co-operative economy. *Economica*, 1970.

Foss, M. A.: The utilization of capital equipment. *Survey of Current Business*, 1963.

Gabor, A. & Pearce, I. F.: A new approach to the theory of the firm. *Oxford Economic Papers*, 1952.

Harcourt, G.: Investment decision criteria, investment incentives and the choice of technique. *Economic Journal*, 1968.

Heathfield, D. F.: The measurement of capital utilization using electricity consumption data for the UK. *Journal of the Royal Statistical Society* (Series A), 1972.

Heathfield, D. F.: Factor productivity in the U.K. engineering industry. In *The economics of technological progress* (ed. Puu and Wibe). Macmillan, 1980.

Lutz, F. & Lutz, V.: *The theory of investment of the firm*. Princeton University Press, 1951.

Marris, R.: *The economics of capital utilization*. Cambridge University Press, 1964.

Meade, J. E.: The theory of labour managed firms and of profit sharing. *Economic Journal*, 1972.

Winston, G. C.: The theory of capital utilization and idleness. *Journal of Economic Literature*, 1974.

Winston, G. C. & McCoy, T. O.: Investment and the optimal idleness of capital. *Review of Economic Studies*, 1974.

Vintage Production Models of U.K. Manufacturing Industry*

Grayham Mizon

Southampton University, England

Stephen Nickell

London School of Economics, England

Abstract

Vintage production models for the U. K. are extended to cover hours worked as a separate element of labour input. The main purpose of the analysis is then to ascertain whether the output of manufacturing, as measured by some index, can be satisfactorily explained as a simple, stable function of a small number of input aggregates.

I. Introduction

A number of studies have already presented estimates of vintage production models for the U. K., in particular those of Hausman (1973), Mizon (1974) and Malcomson & Prior (1979). The models discussed here may be thought of as an extension of these previous exercises, notably in the treatment of hours worked as a separate element of the labour input. The ultimate aim is to discover whether it is possible satisfactorily to explain the output of manufacturing industries, as measured by some index, as a simple, stable function of a small number of input aggregates. In the remainder of the paper we derive and discuss the standard results for vintage production models. This is followed in Section III by the specification of a number of distinct models which may be estimated. In Section IV we then consider the data and results and finish with some general conclusions.

II. Some Results for Vintage Models of Production

Suppose we have a simple vintage model of production of the following form:

$$Q(t) = \left\{ \int_{t-\theta(t)}^{t-1} e^{\lambda v} e^{-\delta(t-v)} \frac{f(k(v))}{k(v)} I(v) \, dv \right\} H(t) \, S \tag{1}$$

---
* This work was financed by the Social Science Research Council. Our thanks are due to Martyn Andrews for computational assistance, and to two referees for valuable comments.

where

$Q(t)$	= output per quarter
$k(v)$	= capital-labour ratio on vintage v
λ	= rate of embodied technical progress
$e^{\lambda v} f(k(v))$	= output per man employed per hour worked on vintage v capital
$I(v)$	= investment in quarter v
$H(t)$	= hours worked per man per quarter
$\theta(t)$	= age of the oldest vintage in use
δ	= rate of decline in productivity of capital stock
S	= shift work factor $= 3S_3 + 2S_2 + S_1$ where S_i is the proportion of capital stock on an i shift system. (For example, a two shift system implies that the capital stock is used for two periods per day by two separate sets of workers.)

In this formulation, where time is measured in quarters, we have implicitly assumed that investment expenditures in any given quarter refer to capital goods which do not come into operation until the succeeding quarter. Furthermore we have assumed that all vintages of capital which are more recent than the oldest vintage in use are themselves in use.

Then, under the assumption of profit maximization we have the following necessary (first-order) conditions.

Marginal return = marginal cost, keeping investment in period t fixed but raising the labour-capital ratio on the t'th vintage. This gives

$$e^{\lambda t}\{f(k(t)) - k(t) f'(k(t))\} \int_{t+1}^{t+L(t)} M(p(v))\, H(v)\, e^{-(r+\delta)(v-t)}\, dv$$

$$= \int_{t+1}^{t+L(t)} e^{-(r-\psi)(v-t)}\, w(v)\, dv \tag{2}$$

where

$w(t)$	= earnings per employee per quarter
$M(p(v))$	= marginal revenue
$L(t)$	= prospective lifetime of t vintage capital
$p(v)$	= price of output at time v
ψ	= rate of increase in the number of employees required to operate a machine as it ages.
r	= rate of interest.

Marginal return = marginal cost raising the level of investment but keeping the capital-labour ratio fixed.

Thus we have

$$S \frac{e^{\lambda t} f(k(t))}{k(t)} \int_{t+1}^{t+L(t)} M(p(v)) H(v) e^{-(r+\delta)(v-t)} dv$$

$$= q(t) + \int_{t+1}^{t+L(t)} e^{-(r-\psi)(v-t)} S \frac{w(v)}{k(t)} dv \tag{3}$$

$q(t)$ = effective price of new capital goods.

Quasi-rent is zero on the marginal unit of capital. That is,

$$M(p(t+L(t))) H(t+L(t)) e^{\lambda t} f(k(t)) e^{-\delta L(T)} = w(t+L(t)) e^{\psi L(t)} \tag{4}$$

or

$$M(p(t)) H(t) e^{\lambda(t-\theta(t))} f(k(t-\theta(t))) e^{-\delta\theta(t)} = w(t) e^{\psi\theta(t)}. \tag{5}$$

If we perform the operation $(2) \div (k(t) \times (3) - (2))$, we have the following equation which defines the optimal capital-labour ratio on each vintage.

$$\frac{f(k(t)) - k(t) f'(k(t))}{f'(k(t))} = \frac{S \int_{t+1}^{t+L(t)} e^{-(r-\psi)(v-t)} w(v) dv}{q(t)}. \tag{6}$$

Furthermore, if we differentiate $(3) \times k(t)$ with respect to t and make use of (2), (3), (4) and (6) we may derive

$$\frac{e^{\lambda t} f(k(t)) M(p(t+1)) H(t+1)}{k(t)}$$

$$= \frac{w(t+1)}{k(t)} + \frac{q(t)}{S} \left\{ r - \psi - \frac{\dot{q}}{q} + (\lambda + \delta + \psi) \frac{f(k(t))}{k(t) f'(k(t))} \right\}. \tag{7}$$

These last three equations will be most useful in simplifying our production models for estimation purposes.

III. Some Basic Models

In order to derive equations which are suitable for estimation, we respecify (1) in discrete time. This gives

$$Q(t) = \left\{ \sum_{v=t-\theta(t)}^{t-1} \frac{(1+\lambda)^v}{(1+\delta)^{t-v-1}} \frac{f(k(v))}{k(c)} I(v) \right\} g(H(t)) + u(t), \tag{8}$$

where $H(t)$ now refers to measured hours worked per quarter per operative and $g(H(t))$ is equal to actual hours per quarter for which capital is worked.

$u(t)$ is a random error term whose stochastic properties we shall discuss later. In this model we assume that investment expenditures, the number of vintages to be used and the capital-labour ratio on the most recent vintage are determined some time previously and may therefore be taken as predetermined. Nevertheless, they may be correlated with past values of the error which may exhibit a high degree of serial correlation. We also suppose that hours of work are selected by the firm in the previous quarter in order to produce some specified level of output. (8) then determines the *ex post* level of output. In addition to the production model, we also have an equation which defines the number of working employees, $N(t)$, namely

$$N(t) = S \sum_{v=t-\theta(t)}^{t-1} (1+\psi)^{t-v-1} \frac{I(v)}{k(v)}. \tag{9}$$

It is worth noting that our above assumptions concerning the prior determination of k and θ imply that the labour input is also predetermined which, given the quasi-fixity of this input, makes good sense.

In order to specify a model whose parameters can be conveniently estimated, we may take differences of (8) and (9). There are two sensible possibilities in this regard, namely to take first differences or to take fourth differences. We begin with the former which is analytically somewhat simpler. From (8) we have

$$Q(t) - (1+\delta)^{-1} \frac{Q(t-1) g(H(t))}{g(H(t-1))}$$

$$= (1+\lambda)^{t-1} \frac{f(k(t-1)) I(t-1) g(H(t))}{k(t-1)}$$

$$- \sum_{v=t-\theta(t-1)-1}^{t-\theta(t)-1} (1+\lambda)^v (1+\delta)^{v+1-t} \frac{f(k(v))}{k(v)} I(v) g(H(t))$$

$$+ u(t) - (1+\delta)^{-1} \frac{g(H(t))}{g(H(t-1))} u(t-1) \tag{10}$$

and

$$\frac{1}{S} (N(t) - (1+\psi) N(t-1)) = \frac{I(t-1)}{k(t-1)} - \sum_{v=t-\theta(t-1)-1}^{t-\theta(t)-1} (1+\psi)^{t-v-1} \frac{I(t)}{k(v)}. \tag{11}$$

Next, multiply (10) by $M(p(t))$ and (11) by $Sw(t)$ and subtract

$$M(p(t)) \left[Q(t) - (1+\delta)^{-1} \frac{Q(t-1) g(H(t))}{g(H(t-1))} \right]$$

$$= M(p(t)) g(H(t)) (1+\lambda)^{t-1} \frac{f(k(t-1)) I(t-1)}{k(t-1)} + w(t) N(t)$$

$$-w(t)(1+\psi)N(t-1)Sw(t)\frac{I(t-1)}{k(t-1)}$$

$$-\sum_{v=t-\theta(t-1)-1}^{t-\theta(t)-1}\frac{I(v)}{k(v)}\{(1+\lambda)^v(1+\delta)^{v+1-t}M(p(t))g(H(t))f(k(v))$$

$$-Sw(t)(1+\psi)^{t-v-1}\}+M(p(t))(u(t)-(1+\delta)^{-1}\frac{g(H(t))}{g(H(t-1))}u(t-1)). \quad (12)$$

Note that for the term in parentheses {} the vintage is very close to that which is the oldest in use and hence, from (5), this term is approximately zero. Eq. (12) may thus be rewritten

$$Q(t)-(1+\delta)^{-1}\frac{Q(t-1)g(H(t))}{g(H(t-1))}-(1+\lambda)^{t-1}\frac{f(k(t-1))I(t-1)g(H(t))}{k(t-1)}$$

$$-\frac{w(t)}{M(p(t))}N(t)+1+\psi)\frac{w(t)}{M(p(t))}n(t-1)+\frac{Sw(t)}{M(p(t))}\frac{I(t-1)}{k(t-1)}$$

$$=u(t)-(1+\delta)^{-1}\frac{g(H(t))}{g(H(t-1))}u(t-1). \quad (13)$$

This may be used as the basis of an estimable equation. An alternative strategy, which is that used by Malcomson and Prior (1979), is to collect the terms in $I(t-1)$ in (13). These are

$$\left\{\frac{Sw(t)}{k(t-1)M(p(t))}-(1+\lambda)^{t-1}\frac{f(k(t-1))}{k(t-1)}g(H(t))\right\}I(t-1)$$

and note that (7) implies that the expression in parentheses is

$$-\frac{q(t-1)}{M(p(t))}\left\{r-\psi-\frac{q(t)-q(t-1)}{q(t-1)}+(\lambda+\delta+\psi)\frac{f(k(t))}{k(t)f'(k(t))}\right\}$$

and hence (13) may be written as

$$Q(t)-(1+\delta)^{-1}\frac{Q(t-1)g(H(t))}{q(H(t-1))}-\frac{w(t)}{W(p(t))}(N(t)-(1+\psi)N(t-1))$$

$$-\frac{q(t-1)I(t-1)}{M(p(t))}\left\{r(t-1)-\psi+(\lambda+\delta+\psi)\frac{f(k(t))}{k(t)f'(k(t))}-\frac{q(t)}{q(t-1)}+1\right\}$$

$$=u(t)-(1+\delta)^{-1}\frac{g(H(t))}{g(h(t-1))}u(t-1). \quad (14)$$

This may not seem particularly advantageous until it is noticed that if $f(k(t))$ is assumed to be Cobb-Douglas, the expression $f(k)/kf'(k)$ is a constant and the unobservable, $k(t)$, is thereby eliminated.

Alternative forms may be derived from (8) and (9) by taking fourth differences. Following precisely the strategy used to derive (13), we obtain after some manipulation

$$Q(t)-(1+\delta)^{-4}Q(t-4)\frac{g(H(t))}{g(H(t-4))}-\sum_{i=1}^{4}\frac{(1+\lambda)^{t-i}}{(1+\delta)^{i-1}}\frac{g(H(t))f(k(t-i))}{k(t-i)}I(t-i)$$

$$-\frac{w(t)}{M(p(t))}(N(t)-(1+\psi)^{4}N(t-4))+\frac{Sw(t)}{M(p(t))}\sum_{i=1}^{4}(1+\psi)^{i-1}\frac{I(t-i)}{k(t-i)}$$

$$=u(t)-(1+\delta)^{-4}\frac{g(H(t))}{g(H(t-4))}u(t-4). \tag{15}$$

An equivalent fourth difference form may be generated corresponding to (14) which we do not spell out since it turns out to be empirically unsatisfactory. We now have three basic equations which may be used for estimation purposes, namely (13), (14) and (15). In order to make these operational, we must now specify functional forms for g, M and f and furthermore we must eliminate the unobservable, k. Starting with the latter problem, we may use (6) to estimate k. If we assume that the firm's expectations concerning future wage rates are based on some expectation concerning the future rate of inflation, we may let $w(v)=w(t)(1+\gamma(t))^{v-t}$ where $\gamma(t)$ is the expected quarterly rate of inflation at time t. Furthermore if we assume static expectations concerning the rate of interest and fixed expectations about the lifetime of capital goods (i.e. $L(t)=\theta^*$, constant), then (6) becomes

$$\frac{f(k(t))-k(t)f'(k(t))}{f'(k(t))}=\frac{Sw(t)}{q(t)}\frac{(e^{(\gamma-r+\psi)(\theta^*-1)}-1)}{(\psi+\gamma-r)}e^{(\gamma-r+\psi)}$$

$$=Sc(t),\text{ say,} \tag{16}$$

where c is a function of the unknown parameters ψ and θ^*. If we assume f has the Cobb-Douglas form, that is

$$f(k)=Ak^{\alpha},$$

(16) implies

$$k(t)=\frac{S\alpha}{1-\alpha}c(t),\quad\frac{f(k(t))}{k(t)}=AS^{\alpha-1}\left(\frac{\alpha}{1-\alpha}\right)c(t)^{\alpha-1}. \tag{17}$$

On the other hand, if we assume a CES form, so

$$f(k)=A(\alpha k^{-\varrho}+(1-\alpha))^{-1/\varrho}$$

where the elasticity of substitution is given by $\sigma=(1+\varrho)^{-1}>0$, then

$$k(t)=\frac{\alpha}{1-\alpha}S^{\sigma}c(t)^{\sigma},\quad\frac{f(k(t))}{k(t)}=\frac{A}{\alpha}(\alpha^{1-\varrho}+(1-\alpha)^{1-\varrho}S^{\sigma\varrho}c(t)^{\sigma\varrho})^{-1/\varrho}. \tag{18}$$

Turning now to the forms of g and M, we make the following assumptions. Since the hours input may have seasonal components which are not reflected in the measured data, we suppose

$$g(H(t)) = S(s_i H(t)^\beta),$$ (19)

where s_i is the value of the seasonal parameter in the *ith* quarter. We also allow $H(t)$ to have an exponent since measured fluctuations in paid hours may well understate true fluctuations in hours actually worked. The marginal revenue, M, we simply assume to be proportional to price, so $M(p(t)) = p(t)/1+\varphi$ where φ may be thought of as a mark-up on *marginal* cost.

Finally, before turning to a consideration of the data and results, it is worth briefly considering how we might expect the error term to behave. Suppose the error term $u(t)$ has a seasonal component s_i ($i = 1, ..., 4$ refers to the quarter) and a mean zero random element $v(t)$, so

$$u(t) = s_i + v(t)$$

with $E(v(t)) = 0$. Then it is very likely that $v(t)$ will be strongly serially correlated since we should expect unusually high or low levels of output due to unmeasured inputs and the like to show a high degree of persistence. Thus we would expect $v(t)$ to satisfy

$$v(t) = \varrho v(t-1) + \varepsilon(t),$$ (21)

where $\varepsilon(t)$ is white noise and ϱ is close to unity. Since $H(t)$, $H(t-1)$ and $H(t-4)$ are all likely to be very close, we have, in the first difference case, an error $\eta_1(t)$ of the form

$$\eta_1(t) = u(t) - (1+\delta)^{-1} \frac{g(H(t))}{g(H(t-1))} u(t-1)$$

$$\simeq s_i - (1+\delta)^{-1} s_{i-1} + v(t) - (1+\delta)^{-1} v(t-1)$$

$$= \left\{ s_i - (1+\delta)^{-1} s_{i-1} \right\} + v(t-1) [\varrho - (1+\delta)^{-1}] + \varepsilon(t).$$

The first term in parentheses on the right is simply an additive seasonal dummy. As far as the second term is concerned, if ϱ is indeed close to unity, this term will be close to zero and we can expect to find little serial correlation in the residuals. In the fourth difference case we have an error, $\eta_4(t)$, of the form

$$\eta_4(t) = u(t) - (1+\delta)^{-4} \frac{g(H(t))}{g(H(t-4))} u(t-4)$$

$$\simeq s_i(1 - (1+\delta)^{-4}) + v(t-4) [\varrho^4 - (1+\delta)^{-4}] + \varrho^3 \varepsilon(t-3)$$

$$+ \varrho^2 \delta(t-2) + \varrho \varepsilon(t-1) + \varepsilon(t).$$

Table 1

ϱ	1	0.9	0.8	0.7	0.6
ω	0.75	0.74	0.71	0.655	0.58

Again if ϱ is close to unity and δ is small we should expect an additive seasonal dummy of negligible importance and the second term on the right also to be close to zero. This leaves

$$\eta_4(t) \simeq \varrho^3 \varepsilon(t-3) + \varrho^2 \varepsilon(t-2) + \varrho\varepsilon(t-1) + \varepsilon(t).$$

Since a first-order autoregressive error is an infinite geometric moving average we may expect to reasonably approximate this error by assuming

$$\eta_4(t) = \omega\eta_4(t-1) + \xi(t)$$

where $\xi(t)$ is white noise and ω is given by

$$\omega = \frac{E(\eta_4(t)\,\eta_4(t-1))}{E(\eta_4(t)^2)}$$

or

$$\omega = \frac{\varrho^5 + \varrho^3 + \varrho}{\varrho^6 + \varrho^4 + \varrho^2 + 1}. \tag{23}$$

Table 1 indicates that we may expect ω to lie between 0.6 and 0.75 if ϱ is large.

IV. Data and Results

The data, full details of which we set out in the Appendix, is quarterly for U. K. manufacturing and has not been seasonally adjusted. In particular, employment is measured by dividing the series of manhours worked by operatives by the hours series. This generates an employment series which approximates closely the number of operatives actually at work (i.e. not on holiday, etc.) which is, of course, what is required in a production model. The price of capital goods has been adjusted to allow for the present value of investment incentives following King (1972) and Malcomson & Prior (1979). The price output and input series have been adjusted so that the values of output (pQ), of labour input (wN) and of capital input (qI) are measured in units of £10^6 per quarter.

We now turn to some results for various different models.[1] First we consider the fourth difference model given in (15). We shall not present any results based on the first difference model (13) since they were very much the same. The basic model which we estimate assumes the Cobb-Douglas form (17) and (15) becomes

$$Q(t)-(1+\delta)^{-4}Q(t-4)\,H(t)^{\beta}/H(t-4)^{\beta}-\sum_{i=1}^{4}\frac{(1+\lambda)^{t-i}}{(1+\delta)^{i-1}}\,Ks_{i}H(t)^{\beta}c(t-i)^{\alpha-1}I(t-i)$$

$$-(1+\varphi)\frac{w(t)}{p(t)}\,(N(t)-(1+\psi)^{4}N(t-4))$$

$$+\frac{w(t)}{p(t)}(1+\varphi)\sum_{i=1}^{4}(1+\psi)^{i-1}I(t-i)\frac{1-\alpha}{\alpha}\,c(t-i)^{-1}=\eta_{4}(t);$$

$$\eta_{4}(t)=\omega\eta_{4}(t-1)+\xi(t), \tag{24}$$

where $K=A\left(\dfrac{1-\alpha}{\alpha}\right)^{1-\alpha}S^{\alpha-1}$, $c(t)=\dfrac{w(t)}{q(t)}\dfrac{e^{(\gamma-r+\psi)}(e^{(\gamma-r+\psi)(\theta^{*}-1)}-1)}{(\psi+\gamma-r)}$.

$\gamma(t)$, the expected rate of inflation, is generated from a fitted ARMA model of the earnings series which is described in the Appendix and θ^* is set arbitrarily at 30 quarters. This latter parameter has no measurable effect on the results if it takes any value from 20 to 60. When the parameters of this model are estimated by minimising the sum of squared residuals $\Sigma_t \xi(t)^2$, we find that δ and ψ are vastly too large in absolute value to be realistic (e.g. $\delta=0.15$ implying an annual rate of decay of about 43 percent). This forces us to reconsider the structure of (24) and this we do by adding a simple "error correction" term of the form

$$+\beta_1 Q(t-4)\frac{H(t)^{\beta}}{H(t-4)^{\beta}}-\beta_2(1+\varphi)\frac{w(t)}{p(t)}\,N(t-4) \tag{25}$$

to the l. h. s. of (24). The implication of this is that if output is large relative to employment in period t-4, then output would tend to fall back in period t. We see this term as capturing the notion that output can be increased for short periods simply by utilizing greater effort but in the longer run this cannot be sustained. Incorporating this into our model gives us an equation to be estimated of the form

$$Q(t)-b_1 Q(t-4)\,H(t)^{\beta}/H(t-4)^{\beta}-\sum_{i=1}^{4}\frac{(1+\lambda)^{t-i}}{(1+\delta)^{i-1}}\,Ks_{i}H(t)^{\beta}c(t-i)^{\alpha-1}I(t-i)$$

$$-(1+\varphi)\frac{w(t)}{p(t)}\,(N(t)-b_2 N(t-4))$$

---

[1] The programme we used is the NAG library routine due to Gill, Murray and Pitfield. As a check we also used a routine due to Jim Davidson.

$$+ \frac{w(t)}{p(t)} (1+\varphi) \sum_{i=1}^{4} (1+\psi)^{i-1} I(t-i) \left(\frac{1-\alpha}{\alpha} \right) c(t-i)^{-1}$$

$$= \eta_4(t); \quad \eta_4(t) = \omega \eta_4(t-1) + \xi(t). \tag{26}$$

Note that $b_1 = (1+\delta)^{-4} - \beta_1$, $b_2 = (1+\psi)^4 - \beta_2$ where β_1, β_2 are defined in (25). The parameter estimates are presented in Table 2 where the restrictions implicit in model 3 are not rejected by the data. The parameter estimates are sensible although the impact of the investment terms is by no means well determined. Points worth noting are first that we cannot reject the hypothesis of a zero rate of decay in caital stock productivity until scrapping age. Second, the point estimate of β indicates that the elasticity of output with respect to measured hours is greater than unity although not significantly. Third, the rate of embodied technical progress is 1.5 percent per quarter and further experiments revealed no evidence of a decline in this rate during the 1970 s. Fourth, the price mark-up, φ, of between 60 and 80 percent seems rather high until it is realised that this is essentially the mark-up over the cost of operatives which is less than 75 percent of total cost. Fifth, our estimate of ω, the residual autocorrelation coefficient, is between 0.64 and 0.74 indicating a high level of serial correlation in the basic $u(t)$ series (see Table 1). Finally, model 3 forecasts well and appears to remain reasonably stable particularly in the light of its elementary dynamic structure. A number of further results are worth commenting on. If we assume that investment incentives count for nothing in determining the marginal capital-labour ratio and thus remove their present value from our measure of q, the model performs slightly worse in terms of explanatory power (the sum of squares is larger by 1.11), but the parameter estimates remain very much the same. Attempts to replace the Cobb-Douglas with the CES formulation were unsuccessful in the sense that the model became close to unidentified. The stopping point of the program which minimises the sum of squares became highly unstable and depended very much on the starting point. The point with the lowest sum of squares which we found indicated, among other things, an *ex ante* elasticity of substitution greater than 3!

Generally speaking, therefore, our results are satisfactory and in accord with our theoretical model. Nevertheless we feel that a number of issues are worth pursuing to see if we can generate some improvements. The fact that the investment terms in our model do not seem to contribute a great deal indicates the possibility that our estimates of the marginal capital-labour ratio based on equation (6) are simply not good enough. Apart from obvious problems of aggregation, there is the question of the speed at which the firms will adjust the capital-labour ratios on new machines in response to relative prices. One alternative strategy is to assume that the marginal capital-labour ratio remains constant. Equation (26) then reduces to

Table 2. *Parameter estimates for 4th difference putty-clay model (1957(iii)–1976(ii))*

Parameters	Model No.		
	1	2 $\delta=\psi=$const$=0$	3 $b_1=b_2$ $\delta=\psi=$const$=0$
b_1	0.50 (0.11)	0.54 (0.11)	0.51 (0.11)
b_2	0.54 (.015)	0.48 (.013)	0.51 (0.11)
β	1.09 (0.19)	1.15 (0.21)	1.15 (0.21)
φ	0.66 (0.31)	0.63 (0.26)	0.83 (0.068)
α	0.19 (0.19)	0.083 (0.077)	0.082 (0.070)
λ	0.013 (0.0029)	0.015 (0.0050)	0.015 (0.0040)
δ	-0.11 (0.19)	0.0	0.0
ψ	-0.16 (0.17)	0.0	0.0
$10^3 K$	5.16 (17.15)	23.51 (61.8)	29.3 (72.4)
s_1	0.979 (0.017)	0.978 (0.030)	0.979 (0.025)
s_2	0.922 (0.045)	0.959 (0.036)	0.958 (0.032)
s_3	0.963 (0.026)	0.977 (0.030)	0.979 (0.025)
Constant	-5.78 (7.77)	0.0	0.0
ω	0.737 (0.14)	0.66 (0.11)	0.64 (0.11)
RSS	122.55	129.04	130.33
R^2	0.946	0.942	0.942
2 log likelihood	-365.45	-369.37	-370.13
DW	2.07	2.11	2.10
Box Pierce Stat (8 DF)	5.96	9.80	10.2
N	76	76	76

Notes:

(i) *One step forecast performance* (using model 3 estimated with forecast observations omitted).

	1975 (iii)	1975 (iv)	1976 (i)	1976 (ii)
Forecast	94.56	102.69	103.16	103.25
Actual	94.4	103.5	103.4	103.1

(ii) *Parameter stability tests*, four periods $\chi^2(4)=0.43$, eight periods $\chi^2(8)=13.39$. Note that these statistics are corrected for degrees of freedom. This correction is not applied to the equivalent statistics in future models which makes them more stringent.

(iii) Asymptotic standard errors are given in parentheses.

(iv) In spite of the apparent stability of the model, the parameters estimated for the period 1957(iii)–1974(ii) show some not inconsiderable differences from those presented in column 3. In particular we have $b_1=b_2=0.58$ (0.09), $\beta=1.63$ (0.26), $\varphi=0.83$ (0.09), $\lambda=0.025$ (0.014), $\alpha=0.35$ (0.67) and $\omega=0.48$ (0.13). α and β appear to change dramatically but the former is so poorly determined in this equation that it moves by less than half a standard error. The latter, on the other hand, moves by nearly two standard errors.

$$Q(t)-b_1 Q(t-4)\frac{H(t)^\beta}{H(t-4)^\beta}-K_1 s_i H(t)^\beta \sum_{i=1}^{4}(1+\lambda)^{t-i}I(t-i)$$

$$-(1+\varphi)\frac{w(t)}{p(t)}(N(t)-b_2 N(t-4))+K_2\frac{w(t)}{p(t)}\sum_{i=1}^{4}I(t-i)=\eta_4(t);$$

$$\eta_4(t)=\omega\eta_4(t-1)+\xi(t). \tag{27}$$

Table 3. *Estimates of Equation (27) (1957(iii)–1976(ii))*

Parameters		Parameters and tests	
b_1	0.51 (0.10)	Constant	41.72 (13.46)
b_2	0.51 (0.27)	ω	0.967 (0.017)
β	1.31 (0.21)	RSS	102.04
φ	0.37 (0.24)	R^2	0.955
λ	−0.069 (0.024)	2 log L	−351.52
$10^4 K_1$	0.103 (0.157)	DW	2.37
$10 K_2$	0.24 (0.059)	Box-Pierce (8 DF)	8.41
s_1	1.01 (0.030)	Test of autoregressive restriction $\chi^2(8)$	14.25
s_2	0.914 (0.054)		
s_3	0.982 (0.028)		

Notes:
(i) *One-step forecast performance* (using model estimated with forecast observations omitted).

	1975 (iii)	1975 (iv)	1976 (i)	1976 (ii)
Forecast	97.95	104.96	105.21	105.96
Actual	94.4	103.5	103.4	103.1

(ii) *Parameter stability tests*, four periods $\chi^2(4)=22.12$, eight periods $\chi^2(8)=78.9$.
(iii) The test of autoregressive restriction was computed on the basis of estimating a linear model with $\beta=1.31$ and $\lambda=-0.069$ imposed. Note $\chi^2_{0.05}(8)=15.51$.

Note that we have impose $\psi=\delta=0$ in this model. Estimates of this equation are provided in Table 3.

The first thing to note is the dramatic improvement in explanatory power with twice the log likelihood increasing by 17.8 over model 2 in Table 2. Unfortunately one or two parameter estimates now square up less well with our prior expectations. In particular, embodied technical progress now appears to take place at −6.9 percent per quarter. Furthermore, the auto-regression parameter ω takes the value 0.967 which is much too high to be consistent with the story we told at the end of Section III. Also, the autoregressive restriction only barely avoids being rejected against first order lags on all the variables which suggests that the dynamics may be more complex than we have allowed. This is confirmed by the poor forecasting performance of the model and its apparent instability. Such dynamic complexity could arise, for example, if output does not respond immediately and fully to changes in inputs but takes a number of periods to reach its long run level. Once we allow this we are, of course, in some difficulty. The long run relationship is given by equation (8) and this already contains a very long distributed lag. This lag was eliminated but only on the assumption that (8) is true in each time period, not simply in the long run. The consequence of this is that setting up and estimating a convincing dynamic model with (8) as its long run solution is more or less impossible given our degrees of freedom constraint. This leaves us with the possibility of simply estimating an equation defining current output as a long distributed lag of all the relevant input variables. The results from such a model are presented in Table 4 and are based on the following maintained hypothesis:

$$Q(t) = \sum_{j=1}^{6} \alpha_j Q(t-j) + \sum_{j=0}^{6} \beta_j H(t-j) + \sum_{j=0}^{6} \gamma_j \frac{q(t-j)\,I(t-j)}{p(t-j)}$$

$$+ \sum_{j=0}^{6} \delta_j \frac{w(t-j)\,N(t-j)}{p(t-j)} + \sum_{j=0}^{6} \omega_j r(t-j) + \text{trend, seasonals.} \qquad (28)$$

The key point to note is the vast improvement in explanatory power if we allow free dynamics. Compared with the model based on (27) in Table 3 twice the log likelihood has increased by 74.1 on the introduction of only 15 new parameters. Furthermore, the model stability test for eight periods indicates a superior forecasting potential vis a vis model (27) as we move far outside the sample period. This is particularly true in the light of the vastly better fit of this equation within the sample period. Nevertheless, in spite of the good performance of this equation in tracking and forecasting the data, we would not wish to take this equation seriously as a production relation. All it indicates is that rates of interest, employment, investment and hours are correlated with output. In order to generate a convincing production relationship we must impose a lot of prior structure and we would, therefore, revert to the models presented in Table 2 as our most satisfactory estimates of the production parameters.

Finally we present some results based on equation (14) which is, essentially, the model used in Malcomson and Prior (1979). The equation we estimate is

$$Q(t) - a_1 Q(t-1) \frac{H(t)}{H(t-1)} - a_2 \left[\frac{w(t)}{p(t)} N(t) + \frac{r(t-1)\,I(t-1)\,q(t-1)}{p(t)} \right.$$

$$\left. + \frac{I(t-1)\,q(t-1)}{p(t)} - \frac{I(t-1)\,q(t)}{p(t)} \right] + a_3 \frac{w(t)}{p(t)} N(t-1)$$

$$- a_4 \frac{I(t-1)\,q(t-1)}{p(t)} + \text{seasonals} = \eta_1(t); \quad \eta_1(t) = \omega_4 \eta_1(t-4) + \xi(t). \qquad (29)$$

In spite of the seasonals we are forced by the data to include fourth order serial correlation in the residuals. The results are presented in Table 5. They are not very satisfactory in terms of prior expectations about the coefficients with the estimated value of the price mark-up being negative. This contrasts dramatically with the Malcomson and Prior results in Column 3 which are very much in the same area as our original results in Table 2. We do, of course, use different data sets over slightly different sample

Table 4. *Estimates of a restricted version of Equation (28) (1957(iii)–1976(ii)*

Independent variables	Estimates	Independent variables	Estimates
$Q(t-1)$	0.30 (0.11)	$(wN/p)_{t-4}$	−0.44 (0.22)
$Q(t-2)$	−0.13 (0.10)	$(wN/p)_{t-5}$	0.23 (0.20)
$Q(t-4)$	0.20 (0.10)	$(wN/p)_{t-6}$	−0.24 (0.11)
$Q(t-5)$	0.12 (0.10)	$r(t)$	171.4 (67.1)
$H(t)$	0.18 (0.026)	$r(t-3)$	−410.0 (80.0)
$H(t-1)-H(t-2)$	−0.062 (0.028)	$r(t-6)$	−222.7 (134.6)
$H(t-4)$	−0.027 (0.028)	Q_1	−6.01 (0.97
$H(t-6)$	−0.054 (0.024)	Q_2	0.39 (0.91
$(qI/p)_t$	0.69 (0.23)	Q_3	−1.67 (0.95)
$(qI/p)_{t-1}$	−0.37 (0.29)	t	0.53 (0.12)
$(qI/p)_{t-3}$	−0.43 (0.30)	Constant	−15.9 (27.5)
$(qI/p)_{t-4}$	0.75 (0.32)	RSS	38.49
$(qI/p)_{t-5}$	−0.31 (0.23)	R^2	0.997
$(wN/p)_t$	0.69 (0.18)	2 log L	−277.42
$(wN/p)_{t-1}$	−0.56 (0.18)	DW	1.96
$(wN/p)_{t-3}$	0.21 (0.13)	Box-Pierce (8 DF)	6.28

Notes:

(i) *One-step forecast performance* (using model estimated with forecast observations omitted).

	1975 (iii)	1975 (iv)	1976 (i)	1976 (ii)
Forecast	94.46	103.84	101.99	101.43
Actual	94.4	103.5	103.4	103.1

(ii) *Parameter stability tests,* four periods $\chi^2(4)=5.58$, eight periods $\chi^2(8)=10.56$.
(iii) Asymptotic standard errors are given in parentheses.

periods.[2] Furthermore, Malcomson and Prior use instrumental variables estimates on the not unreasonable grounds that $N(t)$ and $p(t)$ are determined simultaneously with $Q(t)$ (although this is not a view of the world which we share).[3] Nevertheless, the model seems to be stable outside the sample period and appears to forecast in a reliable fashion.

V. Conclusions

Our results may be summarised as follows. Using a standard putty-clay model with only limited dynamics we are able to summarize the aggregate quarterly data on output an factor inputs over a twenty-year period with a considerable degree of success. Furthermore, the parameter estimates we

---

[2] In particular it should be noted that we have used a somewhat different structure, separating employment and hours. Furthermore, the terms in the output series vary dramatically with the issues of the monthly digest of statistics from which they are collected.

[3] It is worth noting that the instrumental variable estimates we have computed do not appear to move the results any closer to those reported in Malcomson and Prior. All the coefficients are more or less the same except for $a_2=1+\varphi$ which falls dramatically and becomes insignificantly different from zero (although it is not significantly different from its original value).

Table 5. *Estimates of Equation (29) and related specifications*

Parameters	Model No. 1 Eqn. (29)	2 Eqn. (29) removing $H(t)/H(t-1)$	3 Malcomson-Prior
$a_1 = (1-\delta)$	0.81 (0.06)	0.79 (0.07)	0.95 (0.07)
$a_2 = (1-\varphi)$	0.78 (0.20)	0.86 (0.22)	1.74 (0.075)
$a_3 = (1-\varphi)(1+\psi)$	0.29 (0.11)	0.31 (0.23)	1.63 (0.12)
$a_4 = (1+\varphi)\dfrac{\lambda+\delta+\psi}{\alpha}-\psi$	0.40 (0.17)	-0.31 (0.21)	-0.12 (0.11)
Q_1	-4.66 (1.24)	-5.13 (1.07)	
Q_2	-6.09 (1.15)	-4.59 (0.93)	
Q_3	-10.0 (1.81)	-8.91 (1.64)	
Constant	0.77 (3.66)	1.3 (3.1)	-0.57 (1.13)
ω_4	0.44 (0.12)		$\omega_1 = -0.82$ (0.11)
RSS	129.4	196.7	170.45
Box-Pierce $\chi^2(8)$	3.85	6.72	
Test of A. R. 4 Restriction $\chi^2(4)$	7.86		

Notes:

(i) Asymptotic standard errors are in parentheses.

(ii) Malcomson–Prior's results are taken from the first equation in Table 1 in Malcomson–Prior (1979). The residual sum of squares is obtained from the estimate of the error variance presented in that table. Equation 1 was chosen because it had far and away the lowest error variance (i.e. the highest likelihood). The next lowest residual sum of squares in Table 1 is 209.9.

(iii) One step forecast performance using model 1 estimated omitting the forecast observations.

	1975 (iii)	1975 (iv)	1976 (i)	1976 (ii)
Forecast	94.44	101.73	102.04	102.32
Actual	94.40	103.50	103.40	103.10

(iv) *Parameter stability tests*, 4 periods $\chi^2(4)=2.07$, 8 periods, $\chi^2(8)=6.99$.

obtain are not unreasonable on prior grounds. However, we have some evidence that if we are prepared to allow more freedom in the dynamic specification and to forego any attempt to do all but the most primitive and *ad hoc* interpretations of the parameter estimates, then we may obtain large and significant improvements in the explanatory power of our equations. We would argue, however, that by doing so we are no longer estimating a production relation. Finally, we estimated some models along the lines developed in Malcomson & Prior (1979), but with only modest success.

Data Appendix

Output, Q: Index of industrial production in U.K. manufacturing, unadjusted. 1956(i)–1970(iv) provided by CSO, 1968(i)–1976(ii), *Monthly Digest of Statistics*, September issue.

Investment, I: Plant and machinery investment in U. K. manufacturing industry, unadjusted, *Economic Trends Annual Supplement*, 1976.

Hours, H: Average hours worked per operative per quarter in G. B., unadjusted, based on the index of average weekly hours worked by operatives, *D. E. Gazette.*

Employment, N: Index of total man hours worked per week in manufacturing divided by the hours worked per operative, H.

Earnings, w: This series was based on the Index of Average Weekly Earnings, G. B., in *Economic Trends Annual Supplement*, 1976, and the Average Weekly Earnings per person in the *Historical Abstract of British Labour Statistics.*

Effective Price of Capital Goods, q: Derived from the current and constant price investment series in *Economic Trends Annual Supplement*, 1976. The correction for taxes and allowances is based on the formula provided in King (1972) with the data collected from the sources described in King but updated with help from Anderson and Trivedi (1974).

Output Price, p: Wholesale price index for manufacturing output.

Rate of Interest, r: Gross redemption yields on long dated Government Securities. *Financial Statistics* and *Bank of England Statistical Abstract 1.*

Expected Rate of Inflation, γ: This is defined by $\dfrac{w(t, t+1)}{w(t)} - 1$ where $w(t, t+1)$ is the fitted value calculated from an ARIMA model of the w series of the form

$$(1-L)^2 (1-L^4) w(t) = (1+\beta_1 L + \beta_2 L^2 + \beta_3 L^3 + \beta_4 L^4) \varepsilon(t).$$

Full details of these series are provided in Andrews (1978).

References

Anderson, G. & Trivedi, P.: Some series useful in investment equations. S. E. M., Source Paper S. 18, 1974.

Andrews, M.: Quarterly data of U. K. manufacturing industries, 1948–76. Working Paper, L. S. E. Econometrics Programme, 1978.

Hausman, J. A.: *Theoretical and empirical aspects of vintage capital models.* Unpublished D. Phil. thesis, University of Oxford, 1973.

King, M. A.: Taxation and investment incentives in a vintage investment model. *Journal of Public Economics 1,* 121–147, April 1972.

Malcomson, J. M. & Prior, M. J. The estimation of a vintage model of production for U. K. manufacturing, *Review of Economics Studies 46,* July 1972.

Mizon, G. E.: The estimation of non-linear econometric equations: An application to the specification and estimation of an aggregate putty-clay relationship for the United Kingdom. *Review of Economic Studies 41,* 353–369, July 1974.